A Guide to Quantitative History

R. DARCY
and
RICHARD C. ROHRS

Westport, Connecticut
London

Library of Congress Cataloging-in-Publication Data

Darcy, R. (Robert)
    A guide to quantitative history / R. Darcy and Richard C. Rohrs.
       p.   cm.
    Includes bibliographical references and index.
    ISBN 0–275–94897–8 (alk. paper).—ISBN 0–275–95237–1 (pbk.)
    1. History—Statistical methods.   I. Rohrs, Richard C.
  II. Title.
  D16.17.G84 1995
  907′.2—dc20   93–50069

British Library Cataloguing in Publication Data is available.

Library of Congress Catalog Card Number: 93–50069
ISBN: 0–275–94897–8
     0–275–95237–1 (pbk.)

First published in 1995

Praeger Publishers, 88 Post Road West, Westport, CT 06881
An imprint of Greenwood Publishing Group, Inc.

Printed in the United States of America

The paper used in this book complies with the
Permanent Paper Standard issued by the National
Information Standards Organization (Z39.48–1984).

10 9 8 7 6 5 4 3 2 1

TO OUR PARENTS

Contents

Acknowledgments   ix

CHAPTER 1 - Introduction   1

CHAPTER 2 - Organizing Variables for Analysis and
             Sampling Historical Data   7

CHAPTER 3 - Simple Descriptive Statistics   37

CHAPTER 4 - Inferential Statistics: The Basics of
             Probability, Distributions, Significance
             Testing, and Confidence Intervals   59

CHAPTER 5 - t-Test   91

CHAPTER 6 - Cross-Classification   109

CHAPTER 7 - Analysis of Variance   137

CHAPTER 8 - Regression Analysis   175

CHAPTER 9 - Multiple Regression   195

CHAPTER 10 - Measurement: Scales, Indices,
              and Historical Demography   233

Appendix   271

Notes   291

Works Cited   305

Index   315

Acknowledgments

In the process of writing this book we have incurred many debts. Richard Jensen, historian at the University of Illinois-Chicago Circle, and Leroy Folks, statistician at Oklahoma State University, were particularly helpful. Their comments on an initial draft of our manuscript significantly improved it. James Huston (historian at Oklahoma State University), Mark Kornbluh (historian at Michigan State University), and Wijbrandt van Schuur (methodologist at the State University of Groningen) also read the manuscript and provided valuable suggestions. Bill Parle and John Hoss provided timely help with computer software and Karen Murphy and Ann Moffat helped with the figures.

Saundra Mace took our manuscript and with a patience that must be measured in kilotons turned it into what you are now reading. Thank you Saundra.

Ultimately, those who endure the most in a project like this are the authors' families. The patience and endurance of Lynne (Bob's wife) and their children, Mary Frances and Catherine Rose, and Lynn (Rick's wife) and their children, John and Monica, made our work possible.

1

Introduction

This book is intended to introduce statistics and data analysis techniques to historians who do not have an extensive background in mathematics. Today, computers do most of the statistical work, and convenient statistical packages make even the most sophisticated analysis easy. Knowing what the statistics mean, when to use them, and their strengths and limitations, however, is another matter. Here, we carefully lead the reader through all the calculations and explain what is being done and why. The end result should be more confidence in using and interpreting statistics.

Traditionally, historians have used literary evidence in their study of the past. This source was considered the ideal; recorded by contemporaries, these diaries, letters, memoirs, and so forth were considered to be the most authoritative sources of historical information. In the late nineteenth century, however, Frederick Jackson Turner and others employed some nonliterary sources in their research. Supplementing traditional methodology with the techniques of statisticians, geographers, economists, sociologists, and political scientists, they painstakingly analyzed data by hand. By present standards some of their research was elementary; other work demonstrated remarkable sophistication.[1]

Beginning in 1929, a group of French historians, known as the Annale School, rejected concentration on "the transient, the unique and the individual." Instead, the Annalists advocated examination of the enduring structure of the past—"*la longue durée*." This study of "the whole of human activity" also required new sources and methods. Their journal—*Annales d'histoire: économique et sociale*—and work by historians such as Fernand Braudel illustrated their ideas.[2]

American historians have continued to challenge the reliability of literary evidence. First, they suggested that these sources only reflected the opinions of the literate elite—a small percentage of the total population at any one time. Second, this evidence was impressionistic; it represented only one's impression of what happened. Finally, it was frequently inaccurate. This challenge to the reliability of literary sources coincided with greater interest in groups, which, because of their numbers and diversity, defied traditional research methods. There was, then, a desire to explore neglected groups that had left little extant literary evidence but a great deal of information in other forms.

In the United States, the application of social science research techniques became more popular during the 1950s. Initially economic and political historians, and later others, explored the research methods of other disciplines. Gradually there formed an informal network of scholars who advocated this type of research. Besides employing these techniques, they examined different sources and asked different questions than did most of their predecessors. Utilizing alternative sources now allowed them to go beyond their "preoccupation with exceptional individuals to concentration on the life and times"[3] of "the oppressed and inarticulate."[4] Some historians also adopted a more "systematic research design" that tested hypotheses and allowed for greater accuracy than was possible with previous reliance on literary evidence.[5] Some even suggested that historians could now do scientific research. Lee Benson, for one, predicted that in the future "the main business of historians . . . [will be] to participate in the overall scholarly enterprise of discovering and developing general laws of human behavior."[6]

One of the centers of this new approach was the University of Iowa. Although Allan Bogue, a faculty member there at the time, has denied that there had been "an Iowa School" of quantification, there can be no doubt that some members of the University of Iowa's history department were early advocates of quantitative historical research. Scholars such as William Aydelotte, Bogue, and Samuel Hays had a significant impact. In addition, their graduate students—Robert Dykstra, Joel Silbey, Robert Swierenga, and others—produced studies that utilized these new sources of data and methodologies. Unwilling to assume credit for these developments, Bogue recalled his indebtedness to Benson. Bogue asserted that "both Hays and I were to be conduits through which Benson's ideas flowed."[7]

More structure was evident during the next decade. Conferences now provided opportunities to share research with others. There was also interest in collecting and storing machine-readable data; with funding from various sources, the Inter-university Consortium for Political Research (ICPR) was founded at the University of Michigan in 1962.[8] By the end of the decade, those historians interested in social science research also had their own journal: the *Historical Methods Newsletter: Quantitative Analysis of Social, Economic, and Political Development* (now *Historical Methods*). Within a few years other journals, such as the *Journal of Interdisciplinary History* (1970), *Social Science History* (1976), and the *Journal of Family History* (1976), also began publication.

All this activity resulted in significant changes in our perceptions of the past. The greatest effect was on social, economic, and political history. We now know more about topics such as mobility, urbanization, demography, assimilation, political affiliation, and legislative behavior than ever before. Many sources that were previously ignored because they were too massive have now been examined; they have provided information about heretofore little known topics.

This new approach did not endear itself to everyone. Some opponents criticized any effort that minimized the significance of individuals and focused instead on—what were from their perspective—less-significant groups and issues. Central to this criticism was that the disciples of the "new history" preferred an analytical rather than narrative style. The new fascination with determining causes and consequences of historical events troubled those who preferred the traditional "questions of what and how."[9]

Despite some criticism, quantitative techniques are now accepted within the profession. In J. Morgan Kousser's survey of the status of social science history—or "ssh," as he calls it—he found that, instead of disdain, there seemed to be "growing or continuing acceptance."[10] Kousser concluded that "the opinions of the professoriate offer more ground for optimism about the future . . . than is sometimes believed. . . . Ssh is not about to fade away."[11]

In hindsight, it seems evident that neither the claims of quantifiers nor the dire predictions of their critics have proved accurate. Today, not all historians employ quantitative techniques, and many continue to produce traditional history based on literary sources. Yet the value of exploring all available sources, regardless of their format, to further our understanding of the past has been validated. Likewise, quantification has not accomplished everything its proponents promised years ago. Benson's prediction that historians would be involved in "discovering and developing laws of human behavior" has not occurred. Much of the research completed thus far has concentrated on local and regional areas. We have only recently begun to see work that synthesizes these localized studies. There also have been some errors; some statistical techniques have been misapplied, others misinterpreted. Fear of making such mistakes undoubtedly deters some historians from using these valuable analytic tools.[12]

Technology has also changed significantly during the past century. In the late nineteenth century, Herman Hollerith (1860–1929) developed a method for storing information in machine-readable form to facilitate compilation of the 1890 U.S. Census. Machines sorted and counted the information by interpreting hole punches on these "Hollerith cards." Later as keypunch machines, card sorters, and other processing machines became available, scholars adopted these cards for their own research. In the 1930s, Charles Samenow recorded more than 35,000 court cases on cards for his analysis of judicial decision making.[13] Soon thereafter, Charles Hyneman began an analysis of state legislators in which he used punched cards.[14] By the end of World War II, governments, polling firms, and businesses were generating large amounts of data in this form.

Although punched cards were a comparatively compact way of storing data, they wore out and could become disorganized, misplaced, or otherwise unusable. In addition, they required significant storage space as their numbers grew into the millions. Unfortunately, some very valuable studies were lost as a result.[15] Other data sets lacked clear documentation; it was not always evident what the punches meant. Many of these early data sets were difficult to use, and drawing inferences from them was risky.

Only with the advent of computer technology, therefore, have scholars been able to cope with this volume of data. Along with the "computerization" of data has come an increase in access to computers, the establishment of data archives that make these data available, and the development of simple computer programs to process them. Computers are no longer beyond the experience of most Americans; many of us own and depend on them for word processing and records' management. Graduate school training now frequently includes exposure to statistical techniques. There is also less debate over methodology. Some consensus has been reached on the proper use and interpretation of at least basic statistical procedures.

Statistical techniques need not be sophisticated; one can learn a great deal simply by counting, without the aid of any elaborate statistical procedures. The methods and examples presented here show all calculations. Virtually everything can be done by hand with a certain amount of perseverance. We are not suggesting, however, that one calculate everything by hand; we have worked through examples for demonstration purposes only. One can most easily understand the logic behind statistical procedures by working through the calculations.

Instead of just presenting the results as they might appear on a computer printout, we believe that it is essential to understand how the results were achieved. Besides presenting the most common statistics and their applications, we have also suggested others less frequently used by historians. Yet this book is not intended to be inclusive. A work that discusses in detail all techniques available to or currently employed by historians would be encyclopedic. More specialized books and articles are available for those interested in these more advanced techniques.

A book on statistics, data analysis, and quantitative methods can be presented several ways. Mathematical approaches are typically very logical and complete, but they remain incomprehensible to those without sufficient background. This strategy also tends to be deficient in that it does not address the specific problems associated with historical research. One can understand the mathematical assumptions underlying a technique without having any idea as to why it may apply to the study of history. Frequently, texts present techniques without any reference to their historical context and the work that preceded them. Discussion of this background, we believe, will help historians appreciate a method's uses and why it works the way it does.

At the opposite extreme is the "cookbook" approach. This alternative presents a formula and a verbal description of how and under what conditions one can use a particular statistical technique. It then provides a verbal description of what the results mean. The best a reader can get from this type of presentation is the idea that if one follows the directions correctly and the interpretation parallels what is described, the researcher is safe. Security is also provided when computer packages do all the work; then one need only incorporate the "output" into the text. The result often enough, however, is a presentation that is not persuasive.

Here, we try to steer a course between the mathematical and cookbook approaches. We do this by explaining the historical circumstances that led to the development of each statistical procedure and then carefully lead the reader through the calculations. We also provide historical examples and explain the analysis and interpretation in detail. We do not assume any mathematical background beyond high school algebra. As a result, we calculate even complex procedures so the reader can follow along and, in doing so, will know exactly what we have done. Anyone who is patient and calculates the problems with us should be able to understand the techniques more thoroughly than if we had opted for the cookbook approach. The result, we hope, will be greater confidence and authority in using quantitative analysis in historical research.

We recognize that many of these calculations are tedious and that other methods are available to achieve the same results. Statistical data packages, like SPSS (Statistical Package for the Social Sciences) and SAS (Statistical Analysis System), are accessible for mainframe computers, and versions of these and other statistics packages are also available for personal computers. Pocket calculators—even inexpensive models—can also calculate many simple statistics, especially when the number of cases is relatively small.

Occasionally, we discuss procedures that are not included in the standard statistics packages and cannot be calculated easily on hand calculators. In these instances, we have provided our own computer programs in BASIC. We decided to use BASIC because it is the computer language most often available on personal and mainframe computers. Or one can translate our programs into a more sophisticated language, if necessary. As there are a vast number of different calculators, computers, and statistical software packages—all with new editions, models, and versions appearing regularly—we have tried to avoid references to specific hardware and software. Our interest here is in providing an understanding of the available options and techniques, not the operation and use of particular hardware or software.

Ultimately, our aim is practicality. We present alternative ways of resolving methodological problems, point out the advantages and disadvantages of each, and make specific recommendations. The emphasis is on applying the fundamentals of statistical theory specifically to historical research. We hope that this volume will serve as an introduction for those historians who are interested in using these methodological techniques as well as for those who simply want to gain a better understanding of others' research.

2

Organizing Variables for Analysis and Sampling Historical Data

UNIT OF ANALYSIS, VARIABLES, AND POPULATION

The first step of any analysis is to specify the *unit of analysis,* the *variables,* and the *population* to be studied. The unit of analysis is the *case* that is undergoing analysis. For example, in a study of 500 females, the unit of analysis is a person; in a study of thirty religious denominations, the unit of analysis is a religious denomination; in a study of 400 families, the unit of analysis is a family.

At times, multiple units of analysis are required. Consider a study of marriage. That subject may require two units of analysis: the individual and the couple. Structuring data such that *cases* (particular instances of the unit of analysis) are grouped into couples with one person first and the other second can accomplish this. A computer can then structure the data two ways: as couples, by organizing the two cases together; or as individuals, by organizing them separately.

Variables are characteristics of the unit of analysis. If the unit of analysis is a county, variables might be the state in which it is located, its total population in 1920, and its largest religious denomination. Some variables, such as the population, are already in numerical form. Others are not. For a variety of reasons it is useful to convert non-numerical variables, such as the name of the state and the county's largest religious denomination, into numbers. Conversion into numbers simply facilitates computer processing. The assignment of these numbers can be arbitrary and requires the preparation of a *code book* that identifies the meaning of numerical codes.

The *population* is the set of cases to be studied. It is important that we define the population explicitly; the researcher must determine in advance which cases are eligible for inclusion and which are not. Difficulties arise when the population is not properly defined or when one studies one population but generalizes to another. Often in historical research, there are only a limited number of cases available. For example, we may want to explore the experience of apprentices in the American colonial period by using their diaries. We must describe this population carefully and acknowledge that our conclusions about "colonial apprentices" are based on a few unique individuals whose diaries have been preserved.

Election surveys are an example of studying one population while generalizing to another. Polling organizations frequently make different predictions on the outcome of the same election. One organization may survey the population of adult citizens aged eighteen and older, another the population of registered voters, and a third the population of likely voters. The predicted outcome will vary because the analyses are being made on three different populations. In recent presidential elections, only 50–60 percent of the adult citizens cast votes, but between 70 and 80 percent of the registered voters did. Thus, a survey of all adults may predict a different outcome than a survey of likely voters.[1]

TYPES OF VARIABLES

As statistical analysis of variables involves the manipulation of numbers according to some procedure or formula, it is useful to make some observations about numbers and variables first.[2]

There are two types of variables: discrete and continuous. A *discrete variable* is one that can assume only certain values; a *continuous variable* can assume any value in a range. The number of children in a family, for example, is a discrete variable, as only integers (positive, whole numbers) are appropriate. The height of the tallest child is a continuous variable, as it can be any value within a certain range. In theory at least, one can measure height to any degree of accuracy. In practice, the distinction between discrete and continuous variables occasionally becomes blurred. A person's age is commonly treated as a continuous variable although age is typically recorded in integers. A person fifty-one days short of his or her forty-eighth birthday is described as 47 years old, not 47.860.

It is also useful to distinguish between variables that are categorical and those that are not. In practice that distinction is also sometimes blurred. A categorical variable is a discrete variable designed to group cases together into a relatively small number of categories. Classifying adults' ages, for example, as young, middle-aged, and elderly makes age a *categorical variable,* while actual age in years is not.

Another way to classify variables is by the level of measurement

achieved. The level of measurement determines which statistical procedures are appropriate and which are not. Here our interest is in three levels:

1. Numbers are used as names or *tags* that differentiate one thing or set of
   things from another thing or set of things. The numbers on automobile
   license plates, for example, differentiate one automobile from another. One
   can also use numbers to represent categories and to differentiate one from
   another. For example, "1" can be used to represent Protestants and "2"
   Roman Catholics.

2. Numbers can indicate *order.* One can assign ordinal numbers such as first,
   second, or third to things or groups of things to indicate their position
   relative to one another. For example, one can rank the top twenty-five
   basketball teams first, second, third, down to twenty-fifth. One can also
   order children in a family as firstborn, secondborn, and so on.

3. Numbers can indicate *distance.* One can assign numbers to things or
   groups of things in such a way as to indicate how far, on some scale, a
   thing or group of things is from another thing or group of things. For
   example, a task taking five hours takes two more hours than one taking
   three hours; a team that scores 105 points in a basketball game scores one
   more point than a team scoring 104 points.

Numbers, then, can be tags, can indicate order, and can indicate distance, depending on how one uses them. But they do not necessarily have
all these properties at the same time. The properties are hierarchical. If one
uses a number to indicate distance, it also implies order and serves as a tag.
For example, if one uses numbers to indicate the population of a city, then
the numbers also imply order: a city with 1,500,000 people is larger than one
with only 1,000,000. The numbers are also tags either for things or groups
of things in that a number can be used to label a group, such as all cities of
1,500,000 or more. Likewise, numbers assigned to indicate order can also
serve as tags. "First" or "Number One in the Nation" can identify a particular team in addition to indicating the team's relative status. Thus, numbers
with the property of distance also imply order and serve as tags; numbers
that indicate order also serve as tags. The reverse, however, is not necessarily so. Numbers that imply order may or may not imply distance, and
numbers that are tags may not provide order and distance information. We
call variables in which the numbers are just names or tags and convey no
order or distance information *nominal variables*. Variables in which numbers convey order (and hence also serve as tags) are *ordinal variables*.
Variables in which numbers convey distance information (and hence also
convey order and serve as tags) are *interval variables*.[3]

As statistics are designed to exploit a variable's arithmetic properties, there are different statistics for nominal, ordinal, and interval variables. A historian selecting an incorrect statistic risks meaningless results if the assumed properties for numbers are not present. Or the statistic can fail to exploit all the information available and, therefore, reveal less than could be learned. How one assigns numbers to observations determines the numerical properties of the variable and what statistics are meaningful. We need to examine each type of variable in greater detail.

Nominal Variables

Consider the nominal variable "marital status." An individual might be one of the following:

single, never married

engaged to be married, never before married

widowed, not remarried

widowed and remarried

divorced and not remarried

divorced and remarried

married but separated and not living with spouse

married and living with spouse

One can assign numbers to represent a person's marital status, but as there is no order or distance information, the numbers are nominal-level names or tags. They are merely a code or shorthand for a more elaborate verbal description. In this case, assigning specific numerical tags is arbitrary. The eight categories could be numbered one to eight or shuffled about in any order and numbered. It does not matter, because the numerical scheme does not imply order. This type of variable groups several cases into a category designated by a number; it is a categorical variable.

A nominal variable should have two properties: each of the categories should be mutually exclusive and exhaustive. Then the researcher can assign each observed case to one and only one category. If, for example, the only categories are married and divorced, it would be possible that a person could fit both: a person who was divorced but has remarried. The scheme married or divorced combines both present and previous marital status and, therefore, risks creating categories that are not mutually exclusive. The solution is obvious: construct variables that are conceptually simple and then add additional variables (in this case, previous marital status) if necessary. The codes assigned to nominal variables should also be exhaustive, in the sense that there should be a category for every possible case. If, for example, the coding scheme only allows for "married" or "single," then what numerical code do you assign widows, divorced people, and separated people? The scheme is not exhaustive. The solution is either to develop definitions of married to include all people who were ever married or to expand the categories to include other possibilities.

Ordinal Variables

A second variable type is ordinal. Unlike a nominal variable, these numbers imply an order or progression. There are two types of ordinal variables, grouped and ranked. As with nominal variables, the *grouped ordinal variables* collect several cases in each of the categories designated by a number. High school class (freshman, sophomore, junior, senior) is an example of a grouped ordinal variable. As with a nominal variable, each category must be mutually exclusive and exhaustive. But here one can also use the numbers to imply progression—(1) for freshman, (2) for sophomore, (3) for junior, and (4) for senior. One could also assign the numbers in the reverse order and still imply the same progression; any other order, however, would lose the ordinal nature of the variable. Numbers used to code ordinal-level data, therefore, contain information about the order of cases as well as about the category to which they belong.

With *ranked ordinal variables*, each case has a distinct value (or at least most do; in practice there can be ties). Cases are not grouped into categories. While ranked ordinal variables imply an order, they do not indicate the distance between the numbers. Table 2.1 provides an example. The states of the United States in 1850 are listed in order by the size of their population from the greatest (New York) to the fewest (Florida). In practice there can be a tie; but here each state has a unique position relative to the other states. From this information, it is possible to determine the order of the states by population, but not the exact difference between any of them.

Interval Variables

A third type of variable is interval. Numbers associated with interval variables contain meaningful distance information in addition to the implied

Table 2.1
States in Ranked Order by Population, United States, 1850

Ranking	State
1	New York
2	Pennsylvania
3	Ohio
4	Virginia
5	Tennessee
6	Massachusetts
7	Indiana
8	Kentucky
9	Georgia
10	North Carolina
11	Illinois
12	Alabama
13	Missouri
14	South Carolina
15	Mississippi
16	Maine
17	Maryland
18	Louisiana
19	New Jersey
20	Michigan
21	Connecticut
22	New Hampshire
23	Vermont
24	Wisconsin
25	Texas
26	Arkansas
27	Iowa
28	Rhode Island
29	California
30	Delaware
31	Florida

Source: U.S. Interior Department, Census Office, *The Seventh Census of the United States, 1850* (Washington, DC: Robert Armstrong, 1853), xli.

order and tag information. Usually, interval-level variables allow the most powerful statistical analysis.

Age is an example of an interval variable. With a person's actual age (defined as the number of birthdays passed since birth), we know that a person who is twenty-five is not the same age as a person who is twenty-four (category information at the nominal level), and is older than a person who is twenty (order information). In addition, we know that the first person is five years older than the third person: 25 - 20 = 5 (distance information).

The key to understanding the choice of statistics involves arithmetic operations. For nominal variables, statistics are based on *counting* the number of cases in each category, because the numbers merely serve to tag or identify distinct categories. For ordinal variables, statistics involve counting and determining where the middle case is or how the cases are distributed from high to low. For interval variables, it is possible to add and subtract the assigned numbers and perform multiplication, division, and exponentiation.

HISTORICAL SAMPLING

Frequently, historians are confronted with too much information. Many do prefer to study all extant cases; unless a dedicated and competent labor force and sufficient funding is available, however, *sampling* can be a helpful approach. There is no uniform rule as to what constitutes too many cases; that depends on the availability of data, the variables, and the time and resources allotted to the project. Researchers must evaluate each situation independently. Generally, however, if the number of cases exceeds 1,000 or collecting the data is impractical, one should consider sampling. Use of the proper sampling methods with a sample that is sufficiently large can accurately portray the entire population.

There are several commonly held fallacies about sampling. Some people believe that large numbers of cases, however selected, are better than a smaller, random sample. They are not. Do not be impressed by the large numbers. Even with random samples, a smaller one can be superior because the tedious coding process for a larger sample can increase clerical errors.[4] Another fallacy is that, if a group of cases match the population on some "key" demographic characteristic, they will be "typical" of the population in other ways as well. Consider the following example. One could calculate the percentage of men and women and blacks and whites in a population, and then select cases for a sample that would match those percentages. There is, however, no assurance that a sample selected in this manner would accurately reflect other characteristics. Typically such "convenience samples" select the most accessible cases and, therefore, are biased toward characteristics associated with accessibility.

The goal is to select a sample that one can be confident resembles the population from which it was drawn. This is accomplished through probability sampling that randomly selects cases according to the laws of chance. This means the researcher does not determine the selection of particular cases and the cases do not select themselves. For example, apprentices in colonial America who kept diaries selected themselves, in a sense—by writing diaries—and are not likely to be typical of all apprentices of the period. And while any researcher may find it more convenient to locate information concerning prominent individuals, these people may not be typical of the population of interest.

The benefits of proper sampling and the disadvantages of improper techniques were illustrated in dramatic fashion during the 1936 presidential campaign. *Literary Digest*, a popular magazine of the time, predicted the outcome of elections by mailing out "ballots" to individuals identified as telephone and motor vehicle owners and magazine subscribers. Before the election of 1936, *Literary Digest* mailed out 10,000,000 ballots. Respondents were asked if they intended to vote for the Republican challenger, Alf Landon, or the Democratic incumbent, Franklin Roosevelt. In contrast, George Gallup tried a different approach in a pre-election survey for *Fortune*. He randomly sampled 45,000 individuals—a much smaller sample than that of the *Literary Digest*. Based on more than 2,000,000 ballots returned to *Literary Digest*, that magazine predicted that Landon would receive 54 percent of the total vote. The *Fortune* survey predicted that Roosevelt would win with 59 percent of the vote. In fact, Gallup had also predicted *Literary Digest's* prediction—a closely held secret—by mailing out ballots to a sample of 3,000 of the 10,000,000 individuals who were sent ballots by *Literary Digest*. Subsequent events proved both of Gallup's predictions correct.[5]

The *Fortune* survey demonstrated that a small, properly administered sample could be more accurate than one that was larger but ill-conceived. The inadequacy of the *Literary Digest* sample is now obvious; while massive in size, respondents were not typical of all voters. In 1936, because of the Depression, many Americans were poor. People who subscribed to magazines and owned automobiles and telephones were not representative of the entire population.

There are many different methods of selecting random samples. Here we will discuss three: *simple random samples, skip interval samples*, and *stratified cluster samples*.

Simple Random Samples

A simple random sample is one in which a predetermined number of cases (m) are selected from a population with M cases. In the population, each case is unique; that is, it is not listed more than once. In a simple random sample, each case has an equal opportunity of being selected—and, once chosen, cannot be selected again.[6]

Historians frequently encounter lists of a particular population. These lists may be of individuals who served in the House of Representatives, the members of the Long Parliament, or individuals enumerated in the 1880 manuscript census of Indiana. In some instances, an actual list may be available; in others, there is no list, but specific cases can be uniquely identified by a number (e.g., the 512th divorce case). Several procedures can be employed to select a sample from this type of population.

When the cases are numbered sequentially, the simplest method is to use a computer program to generate a set of random numbers. The researcher must first specify the total number of cases in the population and then the size of the sample. A computer program can generate a series of appropriate numbers that will comprise the sample. One example of such a program (in BASIC) is given as Program 2.1.

At other times the list may not be numbered sequentially. Consider a city directory with sixty-five pages; each page is divided into three columns, and each column contains a maximum of fifty names. The exact total number of names (M) is unknown but can be estimated to be less than 9,750 (65)(3)(50), because not all the columns on all the pages are full. The total

Program 2.1
A BASIC Program to Generate a Set of Random Numbers

```
10    PRINT "INPUT THE SAMPLE SIZE"
20    INPUT X(2)
30    PRINT "INPUT THE POPULATION SIZE"
40    INPUT X(1)
50    PRINT "RANDOM NUMBERS"
60    FOR E=1 TO X(2) STEP 1
70    S(1)=INT(RND*(X(1))+1)
80    PRINT S(1)
90    NEXT E
100   END
```

contents of the book (N) consist of two parts: the names of interest (M) and blanks (B) where there are no names. Thus, N = M + B.

Suppose that the researcher decides to select a random sample of 200 names. Because some of the space in the city directory is blank, the sample needs to be increased to ensure that 200 actual cases will be included. Thus, the sample of names (n) will consist of names (m = 200) and blanks (b): n = m + b. Unfortunately, b is unknown so we must use our judgment to estimate that, say, a sample of 250 will provide approximately 200 cases. It is important that the cases included in the sample be left in the order selected. If the sample of 250 cases is sorted into numerical order and the sample is suspended after locating the first 200 nonblank cases, names in the first part of the city directory will have a greater chance of selection than later cases.

To generate a simple random sample of 200 cases from 9,750 possible names, we must identify 250 cases in random order by page, column, and position in the column. We will then include the first 200 nonblank names in the sample. A BASIC program for selecting such a sample is shown as Program 2.2. One can modify the program to accommodate different starting pages and other factors. After inputting a sample size of 250, sixty-five

Program 2.2
A BASIC Program to Generate a Set of Random Numbers by Page, Column, and Line

```
 10   PRINT "INPUT THE SAMPLE SIZE"
 20   INPUT X(4)
 30   PRINT "INPUT THE NUMBER OF PAGES"
 40   INPUT X(1)
 50   PRINT "INPUT THE NUMBER OF COLUMNS"
 60   INPUT X(2)
 70   PRINT "INPUT THE NUMBER OF NAMES IN THE COLUMN"
 80   INPUT X(3)
 90   PRINT "PAGE","COLUMN","CASE"
100   FOR E=1 TO X(4) STEP 1
110   S(1)=INT(RND*(X(1))+1)
120   S(2)=INT(RND*(X(2))+1)
130   S(3)=INT(RND*(X(3))+1)
140   PRINT S(1),S(2),S(3)
150   NEXT E
160   END
```

pages, three columns, and fifty names per column, the program might produce the results shown in Table 2.2 (only the first ten examples are listed). To simplify the process of locating specific cases in a column, you can prepare a guide rule that numbers every fifth name. This will facilitate the location of cases and reduce the possibility of errors.

After the sample of nonblank cases (m) is drawn from the first n (all nonblank and blank cases) in the sample, the total number of nonblank names can be estimated[7] as:

$$M = \frac{(m-1)N}{(n-1)}$$

where M is the number of nonblank names
 m is the number of nonblank names sampled
 n is the total number of items sampled before the m (nonblank names were located (n = m + b)
 N is the total possible number of cases
  (65 X 3 X 50 = 9,750 = N = M + B)

For example, if locating m = 200 names required going through the first n = 236 items of the sample, then the total number of M names is estimated to be:

$$M = \frac{(m-1)N}{(n-1)}$$
$$= \frac{(200-1)9,750}{(236-1)}$$
$$= 8,256.4$$

As much historical research is based on the manuscript schedules of the decennial censuses of the United States, consideration of a sampling strategy for that source is particularly important. The manuscript schedules for each state are comprised of one or more volumes. Each volume is then divided into counties, and the counties into enumeration districts, geographical regions, precincts, towns, beats, or wards. On each page individuals— listed by households—are numbered sequentially and the numbers start again on each page. A random sample as presented above is therefore impractical, because not every individual has been assigned a unique identification number. One solution is to establish an artificial sequence of numbers. By

Table 2.2
Sample Output from Program 2.2

Page	Column	Case
32	1	16
18	3	40
29	2	50
39	3	28
54	3	19
59	1	7
46	1	3
29	3	48
21	2	17
35	3	45

adding together the last page number of each volume, one can generate a sequential list of page numbers for the entire population. Multiply this number by the number of lines on a page and one gets a range of numbers to be assigned to each individual cited in the census. Random numbers within that range can then be generated and converted to volume, page, and line numbers.[8]

A computer program can eliminate much of the tedium of this procedure by producing random volume, page, and line numbers directly. BASIC Program 2.3 prompts the user for some necessary information and then produces a set of random numbers for sampling within a state.

Program 2.3
A BASIC Program to Generate Random Numbers by Volume, Page, and Line

```
10   DIM P(100)
20   PRINT "INPUT THE NUMBER OF VOLUMES FOR STATE"
30   INPUT S(1)
40   PRINT "INPUT THE NUMBER OF LINES ON A PAGE"
50   INPUT S(2)
60   PRINT "INPUT DESIRED SAMPLE SIZE"
70   INPUT S(3)
```

```
 80   M=0
 90   FOR E=1 TO S(1) STEP 1
100   PRINT "INPUT THE ENDING PAGE IN VOLUME ",E
110   INPUT P(E)
120   M=M+P(E)
130   NEXT E
140   PRINT "VOLUME","PAGE","LINE"
150   FOR F=1 TO S(3) STEP 1
160   R(1)=INT(RND*M)+1
170   U(1)=0
180   U(2)=0
190   FOR G=1 TO S(1) STEP 1
200   U(1)=U(1)+P(G)*S(2)
210   IF U(1)>R(1) GOTO 240
220   U(2)=U(1)
230   NEXT G
240   A(1)=G
250   A(2)=INT((R(1)-U(2))/S(2))
260   A(3)=INT((((R(1)-U(2))/S(2))-A(2))*S(2))+1
270   PRINT A(1),A(2),A(3)
280   NEXT F
290   END
```

Skip Interval Samples

The way a population is organized may make sampling procedures other than simple random sampling both necessary and desirable. We can simplify the selection of cases for inclusion in a sample if, for example, the cases are in random order. Then the first 200, or the last 200, or the middle 200 cases will constitute a random sample. Departures from a simple random sample are risky, however. What is the basis for assuming the cases are in random order? How can this be verified? There are actually many patterns to what might appear to be random assemblages.

Skip interval samples are a possible sampling strategy if the population is already in some order that is random or not cyclical. A population list would be cyclical if, for example, every second person was a male or every eleventh person was a sergeant. This procedure involves using a randomly selected starting point and a skip interval. There are several steps to this process.

First, it is necessary to determine the total number of cases in the population. If this information is not available, make an estimate. It is unnecessary to know the population size exactly; a reasonable approximation will do.[9]

Next, determine the size of the desired sample. A sample should be sufficiently large so there are enough of the smallest group of interest to provide reliable estimates of that group's characteristics.[10] Consider the following example. If the research project calls for comparing the occupations of Chicago whites and African-Americans in 1910, determine the size of the sample by calculating the percentage of the African-American population. If African-Americans accounted for 10 percent of the 1910 population of Chicago, then approximately 50 African-Americans should be found in a sample of 500 if selected randomly.

Then, calculate the skip interval. Divide the total number in the population (M) by the sample size (m). For example, if there is a population of approximately 100,000 and a desired sample of 500, the skip interval will be:

$$\text{skip interval} = \frac{M}{m}$$
$$= \frac{100,000}{500}$$
$$= 200$$

Finally, determine a random starting point. Following the example calculated above, the researcher will select every 200th case in the population. There are 200 possible samples, however, one for each of the 200 starting places. One sample of 500 could be created by selecting the first case, then the 201st case, and so on. Other samples could be drawn by starting with the second case and then the 202nd case, the third case and then the 203rd case, and so on. How then does one determine the starting point? That is done by selecting a random number between 1 and the skip interval value—in this case, 200. One way to select a random starting point is to use a pocket calculator. Take some number (the seed) that is always changing—perhaps the time at, say, 3:20 p.m. Then multiply the seed by π (3.14159). The last three digits of the product—in this case 088—provide a random starting point. This process may have to be repeated several times before a number in the desired range is calculated. In this instance, we begin with 88 and include every 200th case (88, 288, 488, 688, 888, etc.) until we have attained a sample of 500 cases.

Stratified Cluster Samples

Frequently, historians do not have a list of cases and, in fact, may have only a vague notion about where the cases may be located. Consider research on Germans living in Texas in 1870. The researcher might know that there were thousands of Germans, but no list of them is available. Here we use a stratified cluster sample. The published census for 1870 provides the number of German-born individuals residing in each one of the 141 Texas counties. Out of a total state population of 818,579, there were 23,985 or 2.93 percent who were German-born. The 1870 manuscript census for Texas is contained in twenty volumes, each with between 400 and 650 pages. Each page contains a front and back side (the front is numbered), and each side contains forty lines. No more than one person is enumerated per line. In some counties, individuals are listed on only one side of the page; another county may occupy the other side, or it may be blank. Age, sex, occupation, value of real estate and personal property, place of birth, citizenship of mother and father, literacy, and other information are recorded for each individual. In addition, we can determine information about the entire household from accompanying data on household members who are listed on adjacent lines.

These data present two problems. The 1870 population of Texans born in Germany—23,985—is probably too large to be included in a data set. Ironically, however, the German-born population is also too small to be easily detected among the total population of Texas; the researcher must, therefore, read through much unrelated material to locate the desired cases.

Stratified cluster samples provide a solution to both of these problems. The first step is to divide the entire population into distinct divisions called *strata*. These strata should divide the population with no overlap, so that each German-born person falls into one but only one stratum. Here we will use the county as the stratum. Of the 141 counties (see Table 2.3), nineteen contained the overwhelming majority of the German-born population (83.44 percent).

We selected the nineteen strata to include the largest proportion of Germans while minimizing the number of strata sampled and maximizing the proportion of Germans within a stratum. Thus, Shackleford County (9.23 percent German) was not included because it would add only forty-two Germans while increasing the number of strata to be sampled. Lavoca County was excluded because its 257 Germans amounted to only 2.8 percent of that county's population.

By dividing the State of Texas into twenty strata—one each for nineteen counties and one for the remaining 122 counties—we can undertake a more efficient search for Germans. Each stratum will provide a distinct

Table 2.3
German-born Population of Texas in 1870

County	German-born	Percent of County	Proportion of All German-born	Quota
Austin	2111	13.99	.0880	88
Bastrop	937	7.62	.0391	39
Bexar	1829	11.40	.0763	76
Bexar District	122	11.33	.0051	5
Calhoun	369	10.72	.0154	15
Colorado	776	9.32	.0324	32
Comal	1878	35.50	.0783	78
DeWitt	844	13.10	.0352	35
Fayette	2128	12.62	.0887	89
Galveston	1923	12.58	.0802	80
Gillespie	1245	34.91	.0519	52
Guadalupe	736	10.11	.0307	31
Harris	1834	10.56	.0765	77
Karnes	230	13.49	.0096	10
Kendall	386	25.13	.0161	16
Mason	148	21.83	.0062	6
Medina	336	16.17	.0140	14
Victoria	480	9.88	.0200	20
Washington	1701	7.36	.0709	71
All others	3972	.61	.1656	166
Total	23985	2.93	1.0002	1000

Source: U.S. Interior Department, Census Office, *9th Census, 1870: The Statistics of the Population of the United States,* 3 vols. (Washington, DC: Government Printing Office, 1872), vol. 1, 372–373.

sample of German-born Texans. Then from the twenty stratum samples, we will construct another sample that is representative of all German-born residents of Texas.

The first step is to establish a *quota* for each of the twenty strata. A quota is the number of German-born individuals who will be sampled from each stratum. Determine the quota by multiplying the proportion of German-born residents living in each stratum by the sample size.

$$quota = \frac{German\text{-}born\ in\ stratum}{total\ German\text{-}born\ inhabitants\ of\ the\ state}\ (sample\ size)$$

For Austin County,

$$\text{quota} = \frac{2,111}{23,985} (1,000)$$

$$= 88$$

The quota for Austin County (88) is the number of German-born individuals who will be sampled from that stratum. The quotas for the various strata are presented in Table 2.3.

The next problem concerns locating these German-born individuals in the manuscript census. Because they are interspersed with non-Germans, we cannot sample them directly. Instead, the researcher must sample clusters of individuals and select all the German-born individuals in that cluster. The most convenient way to sample clusters of individuals is by using the page numbers of the manuscript census. For each stratum, we can generate a random sample of page numbers, and we then scan these pages for German-born individuals until the quota for that stratum has been attained. There are two important considerations. First, the sampled pages must not be sorted numerically; as the sampling will stop once we have achieved the quota, the pages at the end of the stratum will receive short shrift. The last pages must have as equal a chance of being selected as the early pages. Next, we must select all Germans on the page, even if that means exceeding the quota. If one stops in the middle of the page, individuals higher on the page will have a better chance of being sampled than those lower down. As entries within a household are typically ordered by husband, wife, and children from oldest to youngest, failing to include all Germans on a page might underrepresent wives and younger children.

A BASIC program to sample the pages of the manuscript census within a stratum is presented in Program 2.4.

Program 2.4
A BASIC Program to Generate a Set of Random Numbers for a Stratified Sample

```
10   PRINT "INPUT THE NUMBER OF STRATA TO BE SAMPLED"
20   INPUT S(1)
30   PRINT "INPUT ESTIMATED NUMBER OF PAGES TO BE
     SAMPLED FOR STRATUM"
40   INPUT S(2)
50   FOR E=1 TO S(1) STEP 1
```

```
60   PRINT "INPUT NUMBER OF VOLUMES FOR STRATUM ", E
70   INPUT S(3)
80   M=0
90   FOR F=1 TO S(3) STEP 1
100  PRINT "INPUT VOLUME NUMBER OF A VOLUME"
110  INPUT T(1,F)
120  PRINT "INPUT BEGINNING PAGE FOR STRATUM IN VOLUME"
130  INPUT T(2,F)
140  PRINT "INPUT ENDING PAGE FOR STRATUM IN VOLUME"
150  INPUT T(3,F)
160  M=M+(T(3,F)-T(2,F))+1
170  NEXT F
180  DIM A$(25)
190  PRINT "INPUT NAME OF STRATUM"
200  INPUT A$
210  PRINT "INPUT QUOTA FOR STRATUM"
220  INPUT T(4,F)
230  PRINT A$,"   QUOTA = ",T(4,F)
240  PRINT "VOLUME","PAGE"
250  FOR F=1 TO S(2) STEP 1
260  R(1)=INT(RND*M)+1
270  U(1)=0
280  U(2)=0
290  FOR G=1 TO S(3) STEP 1
300  U(2)=U(2)+((T(3,G)-T(2,G))+1)
310  IF R(1)<U(2)+1 GOTO 340
320  U(1)=U(2)
330  NEXT G
340  R(2)=R(1)-(U(1)+1)+T(2,G)
350  PRINT T(1,G),R(2)
360  NEXT F
370  NEXT E
380  END
```

The prompts included in Program 2.4 require some additional explanation:

1. "INPUT THE NUMBER OF STRATA TO BE SAMPLED"—Enter the total number of strata included in the sample; in our example, we had 20.

2. "INPUT ESTIMATED NUMBER OF PAGES TO BE SAMPLED FOR STRATUM"—Calculate this number by dividing the quota for each stratum by the product of the number of lines per page and the proportion of the subject in that stratum. Consider the example of Austin County from Table 2.3. In that instance, 88 (the quota for Austin County) will be divided by the product of 40 (the number of lines per page of the manuscript census) and

.1399 (the proportion of Germans in that stratum). The quotient is 15.725, rounded to 16. The number of pages should be increased by 25 percent to ensure enough pages to reach the quota (25 % of 16 = 4). You would, therefore, respond to this prompt with the number 20 (16 + 4 = 20).

3. "INPUT NUMBER OF VOLUMES FOR STRATUM x"—You must identify the number of volumes of the manuscript census containing stratum 1, then stratum 2, stratum 3, and so on. For example, all of Kendall County is located in one volume. Enter: 1.

4. "INPUT VOLUME NUMBER OF A VOLUME"—Kendall County is located in volume 12. Enter: 12.

5. "INPUT BEGINNING PAGE FOR STRATUM IN VOLUME"—Here you are asked for the page number on which each stratum in the volume begins, one at a time. Kendall County begins on page 113 of volume 12. Enter: 113.

6. "INPUT ENDING PAGE FOR STRATUM IN VOLUME"—Here you are asked to provide the last page of each volume of each stratum one at a time. Kendall County ends on page 136 of volume 12. Enter: 136.

7. "INPUT NAME OF STRATUM"—Here enter: Kendall County.

8. "INPUT QUOTA FOR STRATUM"—The quota for Kendall County is 16. Enter: 16.

While this process is time consuming (particularly for states with a large number of counties), the effort will result in a random sample for an entire state.

Because the researcher does not know exactly how many cases will be sampled from each stratum (the quota is a minimum), developing a sample for the entire state of Texas will require *weighting* cases in each stratum to ensure the proportion of cases from the various strata in the total population are proportionate to the German-born in the strata. After the twenty strata samples are completed, we must compute weights. These weights are assigned to each case in each stratum and are entered as a distinct variable in the computer file. Most standard data analysis software has provisions for weighting data. If the quota for Austin County is eighty-eight, but we have actually sampled ninety-two German-born residents, then the weight for each case in that county would be:

$$weight = \frac{quota\ for\ stratum}{actual\ number\ sampled\ for\ county} = \frac{88}{92} = .957$$

If each case from Austin is given this weight, then the contribution of Austin County to the sample for the entire state will be proportionate to the number of German-born residents of that stratum.[11]

DATA CODING

Once a sample has been selected, it is necessary to prepare a code book before entering data into a computer file. A code book is a description of the data—where it came from, the method of selecting cases, and a list of variables and their numeric codes. As data are often analyzed years after having been gathered, a code book is useful not only to the person who originally collected the data, but also to others. Portability is also important. A coding scheme tailored to a specific computer or software package may prove difficult to transfer. Flexibility is desirable to allow later analysis. Furthermore, it is useful if others, with different computers and software, are able to analyze the data for their own projects. We have presented an example of part of a code book in Table 2.4.

Several things can be noted. First, each variable is assigned a number. This is done to locate variables conveniently and to simplify the naming of variables for computer software. Each case is also assigned a unique identification number. This allows the researcher to identify and return to the original data source when necessary. Usually a missing value for each variable is defined for instances when information is unavailable or illegible. Normally, the same missing data value or symbol is assigned to all variables. In selecting this symbol, make sure to avoid any potentially valid values.

Coding can become very sophisticated. When coding the states of the United States, for example, several options are available. One could prepare an alphabetical list of all the states and assign numbers sequentially from 01 for Alabama to 50 for Wyoming. Another option is to group the states by region and assign the first two digits of the code to the region and the remaining digit to the state within the region. See variable 5 in Table 2.4 where New England is coded "10" and Connecticut "1," Maine "2," and so on. This alternative permits the researcher to group regions or states or both, depending on the requirements of the analysis.

Religious denominations can be coded in a similar way. One possibility is to list them alphabetically and assign sequential numbers. The Institute for Social Research developed a more useful scheme (see Table 2.5). Fifty-four denominations were grouped into four major divisions (Protestant, Roman Catholic, Jewish, and Other), some of which were divided into further subdivisions. A three-digit code for each denomination is then used to allow denominations to be grouped in a variety of ways.

The key concern is to balance coding all available information, much of which may not be used, and the time and resources available for the project.

For some purposes a coding scheme of "(1) Protestant; (2) Not Protestant" will be adequate. If in doubt, researchers should code all the available information.

The variable "occupation" causes a different problem. It is virtually impossible to anticipate, prior to coding, all the different occupations to be encountered. Fortunately, the experience of previous researchers provides us with some assistance. A researcher can select from a variety of prearranged occupational groupings, depending on his or her interests.[12] One may, for example, identify occupation as simply "(1) white collar; (2) blue collar." Another option is to employ the detailed list of occupational categories listed in the decennial census. There, occupations are first grouped into a general category such as Agricultural, Forestry, and Animal Husbandry (see Table 2.6), and then specific occupations are listed under each general category. How detailed one makes the coding scheme depends on the intent of the research. Some projects will require identification of specific occupational categories; on other occasions, groups of occupations will suffice.

Remember that, while the computer can easily collapse specific categories into more general classifications, it cannot re-create data that were never coded. Consider, for example, coding the fifty states of the United States. If the initial decision was to code states only by region, it would be impossible to do any analysis based on individual states without first returning to the original sources and entering the new information. Conversely, however, if a distinct code were assigned to each state, it would be easy to collapse groups of states into regions later.

One must also remember to select occupational categories that are appropriate for the historical period under consideration. A code book for the study of nineteenth-century Michigan need not include nuclear physicists and astronauts. But a study of twentieth-century Connecticut should not exclude blacksmiths and sailors.

These various approaches to coding occupations, however, only identify the occupation of individuals; such approaches are not applicable to research on social mobility. For mobility studies, occupational coding must also incorporate some notion of hierarchy so that the researcher can assess the extent of vertical mobility over time. Occupational coding for this type of study must, therefore, also include some sense of potential wealth, prestige, and social rank. The placement of occupations into general categories then becomes even more crucial. One coding scheme that locates two occupations in the same category would indicate no social mobility, while an alternative scheme that locates the two occupations in separate categories would yield different results. Michael Katz,[13] Theodore Hershberg and Robert Dockhorn,[14] and Patrick Horan[15] have suggested three possible coding schemes for the study of social mobility.

Table 2.4
A Partial Code Book of Biographical Data of U.S. Supreme Court Justices

Variable No.	Variable Name	Col/s.	Code No. and Name
1	ICPR Study Number	1-4	
2	Justice Identification Number	5-6	Each Supreme Court justice is assigned a unique two-digit number. These are listed in the actual code book.
3	Party Identification	7-8	01 Federalist 02 Jeffersonian Republican 03 National Republican 04 Jacksonian Democrat 05 Whig, American ("Know Nothing"), or Republican 06 Northern Democrat 07 Calhoun or States'-rights Southern Democrat 08 Liberal Southern Democrat 09 Southern Democrat or Conservative Northern Democrat 10 Liberal Republican 98 Unknown or Independent
4	Reputation as a Frequent Dissenter	9	1 Had such a reputation 2 Did not have such a reputation
5	State Appointed From	10-12	New England 101 Connecticut 103 Massachusetts 105 Rhode Island 102 Maine 104 New Hampshire 106 Vermont Middle Atlantic 111 Delaware 113 New York 114 Pennsylvania 112 New Jersey East North Central 121 Illinois 123 Michigan 125 Wisconsin 122 Indiana 124 Ohio

28

West North Central
131 Iowa
132 Kansas
133 Minnesota
134 Missouri
135 Nebraska
136 North Dakota
137 South Dakota

Solid South
140 Virginia
141 Alabama
142 Arkansas
143 Florida
144 Georgia
145 Louisiana
146 Mississippi
147 North Carolina
148 South Carolina
149 Texas

Border States
151 Kentucky
152 Maryland
153 Oklahoma
154 Tennessee
155 Washington, DC
156 West Virginia

Mountain States
161 Arizona
162 Colorado
163 Idaho
164 Montana
165 Nevada
166 New Mexico
167 Utah
168 Wyoming

Pacific States
171 California
172 Oregon
173 Washington

External States
180 Alaska
181 Hawaii

6   Ethnic Background   13-15
301 English or Welsh
302 Irish
303 Scotch (Irish)
310 Austrian
312 French
315 German
317 Dutch
318 Swiss
329 Scandinavian
331 Czech
336 Polish
337 Russian
351 Italian
352 Spanish or Portuguese
699 African
888 Other

Source: John R. Schmidhauser, compiler, "United States Supreme Court Justices Biographical Data, 1789–1958," ICPSR No. 7240, Inter-university Consortium for Political and Social Research, University of Michigan, Ann Arbor, 1972.

Table 2.5
Code Book of Religious Denominations

Division/Subdivision	Code No. and Name

Protestant, General

        100 Protestant, no denomination given

        101 Non-denominational Protestant Church

        102 Community Church (no denominational basis)

        109 Other Protestant (not listed below)

Protestant, Reformation Era

        110 Presbyterian

        111 Lutheran (except Missouri Synod)

        112 Congregational

        113 Evangelical and Reformed

        114 Reformed, Dutch Reformed, or Christian
            Reformed

        115 United Church of Christ

        116 Episcopalian, Anglican, Church of England

Protestant, Pietistic

        120 Methodist

        121 African Methodist Episcopal (AME)

        122 United Brethren or Evangelical Brethren

        123 Baptist (except Southern, Primitive, Free Will,
            Missionary, Fundamentalist or Gospel Baptist)

        124 Disciples of Christ

        125 "Christian"

        126 Mennonite Amish

        127 Church of the Brethren

Protestant, Neo-fundamentalist

        130 United Missionary or Protestant Missionary

        131 Church of God; Holiness

        132 Nazarene or Free Methodist

        133 Church of God in Christ

        134 Plymouth Brethren

        135 Pentecostal or Assembly of God

        136 Church of Christ

        137 Salvation Army

        138 Primitive, Free Will, Missionary, Fundamental-
            ist, or Gospel Baptist

Table 2.5, continued

139 Seventh Day Adventist
140 Southern Baptist
141 Missouri Synod Lutheran
149 Other Fundamentalists

Neo-traditional Christian

150 Christian Scientists
151 Spiritualists
152 Latter Day Saints, Mormons
153 Unitarian or Universalists
154 Jehovah's Witnesses
155 Quakers
156 Unity

Catholic

200 Roman Catholic

Jewish

300 Jewish

Greek Rite Catholic

700 Greek Rite Catholic

Eastern Orthodox

710 Greek Orthodox
711 Russian Orthodox
712 Rumanian Orthodox
713 Serbian Orthodox
719 Other Eastern Orthodox

Non-Christians, Other than Jewish

720 Mohammedans
721 Buddhists
722 Hindu
723 Bahai
728 Agnostics, Atheists
729 Other Non-Judeo-Christian Religions
790 Other Religions
998 None, no preference, do not know preference
999 Not available, not applicable

Source: Center for Political Studies, "American National Election Survey, 1970," ICPSR No. 7298, Inter-university Consortium for Political and Social Research, University of Michigan, Ann Arbor, 1971.

Table 2.6
Example of Occupational Categories Grouped under a General
Category in U.S. Census, 1910

General Category	Occupational Category
Agricultural, Forestry, and Animal Husbandry	

Dairy Farmers
Dairy Farm Laborers
Farmers

Farm Laborers
    Farm Laborers (home farm)
    Farm Laborers (working out)
    Turpentine Farm Laborers

Farm, Dairy Farm, Garden, Orchard, etc., Foremen
    Dairy Farm Foremen
    Farm Foremen
    Garden and Greenhouse Foremen
    Orchard, Nursery, etc., Foremen

Fishermen and Oystermen
Foresters

Gardeners, Florists, Fruit Growers, and Nurserymen
    Florists
    Fruit Growers and Nurserymen
    Gardeners
    Landscape Gardeners

Garden, Greenhouse, Orchard, and Nursery Laborers
    Cranberry Bog Laborers
    Garden Laborers
    Greenhouse Laborers
    Orchard and Nursery Laborers

Lumbermen, Raftsmen, and Woodchoppers
    Foremen and Overseers
    Lumbermen and Raftsmen
    Teamsters and Haulers
    Woodchoppers and Tie Cutters

Owners and Managers of Log and Timber Camps
Stock Herders, Drovers, and Feeders
Stock Raisers

Other Agricultural and Animal Husbandry Pursuits
    Apiarists
    Corn Shellers, Hay Balers, Grain Threshers, etc.
    Ditchers
    Poultry Raisers and Poultry Yard Laborers
    Other and Not Specified Pursuits

Source: Bureau of the Census, *Thirteenth Census of the United States Taken in the Year 1910,* 11 vols. (Washington, DC: Government Printing Office, 1914), vol. 4, 96.

Hershberg and Dockhorn devised one such scheme for the Philadelphia Social History Project. While theirs may appear to be an overly complex solution, it illustrates the variety of possible approaches. Each occupation was assigned a twenty-three-digit code that was comprised of eight subcodes. The code for a retired merchant, for example, was 00264 0205 3 260206 162 99 1 1. The first five digits identified each occupation. The following four-digit sequence consolidated all variant spellings of the same occupation; thus, "merchant" and "merchent" were assigned the code 0205. The next single-digit code identified the sector of the economy in which each occupation belonged. In this case, code 3 was for "commerce and service." Three two-digit subcodes comprised the next six-digit code: 26 stood for the industry (here, "general commercial"), 02 for subdivisions within each industry (here, "unspecified commercial"), and 06 for minor subdivisions within each major subdivision (here, "merchant"). The next three-digit code identified the function assigned to that occupation. This allowed all merchants—whether retired, or in fish marketing, or large or small—to be grouped together. This eliminated the need for recoding. The next two-digit code stood for the workplace. In this case, 99 meant "residual." The first of the next two single-digit codes identified the individual's current status in the job cycle: 1 indicated "retired." The final code identified a vertical occupational status. In this case, 1 signified that the individual occupied a "high white-collar/professional" status.[16] With this type of intricate coding scheme, one can analyze social mobility in a variety of different ways. Often, however, a far more direct coding scheme will be adequate. The application of Marxist doctrine to the study of history has also led to the encoding of occupations by class thus opening up the "vast empirical terrain [of census data] to Marxist analysis."[17]

Another important aspect of coding involves compatibility with other scholars. This permits the comparison of results and can greatly simplify the technical aspects of a presentation. For a scholar of medieval Italy, it may be simpler to indicate that occupation is coded using the method employed by David Herlihy and Christiane Klapisch- Zuber in their analysis of households in the Florentine *Catasto* than to develop some novel scheme.[18] Likewise, consider the collaborative effort of Theodore Hershberg and four other historians in compiling data on occupation and ethnicity in five nineteenth-century cities in the United States and Canada. All five agreed to use some of the same variables in their respective studies. They defined their population identically to include only males over age eighteen and then adopted the same coding scheme for age, ownership of real property, ethnicity, and occupation.[19] This cooperative approach provided an opportunity for comparison that would have been impossible if they had worked independently. They were also able to reach broader conclusions than if each studied one city in isolation.

Another difficulty associated with coding involves "drift." Frequently one or more people code data over an extended period of time. While coding most variables does not require making judgments because the selection of the appropriate numerical code is obvious, there are some variables that necessitate decisions. Consider the problem of voter registration books. In responding to the question "What is your occupation?" a voter or registrar may have incorrectly provided the place of employment instead of occupation. This discrepancy may not always be coded in the same way by different coders. It may be given a missing data code, or the occupation may be deduced from the place of employment. It is essential that coding be consistent and that the researcher design codes in such a way as to anticipate and avoid such problems.

CHECKING DATA

The quality of any research project is dependent in part on the accuracy of the data.[20] After entering data, it is necessary to eliminate as many of the errors as possible. Consider the following example. Examination of a portion of the 1950 census of the United States revealed some rather unexpected demographic characteristics. The Census Bureau reported a surprising number of widows among American teenagers. Another anomaly occurred in the size of several age cohorts of American Indians. It was later discovered that some of the data had been entered in the wrong columns of the computer cards. The coded value of one variable entered in an adjoining column meant something entirely different and consequently altered the results.[21]

There are other examples of similar problems associated with the manuscript census. Nancy Shoemaker has uncovered several other errors in the enumeration of American Indians. One difficulty involved "age heaping," the practice of identifying age by decade (30, 40, 50, etc.) rather than the exact age. She also discovered that census enumerators imposed Euro-American standards—at variance with Indian culture—for determining heads of household and the relationship of others to them.[22]

One way to clean data is to check all the responses for each variable. A software program that lists the categories coded for each variable and the number of observations coded into each category can accomplish this. This will reveal codes or characters not assigned to that variable. One can then locate the specific incorrect case with a software routine that selects and lists identification numbers of cases having invalid values.

Mathematical and logical checks are other methods of data verification. Often, numerical data have previously been totaled. One can, therefore, compare the sum of a variable in the new data file with existing totals. For example, if votes by precinct are being entered, they should tally with the published totals for the county. If they are not the same, it is necessary to determine the source of the difference and which source of data is most valid. Be advised, however, that there are other reasons besides errors in data entry for discrepancies; election results, for example, are sometimes revised after publication. Logical checks can also be useful. A data set of congressmen who served in the 1820s should not include any graduates of the University of Illinois, which was chartered in 1867. This type of inaccuracy can be identified by running the data through standard computer analysis packages or by cross-tabulating variables.

3

Simple Descriptive Statistics

When analyzing a large number of cases, historians need a way to describe their characteristics simply. This is the value of descriptive statistics. Statistics of central tendency and dispersion will satisfy the needs of most historian researchers. Statistics of central tendency—mean, median, and mode—characterize the "typical" member on a single variable. Statistics of dispersion—standard deviation, variance, and percent—indicate how typical of the group the typical member is by measuring the group's homogeneity.

Specific statistics were developed within a scientific context and are defined mathematically. Confusion arises with attempts to interpret the calculations in words or provide them with some contextual meaning. Words like "average," "dispersion," and "normal" have their own history during which they have acquired a variety of meanings and usages. Statisticians, meanwhile, have given technical meanings to a number of these ordinary words. Historians must be alert to these special statistical meanings. One must also exercise care for technical usage when presenting results.

It is important to know what statistics to use in a particular context, what they mean in that context, and how to describe results clearly in order not to mislead others. For these reasons, the focus here is on the development and meaning of statistics and not just on formulas and calculations.

SAMPLE AND POPULATION

Before introducing measures of central tendency and dispersion, some comments on the concepts of *sample* and *population* are necessary. Inferential statistics, analysis of variance, and other topics discussed in subsequent chapters involve estimating or making inferences about some unknown parameter (a characteristic of a population) from a sample (a set of observations). We may, for example, toss a coin ten times to see if it is "fair," that is, if in the long run it has a tendency to come up heads and tails an equal number of times.

The unknown *population parameter* in this case is a property of the coin when tossed: its probability of coming up heads. The *sample statistic*, or estimate of the population parameter, is the proportion of heads observed in the ten tosses. The observations are a sample in the sense that they are only some of many possible observations that could have been made. The parameter being determined—whether or not the chance of heads is 1/2— is the population parameter. Population refers to all possible observations of which the sample is a subset.

Most of us think of a population in terms of people. The population of the Parish of Killeshandra, County Cavan, Ireland, in 1891, for example, was the sum total of the people living there at that time. A random sample of that population would be a group of people selected by certain procedures from the census records. The population parameter of interest might be the percentage of the population five years of age and older who were literate. The sample statistic that estimates the population parameter is the percentage of those in the sample five years of age or older who were literate. This use of the terms "sample" and "population" fits the statistician's meaning as well as their ordinary meanings. Here, the sample statistic is used to estimate a population parameter that one could also determine directly.

Suppose, however, that literacy rates among male and female residents of Killeshandra five years of age and older interest us. Of the 2,767 males, 82.15 percent were literate; of the 2,584 females, 85.28 percent were literate. In one sense, these are population parameters for that place and time. But we may find it useful to look at the problem differently. Our question might be whether or not males and females had the same chance of being literate. Now we consider the 5,351 persons five years of age and older as consisting of two samples. Achieving literacy is seen as a random process analogous to a coin toss with a coin heavily biased toward literacy. Each person had a certain chance of becoming literate; some succeeded, some did not. The question is whether males had the same chance as females, that is, whether the population parameter for males and females was the same. Just as tossing a coin ten times and then another ten times might result in a different proportion of heads each time, so too a similar process might result in slightly different male and female literacy rates even though each individual had the same chance for literacy. In this case, the problem is to use the sample information to decide whether or not the two population parameters are the same. We will return in subsequent chapters to this problem of making inferences to populations from sample information.[1]

Statisticians use Greek letters to refer to population parameters, which are usually not directly measured or calculated, and Latin letters to refer to sample estimates, which one calculates from observed data.

STATISTICS OF CENTRAL TENDENCY

There are three statistics of central tendency: the *mode*, the *median*, and the *mean*.

The Mode

J. M. Thompson, in his book *The French Revolution*, presents a table similar to our Table 3.1 and then comments that "it needed no statistician to show that the victims of the Tribunal, in the summer of '94, were no longer common enemies, whether *aristos*, or treacherous generals, or dishonest officials, but ordinary citizens of the professional and working classes."[2]

The mode in Table 3.1 is the category or categories (a classification can be bi-modal, tri-modal, or multi-modal) that occur most often. The mode for each month is shown in italics in Table 3.1. Notice that we used verbal labels and not numbers to identify the various categories in this table. If we used numbers to identify categories, they would serve only as names or

Table 3.1
The Terror of 1794: Victims by Social Class and Month

Period	Clergy	Nobles	Army	Officials	Middle Class	Lower Class	N
April	18	*45*	25	43	42	30	203
May	21	41	34	49	*83*	74	302
June	43	57	25	86	143	*245*	599
July	21	0	40	27	132	*166*	386
Total	103	143	124	205	400	515	1490

Source: J.M.Thompson, *The French Revolution* (New York: Oxford University Press, 1945), 538.

tags to differentiate categories.

Thompson characterizes all the Tribunal victims in a particular month by the most "typical" victim, that is, the most numerous group. This is done to present a complex notion simply. According to Thompson, the victims of the Terror shifted from the upper to the lower classes. The fifty-seven nobles guillotined in June 1794 might well have preferred that all the victims be from among the lower classes. Characterizing the most frequent category minimizes the error when we characterize a group by a single characteristic. Consider the 599 victims killed in June. By saying they were "ordinary citizens," Thompson is correct 388 times (143 + 245 = 388) and incorrect 211 times (43 + 57 + 25 + 86 = 211). If he had characterized the June victims as upperclass, he would have been wrong more often: 388 instead of 211 times. The mode characterizes a group by the most frequent category and, by doing so, misrepresents the fewest cases.

Yet even a simple statistic like the mode can lead to problems. Notice that Thompson grouped (collapsed) several of his original categories together in his verbal description to simplify his conclusion. If we wanted to make a different point about the victims, could we alter the figures? Another scholar might collapse the categories differently and conclude that the modal victim in each month was not a "common enemy," but rather a friend of the Revolution. Differing interpretations of the mode are possible because one can collapse (or combine) categories in various ways.

The solution is to present the data in tabular form and allow the reader to analyze them. How one collapses the categories needs to be identified. The table should illustrate all the results, using the text to highlight certain central points.

The Median

If the cases at hand can be ordered (as they can with ordinal and interval variables), then the middle case—*the median*—is the most typical. As with the mode, this corresponds with an intuitive notion of "typical" or "representative." The median, thus defined, divides a group into two halves of equal size. Consider Table 3.2, derived from Gearóid Ó'Tuathaigh's book *Ireland before the Famine, 1798–1848*. Here, the author grouped the data into four ordinal categories. As the data are percentaged, determining the median is simple. The first step is to calculate the *cumulative percentage* of each category. This is the percentage of cases in a category added to the percentages of cases in all the categories "above." Thus, the cumulative percentages for Irish landholdings in 1841 are (from the top of the

Table 3.2
Irish Landholdings by Size and Year, 1841–1851

Size of Holding	1841		1851	
	Number	Percent	Number	Percent
1–5 Acres	310,436	44.9	88,083	15.5
5⁺–15 Acres	252,799	36.6	191,854	33.6
15⁺–30 Acres	79,342	11.5	141,311	24.8
Above 30 Acres	48,625	7.0	149,090	26.1
Total	691,202	100.0	570,338	100.0

Source: Gearóid Ó' Tuathaigh, *Ireland before the Famine, 1798–1848* (Dublin: Gill and Macmillan, 1972), 206.

table to the bottom) 44.9, 81.5 (44.9 + 36.6), 93.0 (44.9 + 36.6 + 11.5), and 100.0 (44.9 + 36.6 + 11.5 + 7.0). For 1851, the cumulative percentages are 15.5, 49.1, 73.9, and 100.0. The category in which the cumulative percentage first exceeds 50.0 percent contains the median. In 1841 the median is 5⁺–15 acres; in 1851 it is 15⁺–30 acres. The size of the holdings increased between 1841 and 1851. In each instance, half the holdings were larger than the median (or the same size) and half the holdings were smaller (or the same size).

Now let us consider the median for a ranked-ordinal variable: the duration of British cabinets between December 1868 and December 1905 (see Table 3.3).[3] To determine the median duration of a cabinet, it makes no sense to determine the middle case from the data in their present form. Unless we reorder the data, we will get the middle cabinet in a chronological sequence, not in duration. Thus, we must reorganize the cabinets either from longest to shortest or shortest to longest (see Table 3.4).

Balfour's cabinet is in the middle; and therefore, 41 is the median or middle duration. There were five cabinets of shorter duration and five of longer duration. The median has made use of the ordinal aspect of the reorganized list. Cabinet durations, however, also have distance information; that is, we know how much longer one cabinet lasted than another. Take the absolute distance (ignoring the sign of the difference) between the median (41 months) and each individual duration, and then determine their sum.

$$\text{sum of absolute distances} = \Sigma |x_i - \text{median}|$$

where x_i is the ith individual duration (here i varies from 1 to 11)

median is the median of the set of n durations

Σ means add them all up

$|x_i - \text{median}|$ indicates the absolute value of the x_i - median difference

For example, the first cabinet duration is six months, so $x_1 = 6$. The sum of the absolute differences here is:

$$|6 - 41| + |8 - 41| + |15 - 41| + |19 - 41| + |28 - 41| + |41 - 41|$$
$$+ |62 - 41| + |62 - 41| + |72 - 41| + |74 - 41| + |85 - 41| = 279.$$

The total absolute difference between all the durations and the median amounts to 279 months. This is the minimum possible absolute distance any number can have from the set of durations. Any number other than the median would produce a greater absolute difference. Consequently, one can interpret the median here both as the middle case and as the single value closest to all the other values taken together.

Now let us consider an even-numbered list of cabinets. (We will drop the last, Lord Salisbury's Third, for convenience.) With an even number of cases of a ranked-order variable, there is no single middle value. What then is the median? Recall that the median minimizes the total sum of the abso-

Table 3.3
Duration of British Cabinets in Months, December 1868–December 1905

Cabinet	Date Formed	Months
Gladstone's First	December 1868	62
Disraeli's Second	February 1874	74
Gladstone's Second	April 1880	62
Lord Salisbury's First	June 1885	8
Gladstone's Third	February 1886	6
Lord Salisbury's Second	August 1886	72
Gladstone's Fourth	August 1892	19
Lord Rosebery's	March 1894	15
Lord Salisbury's Third	June 1895	85
Balfour's	July 1902	41
Campbell-Bannerman's	December 1905	28

Source: Walter L. Arnstein, *Britain Yesterday and Today: 1830 to the Present*, 4th ed. (Lexington, MA: D. C. Heath, 1983), 417–418.

Table 3.4
Ranked Duration of British Cabinets, December 1868–December 1905

Cabinet	Date Formed	Months
Gladstone's Third	February 1886	6
Lord Salisbury's First	June 1885	8
Lord Rosebery's	March 1894	15
Gladstone's Fourth	August 1892	19
Campbell-Bannerman's	December 1905	28
Balfour's	July 1902	41
Gladstone's First	December 1868	62
Gladstone's Second	April 1880	62
Lord Salisbury's Second	August 1886	72
Disraeli's Second	February 1874	74
Lord Salisbury's Third	June 1895	85

Source: See Table 3.3.

lute differences between itself and all the other values. The two middle cases, then, are the median. Here, the two middle cases are Campbell-Bannerman's cabinet (28 months) and Balfour's cabinet (41 months). The total absolute difference for 28 or 41 or for any number in between—say, 33.33—is the same.

$$|6 - 28| + |8 - 28| + |15 - 28| + |19 - 28| + |28 - 28| + |41 - 28|$$
$$+ |62 - 28| + |62 - 28| + |72 - 28| + |74 - 28| = 235$$

$$|6 - 41| + |8 - 41| + |15 - 41| + |19 - 41| + |28 - 41| + |41 - 41|$$
$$+ |62 - 41| + |62 - 41| + |72 - 41| + |74 - 41| = 235$$

$$|6 - 33.33| + |8 - 33.33| + |15 - 33.33| + |19 - 33.33| + |28 - 33.33|$$
$$+ |41 - 33.33| + |62 - 33.33| + |62 - 33.33| + |72 - 33.33| +$$
$$|74 - 33.33| = 235$$

This is the problem with using the median of an even number of cases. Whether one defines the median as the middle case in an ordered list or as the value that minimizes the sum of the absolute differences between itself and all other values, there is no single unique median when the cases are ranked individually (as opposed to grouped). This makes the median less useful for inferential statistics, as it has no unique value.[4]

For descriptive purposes, however, the median does have advantages.

First, it fits our intuitive notion of "typical" for ordered data, in that it is both the center and the single value "closest" to all the other values taken together. Second, it is not affected (as is the mean) by extreme values.

There are a number of possibilities for resolving the problems associated with the median.[5] We suggest two. First, report both of the two middle values for an even number of cases: the median duration in our example was between 28 and 41 months. Alternatively, compute the half-way point between the two middle cases and report it. In this case, the median duration was 34.5 [(28 + 41)/2] months.

The Mean

The word "*mean*," with its origins in Old English and Gothic, refers to middle, ordinary, or average. It still retains traces of its derivation in phrases such as "He is no mean scholar"—indicating that he is no ordinary scholar.

By the eighteenth century, astronomers and navigators used the word "mean" for their own purposes. When the same observer was employing the same instruments at the same time under similar conditions and was recording repeated observations of the same thing, the results would typically vary. People assumed that these observations contained slight errors due to differences in conditions, frailties of the observer, and limitations of the instruments. How, then, could one determine the correct value? An ad hoc method was adopted to average the observations by calculating their arithmetic mean. The mean was defined as the sum of all the observations divided by the number of observations. Here, it is useful to introduce some mathematical notations. Thus, if x_i was the ith observation and n was the number of observations, then the sample mean—$\bar{x}$—of the observations would be:

$$\bar{x} = \sum x_i / n$$

The population mean would be:

$$\mu = \sum x_i / n$$

where μ is the Greek letter mu.

At this point, the mean was simply a rule of thumb; it lacked a clear interpretation or mathematical justification. Given the error inherent even in careful observations,[6] the mean of several observations was thought to approximate the true value better than one observation.

In the mid-eighteenth century, Thomas Simpson, professor at the Royal Military Academy at Woolwich, England, attempted to justify this method formally. He hypothesized that, if one assumed the errors of measurement to be random (not biased by, say, a poor telescope lens) and each observation to be reasonably close to all the others (i.e., there were no wildly divergent ones), then the *probability of error* was much less with the average of several than with a single observation.[7] This thinking was based on the idea that there was some assumed "true" state of affairs with numerous attempts being made to observe it. The observations consisted of two components: the true state of affairs and an error due to human measurement.

The purpose here was twofold. First, theories such as Newton's celestial mechanics could only be tested and explored with accurate observations. Second, practical problems such as navigation and cartography required accuracy. From the beginning, then, concern with the mean involved error in its probability and magnitude. The problem was to estimate some true value in such a way as to minimize the error.

The theoretical and practical importance of this problem attracted the attention of mathematicians. There were two approaches. The first was to estimate the "true" value from a set of observations in the most *accurate* way by using the method of *least squares*. The second approach concerned the probability that an estimate would have a given degree of error; this involved probability theory. By 1827, the two approaches were synthesized.

Least Squares

As they developed in postmedieval Europe, the Western sciences of astronomy, navigation, and cartography involved making many observations of many things; each observation contained error and was related through theory (e.g., geometry) to other observations. Consider the Ordnance Survey of the British Isles for 1858. There were 920 geographical points whose exact location was observed (with some error in each). Each of these could be related to the others by triangulation. Eventually, there were 1,554 equations containing the 920 estimates. Each of the estimates, however, contained some degree of error, and the results of the triangulation were not exact.[8]

The solution was the method of least squares published in 1805 by Adrien Marie Legendre (1752–1833). He proposed that the best estimate of the "true" values would be those that minimized the sum of squares, that is, the sum of squared errors. As Legendre suggests, " 'The method of least squares reveals, in a manner of speaking, the center around which the results of observations arrange themselves, so that the deviations from that center are as small as possible.' " [9]

There were several benefits of this method. First, it was possible to calculate even with many observations. Second, if there was a perfect fit, the method would find it. Third, the arithmetic mean was the solution in the special case where there were many observations of one unknown. Through the method of least squares, the mean gets a different meaning. It is the single value that minimizes the sum of squared errors for a set of observations. It no longer is an ad hoc technique, but part of a solution to a more general problem.

Recall the data on the British cabinet duration presented in Table 3.4. We have reproduced this order in Table 3.5, along with the calculation of

Table 3.5
Ranked Duration of British Cabinets, December 1868–
December 1905 with Calculations of Error and Squared Error

Cabinet	Months x_i	Error $(x_i - \mu_x)$	Squared Error $(x_i - \mu_x)^2$
Gladstone's Third	6	$(6 - 42.91) = -36.91$	$-36.91^2 = 1362.35$
Lord Salisbury's First	8	$(8 - 42.91) = -34.91$	$-34.91^2 = 1218.71$
Lord Rosebery's	15	$(15 - 42.91) = -27.91$	$-27.91^2 = 778.97$
Gladstone's Fourth	19	$(19 - 42.91) = -23.91$	$-23.91^2 = 571.69$
Campbell-Bannerman's	28	$(28 - 42.91) = -14.91$	$-14.91^2 = 222.31$
Balfour's	41	$(41 - 42.91) = -1.91$	$-1.91^2 = 3.65$
Gladstone's First	62	$(62 - 42.91) = 19.09$	$19.09^2 = 364.43$
Gladstone's Second	62	$(62 - 42.91) = 19.09$	$19.09^2 = 364.43$
Lord Salisbury's Second	72	$(72 - 42.91) = 29.09$	$29.09^2 = 846.23$
Disraeli's Second	74	$(74 - 42.91) = 31.09$	$31.09^2 = 966.59$
Lord Salisbury's Third	85	$(85 - 42.91) = 42.09$	$42.09^2 = 1771.57$
Total	472		8470.93

Note: Mean $= \mu_x = (\Sigma x_i) / n = 472 / 11 = 42.91$;

$$\Sigma (x_i - \mu_x)^2 = 8470.93$$

Source: Authors' calculation from Table 3.4.

the mean, the error, and the sum of squares, or the sum of the squared error. The total sum of squares is 8,470.93. Replacing the mean (μ or $\bar{x}$) in the calculations with any other value will result in a larger sum of squares.

Probability of Error

There are other reasons for using the mean. Mathematicians have studied the probability of making an error of a certain amount. The value used to estimate the "true" value should have the least probability of being in error. This approach focused on the distribution of errors.

In 1809, Carl Friedrich Gauss (1777–1855) demonstrated that the arithmetic mean was "the most probable value of a single unknown observed with equal care several times under the same circumstances"[10] when the error terms were distributed normally. By 1810, Pierre Simon Laplace (1749–1827) presented the Central Limit Theorem: "any sum or mean . . . will, if the number of terms is large, be approximately normally distributed."[11]

To understand this, consider a set of observations of the same thing taken under similar circumstances. Each result may be slightly different because of the error inherent in human observation. Common and even mathematical sense suggested that to combine observations with error would compound the error. That, in fact, was the view of Leonhard Euler (1707–1783).[12] What the work on probability theory showed, however, was the opposite. Take a set of several observations of the same thing taken on different days or by different observers. If the individual observations are plotted, they will be scattered: some will be clustered together; others will diverge from this central cluster. Probability theory demonstrates that, if the means for each set of observations were plotted, they too would show a scatter with some clustering together and others diverging. If the plots of the individual observations and the means taken from them were compared, the plot of the means would be much less scattered and much more clustered near some central "true" value. In practice, as well as in theory, the mean reduces rather than compounds error. It is a far better estimate of the "true" value than taking a single observation.

The mean began as an ad hoc way to represent a number of observations. It had little of the mode's or median's intuitive meaning. Later, however, Laplace was able to refer to the mean as " 'most advantageous' "[13] because it was most accurate "in two senses: smallest expected error and most likely to be near the quantity being estimated."[14] The mean is different from the mode and the median; both of them try to capture a simple, intuitive meaning of "typical." The mean's justification comes not because of its intuitive notion, but because it fits into a broader pattern of statistical reasoning. How can one use and interpret the mean as a summary statistic? Using the earlier example of cabinet duration, one would simply report that the mean (or average) cabinet duration during the period December 1868–December 1905 was 42.91 months. The advantage of the mean over the median is that the former relates to the literature on error. Some cabinet durations are close to the mean; others are quite far away. Often, historians want to explain why some cabinets endured longer than others. The mean and squared error will provide a basis for answering that type of question.

Recall, however, that while the mean is useful, it can also be misleading. Consider Table 3.6 adapted from Karl Marx's discussion of the concentration of wealth in *Capital*. We have supplemented his original table by calculating the mean for each group as well as the mean for the entire group. The overall mean of £694.19 is misleading in that it is not typical of the entire group or any single category. The typical person—the median or modal person—is in the group reporting a mean profit of £317.16. That group represents more than 90 percent of the people. The large profits of a few inflate the overall mean to more than twice the amount of the median and mode. The mean can mislead the reader into thinking that the average person was getting twice the profit than was actually the case.

We have seen that the mean is vulnerable to extreme values. There are several ways to minimize this problem. The first strategy is to discard the

Table 3.6
Mean Derived from Marx Report on Distribution of Income from Profits (in Pounds), Year Ending April 5, 1865

Total Income from Profits (£)	Number of People	Mean (£)
105,435,738	332,431	317.16
64,554,297	24,265	2,660.39
42,535,576	4,021	10,578.36
27,555,313	973	28,319.95
11,077,238	107	103,525.58
251,158,162	361,797	694.19

Note: Mean = $\bar{x}$ = (251,158,162 / 361,797) = £694.19

Source: Adapted from Karl Marx, *Capital: A Critique of Political Economy*, 3 vols. (New York: International Publishers, 1967), vol. 1, 650.

extreme values. If one is interested in examining income of residents of a village, for example, one can separate exceptionally wealthy villagers from the others. This can be done in two ways: by reporting a mean for "small farmers" as well as a separate mean for "large landowners"; or by noting that one case, representing a particularly wealthy person, was discarded and the mean refers to all but that one exceptional case. A second strategy is to use the median for descriptive purposes. Extreme values do not influence the median. Either of these strategies can resolve the problem of extreme values.

Other methods are the *trimean* and *interquartile* means. Basically, these involve either excluding the lower and upper quarters of the data and calculating the mean from the middle half, or calculating a mean in which the data from the middle third of the range are weighted more heavily than the extreme thirds.[15]

MEASURES OF DISPERSION

Commonly employed measures of dispersion are *standard deviation, variance,* and *percentage,* along with *quartiles, percentiles, histograms,* and *bar charts.*

Standard Deviation

We have already learned that the mean is associated with the probability of error. During the mid-nineteenth century, researchers needed to describe not only the central tendency or "typicalness" of a set of observations, but also their homogeneity. In 1893, Englishman Karl Pearson (1857–1936) proposed the standard deviation.

The standard deviation is based on the sum of squares. The problem with the sum of squares as a measure of homogeneity for a set of observations was that it was in squared units (squared months, in the case of cabinet duration) and this made little intuitive sense. Another, more serious problem was that the sum of squares was a function of not only the homogeneity of a set of observations (i.e., the more homogeneous the group, the less the sum of squared error), but also of the number of observations. The more observations, the larger the sum of squares. This, however, could be due to either the error in the observations or the number of observations, or both. Pearson's standard deviation averaged the squared deviations and then calculated their square root, yielding the average error or roughly (but not quite) the amount by which the average observation differed from the mean.

The more the average case differed from the mean, the more heterogeneous the observations were. The less the average case differed from the mean, the more homogeneous the observations were. In notation, the population standard deviation is:

$$\sigma_x = \sqrt{\frac{\Sigma(x_i - \mu_x)^2}{N}}$$

where σ_x (the Greek letter "sigma") is the population standard deviation of the variable x

x_i is the ith observation of the variable x
μ_x is the population mean of the variable x
N is the number of cases in the population
the term $\Sigma(x_i - \mu_x)^2$ is the sum of squares

The sample standard deviation is:

$$S_x = \sqrt{\frac{\Sigma(x_i - \bar{x})^2}{(n-1)}}$$

where S_x is the sample standard deviation of the variable x,
$\bar{x}$ is the mean of x
n is the number of observations

In the case of the cabinet duration (N = 11), the population standard deviation is:

$$\sigma_x = \sqrt{\frac{\Sigma(x_i - \mu_x)^2}{N}}$$

$$= \sqrt{\frac{8470.93}{11}}$$

$$= 27.75$$

Roughly, the average case is 28 months off the mean of 43.

The Variance

In 1918, Sir Ronald A. Fisher introduced the term *variance*, which he defined as the average squared error.[16] The population variance of the variable x is:

$$\sigma_x^{\,2} = \Sigma(x_i - \mu_x)^2 / N$$

where $\sigma_x^{\,2}$ is the variance of the variable x
$\Sigma(x_i - \mu_x)^2$ is the sum of squares
N is the number of cases

The sample variance is:

$$S_x^{\,2} = \frac{\Sigma(x_i - \overline{x})^2}{(n-1)}$$

where $S_x^{\,2}$ is the sample variance
$\overline{x}$ is the sample mean
n is the number of observations in the sample

In the example of cabinet duration, the population variance is:

$$\sigma_x^{\,2} = 8,470.93 / 11 = 770.085$$

The variance is simply the squared standard deviation:

$$\sigma_x^{\,2} = (\sigma_x)^2$$
$$S_x^{\,2} = (S_x)^2$$

For describing data, the variance is of little value to historians, for whom the standard deviation has a more intuitive interpretation. The variance does, however, prove useful in statistical inference.

Quartiles and Percentiles, Histograms, and Bar Charts

Other ways exist for examining the dispersion of interval variables.

Between 1875 and 1885, Francis Galton (1822–1911) experimented with *percentiles* and *quartiles* to reveal the properties of a dispersion of cases.[17] If there are a large number of observations, place them in ascending (or descending) order. Next, divide that ordered array into four groups, each with an equal number of observations (quartiles) or 100 such groups (percentiles). The frequency of cases (or the proportions in each group) reveals how the variable is distributed. A modern version of this would be a *bar graph* or *histogram*. Researchers use these techniques frequently in psychology, marketing, education, and economics. There are several computer programs that will convert any raw data into a bar chart.

Examination of the historical development of histograms and bar graphs will help us appreciate them better. By the first half of the nineteenth century, probability distributions and their relationship to the accuracy and probability associated with the mean were well known. The theoretical development of this, however, depended on the assumption that "errors" were random. For the original intent—namely, the determination of specific values from sets of observations taken under closely similar circumstances— this assumption was satisfactory. The question was, To what extent did social and biological phenomena lend themselves to exploration with these techniques?

In 1846, a Belgian, Adolphe Quetelet (1796–1874), published his famous *Lettres à S.A.R. Le Duc Régnant de Saxe-Cobourg et Gotha sur la Théorie des Probabilités appliquée aux sciences morales et politiques*.[18] These letters were tutorials on probability. One of Quetelet's tables referred to the chest measurements of 5,738 Scottish soldiers. He was interested in the fit of that distribution to the binomial distribution (see Chapter 4). As Table 3.7 illustrates, the fit was very close. Chest measurements centered on a certain value; the farther a measurement was from that value, the less frequently it was observed—just as would be the case with random "error." Other researchers also demonstrated that social and natural phenomena fit the assumptions of probability theory and could be examined and tested with statistical procedures.

In England, Galton took this approach in another direction. In work done between 1869 and 1875, he *assumed* phenomena that were not directly measurable would also fit certain probability distributions. If cases could be ranked, a normal distribution could be assumed and more precise measurement could be assigned; this was the reverse of what Quetelet did.[19] One result was a more precise measurement of intelligence. Assume, for example, that one has devised a test to rank a group of people on intelligence. If intelligence is distributed normally, then one can reorganize the group to fit the normal curve. Most cases cluster about the center

Table 3.7
Distribution of Chest Circumferences of 5,738 Scottish Militia Men, after Quetelet's *Lettres sur la Théorie de Probabilités*

Chest Circumference in Inches	Number	Percent	Expected from Binomial Distribution (Percent)
33	3	.05	.07
34	18	.31	.29
35	81	1.41	1.10
36	185	3.22	3.23
37	420	7.32	7.32
38	749	13.05	13.33
39	1073	18.70	18.38
40	1079	18.80	19.87
41	934	16.28	16.75
42	658	11.47	10.96
43	370	6.45	5.60
44	92	1.60	2.21
45	50	.87	.69
46	21	.37	.16
47	4	.07	.03
48	1	.02	.01
Total	5738	99.99	100.00

Source: Adapted from reprint in Stephen M. Stigler, *The History of Statistics: The Measurement of Uncertainty before 1900* (Cambridge, MA: Belknap Press of Harvard University, 1986), 207. See also note 18. The table presents the data percentaged instead of Quetelet's per 1,000.

(the mean) and fewer at a distance from the center. Now one can remeasure intelligence in terms of distance from the center of the curve. This is an interval-level measurement.[20]

The visual display of data has a purpose connected to a wider theoretical enterprise. However, much modern usage of histograms do not have this purpose: the histograms merely serve as illustrations of what could in fact be better presented in a table. Frequently, they do not add anything and instead proliferate what Edward Tufte calls "chartjunk."[21]

Consider Figures 3.1 and 3.2, based on data in Robert Fogel and Stanley Engerman's *Time on the Cross*. It is very difficult to determine by visual inspection the relative lengths of the bars. There are, in fact, elements of an optical illusion. Given two bars of the same length, the one next to a longer bar appears slightly shorter while the one next to a shorter bar appears slightly longer. In each figure the bars for U.S. Slave, Holland, and France are the same length. In Figure 3.1, however, U.S. Slave appears longer than Holland; while in Figure 3.2, U.S. Slave appears shorter than Holland. Table 3.8 presents the same information in tabular form. Notice how easy it is to determine differences between slave life expectancy and that for other groups. Simple subtraction is easier than trying to judge differences in bar lengths.

Charts can indeed be useful when they simplify complex information or graphically illustrate relationships. Consider the chart showing the strength of Napoleon's armies during his Russian campaign (see Figure 3.3). The changing width of the line dramatically conveys the progressive losses suffered at various stages of the campaign. Historians need to use caution when they work with charts, however. If one can convey the material clearly with a table, a chart is unnecessary. If material is difficult to interpret in tabular form, then a chart may be appropriate.

Table 3.8
Life Expectancy at Birth for U.S. Slaves and Various Free Populations, 1830–1920

Population	Life Expectancy at Birth
U.S. Slave, 1850	36
U.S. White, 1850	40
England and Wales, 1838–1854	40
Holland, 1850–1859	36
France, 1854–1858	36
Italy, 1885	35
Austria, 1875	31
Chile, 1920	31
Manchester, England, 1850	24
New York, Boston, Philadelphia, 1830	24

Source: Adapted from Robert William Fogel and Stanley L. Engerman, *Time on the Cross: The Economics of American Negro Slavery* (Boston: Little, Brown, 1974), 125.

Figure 3.1
Bar Chart of Life Expectancy at Birth for U.S. Slaves and Various Free Populations, 1830–1920

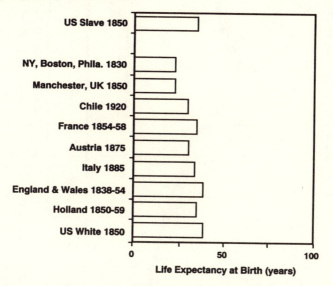

Life Expectancy at Birth (years)

Figure 3.2
Redrawn Bar Chart of Life Expectancy at Birth for U.S. Slaves and Various Free Populations, 1830–1920

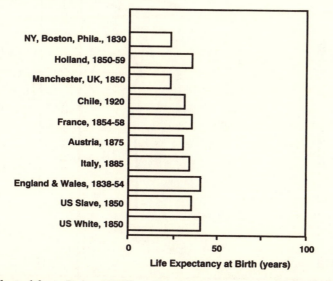

Life Expectancy at Birth (years)

Source: Adapted from Robert William Fogel and Stanley L. Engerman, *Time on the Cross: The Economics of American Negro Slavery* (Boston: Little, Brown, 1974), 125.

Figure 3.3
Figurative Chart of Napoleon's Campaign against Russia

Legend: This map shows the successive losses of men in the French army during the 1812/1813 Russian campaign. The width of the line is proportional to the size of the French army. The lighter line illustrates the advance into Russia; the dark line portrays the French retreat. Temperatures at various times during the retreat are included in the graph at the bottom.

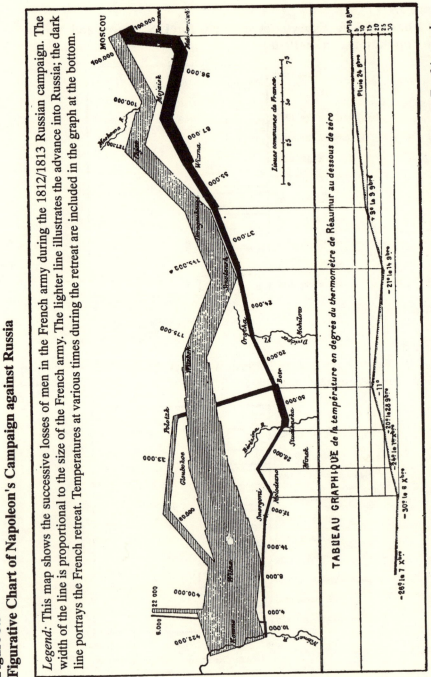

Source: Drawn by M. Minard and published in Etienne Jules Marey, *La Méthode Graphique dans les Sciences Expérimentales et Principalement en Physiologie et en Medecine* (Paris: G. Masson, 1878), 72.

Percentage

Percentage is another way to describe the dispersion of categorical data. To calculate percentage, take the number of cases (the frequency) in a category and divide it by the total number of cases; then, multiply that result by 100. We used this procedure in Table 3.9. Notice that the table reveals the pattern of victims more clearly than the original data presented in Table 3.1. The proportion of victims from among the "common enemies" (clergy, nobles, army, and officials) declined over time, and the proportion from the middle and lower classes increased.

Unfortunately, even such a simple device as a percentage can present problems. Notice that we calculated the percentage of victims from each social class by month. We could also have calculated it by social class (see Table 3.10).

The two tables use the same data yet they provide quite different portrayals of the pattern of executions. From the first table we might conclude that the lower- and middle-class victims rose from 35.5 percent to 77.2 percent of the monthly victims between April and July. From the second table we might conclude that the proportions of clergy, army, and officials were roughly the same for each month. The first looks at the class proportions of each month's victims. Notice that the numbers of the two lowest classes rose during the summer. The second looks at the proportions of each class's victims executed in a given month. Notice that for three of the four upper classes there were as many victims in the later months as the earlier ones. Both generalizations are correct. The problem comes when one calculates the percentages one way, but reaches conclusions the other.

Table 3.9
Illustrating Row Percentages: The Terror of 1794, Victims in Each Social Class as Calculated by Month

Period	Clergy	Nobles	Army	Officials	Middle Class	Lower Class	Total	(N)
April	8.8	22.2	12.3	21.2	20.7	14.8	100.0	(203)
May	6.9	13.6	11.3	16.2	27.5	24.5	100.0	(302)
June	7.2	9.5	4.2	14.3	23.9	40.9	100.0	(599)
July	5.4	0.0	10.4	7.0	34.2	43.0	100.0	(386)

Source: Authors' calculations from data in Table 3.1.

Table 3.10
Illustrating Column Percentages: The Terror of 1794, Victims in Each Month as Calculated by Social Class

Period	Clergy	Nobles	Army	Officials	Middle Class	Lower Class
April	17.5	31.4	20.2	21.0	10.5	5.8
May	20.4	28.7	27.4	23.9	20.8	14.4
June	41.7	39.9	20.2	41.9	35.7	47.6
July	20.4	0.0	32.2	13.2	33.0	32.2
Total	100.0	100.0	100.0	100.0	100.0	100.0
(N)	(103)	(143)	(124)	(205)	(400)	(515)

Source: Authors' calculations from data in Table 3.1

Thompson does this in *The French Revolution*. He calculates percents by months, but then concludes with the generalization that the Terror was increasingly victimizing the "ordinary citizens."

In fact, the Tribunal never lessened its attacks on the upper classes, except for the nobles in July; as many clergy, army members, and officials were victims in July as were in April. While continuing to find victims among the upper classes, the Tribunal simply added more victims from the middle and lower classes.

A WORD OF ADVICE

Simple descriptive statistics are more complicated than they seem. The problem takes two forms: one is understanding how they fit into a wider statistical theory, and the other is interpreting them correctly. One reaction might be to avoid statistics all together. While this might be appropriate in certain circumstances, as a general practice it is shortsighted. A better solution is to devote more time to get familiar with the background of statistical techniques and interpretations.

What advice do we offer an historian contemplating some statistical description? It is best to consider the subject. Statistical presentations should make sense, and there should be no unresolved doubts. Care, consideration, and contemplation are necessary. It is a mistake to treat a statistical presentation as something independent—a display or an embellishment. It should either be an integral part of the main agrument or else be abandoned.

4

Inferential Statistics:
The Basics of Probability, Distributions, Significance Testing, and Confidence Intervals

Many social scientists and some historians consider themselves "cookbook" users of statistics. They want to calculate a correlation, average, or some other statistic, but they do not trouble themselves with the issues of probability or inference. Typically, users of "cookbook" statistics focus on the size of the statistic or report a big or small difference between two groups. This is often a mistake. The question is not how strong a relationship is or how different two groups are, but how likely it is to observe something simply by chance. That is the subject of inferential statistics. It is the means by which we evaluate descriptive statistics and place them in context. An understanding of the basics of probability, distributions, significance testing, and confidence intervals is essential to the proper use and interpretation of descriptive statistics.

Suppose we toss a coin four times with these results: heads, tails, heads, heads (HTHH). We have observed heads come up 75 percent of the time. Can we conclude that the coin is biased toward heads? It is possible, of course, that a particular coin has been minted in such a way that, when it is properly tossed, heads comes up more than tails. Another possible explanation is chance. Here we might assume two things. First, the chances of a coin coming up heads are the same as its chances of coming up tails. Second, the tosses are independent of each other; that is, what happens in one toss has nothing to do with what happens in another toss. These assumptions describe a chance model for the coin toss.

Hypotheses are statements about parameters of the assumed chance model. These hypotheses are of two sorts: the null hypothesis and an alternative. The *null hypothesis* usually states that the parameter is a certain value. In most social science and history applications, the null hypothesis states that there is no difference or no relationship. The *alternative hypothesis* states that, first, the parameter is not that value or, second, it is a greater value or, third, it is a lesser value. The alternative hypothesis specifies a range of values for the parameter of the chance process and can take one of three forms.

In this context, the null hypothesis might be that the probability of heads, P(H), in a single toss is the same as the probability of tails, P(T); that is, P(H) - P(T) = ½ - ½ = 0. The alternative hypothesis might be:

$$(1)\ P(H) \neq P(T) \text{ or } P(H) - P(T) \neq 0$$
$$(2)\ P(H) < P(T) \text{ or } P(H) - P(T) < 0$$
$$(3)\ P(H) > P(T) \text{ or } P(H) - P(T) > 0$$

One task of inferential statistics is to compare observed data with what we would expect if the null hypothesis were correct. How likely is it that we will observe our results if the chance model described by the null hypothesis is correct? There are several ways to answer this question when tossing a coin four times. One is to list all possible outcomes (see Table 4.1).

Table 4.1
Possible Outcomes of Four Coin Tosses

First Toss	Second Toss	Third Toss	Fourth Toss
HEAD	HEAD	HEAD	HEAD
TAIL	HEAD	HEAD	HEAD
HEAD	TAIL	HEAD	HEAD
HEAD	HEAD	TAIL	HEAD
TAIL	TAIL	HEAD	HEAD
TAIL	HEAD	TAIL	HEAD
HEAD	TAIL	TAIL	HEAD
TAIL	TAIL	TAIL	HEAD
HEAD	HEAD	HEAD	TAIL
TAIL	HEAD	HEAD	TAIL
HEAD	TAIL	HEAD	TAIL
HEAD	HEAD	TAIL	TAIL
TAIL	TAIL	HEAD	TAIL
TAIL	HEAD	TAIL	TAIL
HEAD	TAIL	TAIL	TAIL
TAIL	TAIL	TAIL	TAIL

Source: Authors' calculations.

The total number of possible outcomes is r^n (r is the number of possible outcomes in one trial, and n is the number of trials). Thus, $r^n = 2^4 = 16$. Why is that true? The first toss has two possible outcomes. A second toss results in two more outcomes (or 2 X 2), a third toss results in two possible outcomes for each of the previous four possible outcomes, and a fourth toss results in two possible outcomes for each of the previous eight outcomes (or 2 X 2 X 2 X 2 = 16). Given the initial assumptions and the null hypothesis—P(H) = P(T)—each of the sixteen outcomes is equally likely. Our earlier outcome—HTHH—has a 1 in 16 chance of happening, or a probability of .0625. Therefore, 6.25 percent of the time, HTHH should occur by chance in four tosses of a fair or unbiased coin.

If the chances of a particular pattern of four tosses are .0625, what is the probability of two of the four tosses ending in heads? There are six possible ways to get exactly two heads (see Table 4.1). The probability of four tosses producing two (no more, no less) heads is 6/16 = .375. We expect a fair coin to produce exactly two heads in four tosses 37.5 percent of the time.

That is how we expect the chance process described by the null hypothesis—P(H) = P(T)—to behave. Is what we observed compatible with the null hypothesis, or is there evidence for concluding that the coin is biased? The alternative hypotheses that the coin is biased are P(H) ≠ P(T) or P(H) < P(T) or P(H) > P(T). There are several ways to look at that problem; the null hypothesis provides one explanation. What is observed— HTHH— is not impossible if heads and tails each have an equal probability of occurring in any given toss (the null hypothesis). Of course, what we observed is also compatible with other hypotheses—for example, a model of a biased coin that has the chance of heads at .67 and that of tails at .33. In this case, then, four coin tosses were unable to provide evidence against the fair coin hypothesis. Coin tossing simplistically presents the various elements of statistical inference discussed more fully below.

Successive coin tosses are usually not of interest to historians, but many other things behave like successive coin tosses. Examples include the birth of a boy or girl, whether the price of something increases or decreases, and whether a member of Parliament votes yea or nay.

WHAT IS PROBABILITY?

The concept of probability is central to inferential statistics. Although there is disagreement on its definition,[1] that debate does not prevent the concept from being used in everyday life. We all understand general statements of probability. The problem is what "probability," "chance," "likeli-hood," and similar expressions imply about the world.

Probability as a Feature of the Physical World

The physics of Isaac Newton explains events in terms of the determin-istic action of matter on matter: given a certain combination of matter and forces, only one outcome is possible. What does probability mean in the deterministic universe of Newtonian physics? If a coin is tossed, all sorts of forces act upon it. One is the initial impulse generated by the thumb. There are also the forces of gravity of the earth and all other bodies in the uni-verse, molecules of air smashing into the coin, solar and cosmic rays strik-ing it, and a hand ready to catch it. All of these factors affect the coin as it spins upward and then downward. Whether it comes up heads or tails de-pends on all these forces—and perhaps on other, unknown things as well.

With a coin toss it is very difficult to control all of these conditions. If we could duplicate them exactly, in the Newtonian view the outcome would always be the same. But the conditions of each toss are never exactly identical, nor even the same within certain tolerances. The result is that sometimes the coin lands heads up, sometimes tails up. Each particular outcome is determined, but we are unable to predict what will happen in a given toss; it is too complex. As the situation changes constantly, half of the time heads are produced, and half of the time tails are produced, in no particular pattern. From this perspective, probability refers to the net out-come of a complex set of shifting but deterministic factors that we cannot predict because all the appropriate conditions cannot be specified.

Another view, at odds with the Newtonian interpretation, is that the world is either not deterministic or only partially deterministic. This notion maintains that probability is a fundamental property of our world. It holds that we live in a probabilistic universe not governed by laws of cause and effect, at least not completely. This idea originated in the statistical mechan-ics of Ludwig Boltzmann and the subatomic physics of Werner Heisenberg.[2] According to Heisenberg, "the laws of nature determine not the occurrence of an event, but the probability that an event will take place."[3] A number of perspectives in modern physics suggest that Newtonian notions of cause and effect are not applicable at the subatomic level. Even at the molecular level, determinism breaks down in that one cannot determine all aspects of mass, direction, and velocity simultaneously.

With human behavior, the notion of free will suggests that even if there are regularities in human behavior it is not possible to predict individual behavior, but only collective behavior. Emile Durkheim (1858–1917) studied, among other things, trends in suicide. He learned that the number of suicides varied by season and other factors to the extent that one could accurately predict their number in a given place at a given time. What was not possible, of course, was to predict who would commit suicide.[4]

It is unnecessary to take a position on which view of probability is correct. Probability calculations work out the same, either way. And as if the debate about the nature of the universe were not enough, there is also disagreement about probability statements. Basically there are three views: probability as frequency, as equally likely outcomes, and as a reasonable subjective assessment.

Probability as Relative Frequency

From the frequency perspective, the probability (k/n) means that, if there is a set of n outcomes (tosses of a coin), k of these will be of a certain kind (e.g., heads). Thus, probability refers to the frequency of a certain outcome in a set of trials. If one tosses a fair coin a great many times, the ratio of heads to the total number of tosses should approach 1/2 or .5. How many are a great many? The usual response—in the long run—is vague. Elaborations, such as "expectation of the long-run frequency," are no more helpful. Another problem is that heads and tails should be distributed randomly throughout the tries. But what does "random" mean? Any distribution of heads and tails—including 100,000 straight tails followed by 100,000 straight heads—could be random.

Another aspect of the frequency theory of probability concerns the notion that, as the number of trials increases, the proportion should approach some limit. In terms of coin tossing, for example, the idea is that, as the number of tosses becomes larger and larger, the proportion of heads should approach 1/2. But statisticians do not look at probability that way. Each toss of the coin can move the relative frequency closer to, or farther away from, the theoretical limit no matter how many tosses have occurred. Suppose there have already been 1,000,000 tosses with 499,999 heads and 500,001 tails. If the next toss is heads, the relative frequency 500,000/1,000,001 is closer to the limit of 1/2. But if the outcome is tails, the relative frequency 499,999/1,000,001 is farther from the limit. Both outcomes are equally likely.[5]

Probability as Equally Likely Events

The classical (or range) view of probability is associated with Jacob Bernoulli (1654–1705), Pierre Simon Laplace (1749–1827), and John Maynard Keynes (1883–1946).[6] It concentrates on the notion of theoretical outcomes. If there are n possible outcomes and k of them satisfy some condition, then the probability of the condition's being satisfied is k/n. In the case of the coin toss, n equals 2 (there are two possible outcomes for each toss, heads or tails) and k equals 1 (there is one way to satisfy the condition "heads"). The probability of heads is 1/2 or .5. This is a version of the "principle of insufficient reason," proposed by Laplace. It states that, if there is no reason to think one outcome is more likely than another, then treat each outcome as equal to all others.

The rationale offered for this is not satisfactory, however. One problem lies in identifying the possible outcomes. In the case of a coin toss, if we add "landing on its edge," does the probability of heads drop to 1/3? Clearly not. But to what does it drop?

Probability as Subjective Assessment

A third view of probability is that it represents subjective evaluations. One problem with seeing probability as an objective aspect of the universe is that it is obscure why nature obeys the laws of probability.[7] Philosopher and mathematician Frank Ramsey (1903–1930) suggests that we can understand probability in terms of degrees of belief. He asks us to consider the case of unhealthy toadstools.

> Granting that he [any person] is going to think always in the same way about all yellow toadstools, we can ask what degree of confidence it would be best for him to have that they are unwholesome. And the answer is that it will in general be best for his degree of belief that a yellow toadstool is unwholesome to be equal to the proportion of yellow toadstools which are in fact unwholesome.[8]

The idea that probability measures a subjective opinion or belief solves a number of problems and relates to a branch of statistics associated with Thomas Bayes (1702–1761). Many believe, however, that probability cannot be just subjective: too much of reality seems to be probabilistic.[9] Fortunately, we can apply probability to historical data without all of these questions being settled definitively.

BASIC AXIOMS OF PROBABILITY

Our mathematical understanding of probability can proceed because it is abstract and involves properties that are universally accepted. It is only in the interpretation of the results that disagreement arises.

Much of our knowledge of the mathematics of probability originated in the seventeenth-century work of Blaise Pascal (1623–1662) and Pierre de Fermat (1601–1665). These two Frenchmen and Jacob Bernoulli, a Swiss mathematician, worked on problems associated with games of chance. Yet it has only been in the twentieth century that A. N. Kolmogorov, a Russian mathematician, presented the formal axiomatic basis for inferential statistics.[10] Kolmogorov was not the only one to attempt this,[11] but his work has been the most widely recognized.

Axioms are statements about which there is general agreement. They, along with some definitions and assumptions, form the basis of a system. From these axioms, definitions, and assumptions, logic and mathematics are used to make deductions. If the system is a good one, then a few axioms, definitions, and assumptions can be used to describe the basics of probability. And if these axioms are accepted, then the results deduced must also be accepted.

We are not going to present a formal statement of the axiomatic basis of probability; instead, we will discuss some of the basic ideas informally.[12] Consider again a single toss of a fair coin. There is a set of conditions that are realized: a coin appears, is displayed for inspection, tossed a certain way, caught in a certain way, placed on a surface, and uncovered. Every time that set of conditions is realized, an event occurs—say, heads. There are three possibilities: the event will unavoidably occur when the conditions are realized, in which case it is *certain*; the event cannot occur, in which case it is *impossible*; or the event may or may not occur, in which case it is neither certain nor impossible, but *random*. If the conditions are realized, it is *certain* that either a head or tail will occur. If the conditions are realized, it is *impossible* that a head and tail will both occur. If the conditions are realized, it is *random* whether or not a head occurs.

A quantity called a "probability" can be associated with an event. If the event is certain, the probability is one; if the event is impossible, the probability is zero. If the event is random, the probability is greater than zero but less than one. For random events, we can assign probabilities several ways. For example, if the n possible events are assumed to be equally likely, then the probability of any one of them is 1/n (classical probability). If certain conditions are realized n times and the event of interest occurred m of these times, then we can assign the probability m/n to the event (empirical probability). In the case of the coin toss, the probability of heads could be .5 (each possible event is equally likely) or .5007 (the relative frequency of heads that will occur in 10,000 tosses of a certain coin),[13] or some other value. The probability might thus be represented as $P(H) = .5$ or perhaps $P(H) = .5007$.

Combinations of Mutually Exclusive Events

If, given the realization of certain conditions, it is impossible that two or more events can occur simultaneously, they are called *mutually exclusive*. In a single toss of a coin, heads and tails cannot both occur; heads and tails are thus mutually exclusive. *The probability of any one of several mutually exclusive events is the sum of their individual probabilities.*

Consider dice. A die has six sides. As a result of a single toss of a fair die, there are six possible mutually exclusive events, each having an equal probability: 1/6. The probability of the die exposing a one or a two is the sum of their individual probabilities.

$$P(1 \text{ or } 2) = P(1) + P(2) = (1/6) + (1/6) = 2/6 = 1/3$$

Combinations of Independent Events

Two or more events are *independent* of each other if knowing that one occurred provides no insight into predicting whether or not the other has occurred or will occur. If two events are independent, it is conventional to conclude there is no causal connection between them. If they are not independent, then some sort of causal connection exists: one causes the other, for example, or a third causes both.

Now consider several tosses of a coin. How can we view the successive outcomes (first toss, second toss, and so on)? If it is a fair toss of a fair coin, then the outcome of one toss has no effect on the outcome of any other toss. The tosses are independent of one another. If we use P(H) to designate the probability of heads in a toss of a coin and P(HH) to designate the probability of heads in the first and second tosses of a coin, then if the two tosses are independent,

$$P(HH) = P(H) \times P(H) = .5 \times .5 = .25$$

The probability of several independent events all occurring is the product of their individual probabilities.

If the probability of heads in one toss of a fair coin is 1/2, then the probability of getting four heads in four tosses is:

$$(1/2)\,(1/2)\,(1/2)\,(1/2) = 1/16 = .0625$$

Recall in Table 4.1 we enumerated all sixteen possible outcomes for four tosses of a fair coin. We viewed each of the sixteen outcomes as equally likely. As there are sixteen possibilities, each has a probability of 1/16—exactly what the multiplication rule calculates for independent events.

Recall how the addition rule works. What is the probability of getting three heads (no more, no less) in four tosses of a fair coin? Each of the sixteen outcomes of four tosses has a probability of 1/16. There are four outcomes with exactly three heads: THHH, HTHH, HHTH, HHHT. The probability of getting three heads in four tosses of a fair coin is:

$$P(THHH) + P(HTHH) + P(HHTH) + P(HHHT)$$
$$= (1/16) + (1/16) + (1/16) + (1/16) = 4/16 = .25$$

Notice also how some of the other ideas apply. Toss a fair coin four times; there are sixteen possible sequences of heads and tails. The probability of getting any one of the sixteen is:

$$P(HHHH) + P(THHH) + P(HTHH) + P(HHTH) +$$
$$P(TTHH) + P(HTTH) + P(THTH) + P(TTTH) +$$
$$P(HHHT) + P(THHT) + P(HTHT) + P(HHTT) +$$
$$P(TTHT) + P(THTT) + P(HTTT) + P(TTTT) =$$
$$(1/16) + (1/16) + (1/16) + (1/16) + (1/16) + (1/16) +$$
$$(1/16) + (1/16) + (1/16) + (1/16) + (1/16) + (1/16) +$$
$$(1/16) + (1/16) + (1/16) + (1/16) = (16/16) = 1$$

If the probability of exactly three heads (in any order) is 4/16, then the probability of getting something other than exactly three heads is:

$$1 - 4/16 = 12/16 = 3/4 = .75$$

Conditional Probability

The final basic concept is *conditional probability*. The notation $P(H_2|H_1)$ means the probability of heads in the second toss under the condition that the first toss was heads. If the outcomes of each toss are independent, then $P(H_2|H_1) = P(H_2|T_1) = P(H_2) = 1/2$. That is, the chances of heads in the second toss are the same whether or not the first toss was heads.

Continuing with $P(H_2|H_1)$, notice that, of the sixteen possible outcomes of four tosses (n = number of possible outcomes), there are eight ways that heads can occur on the first toss (k_1 = number of ways that heads can occur on first toss) and eight ways that heads can occur on the second toss (k_2 = number of ways that heads can occur on second toss). There are four ways that heads can occur on the second toss if heads occurs on the first toss (r = number of ways that heads can occur on the first when heads occurs on the second toss of four tosses). Recalling that each of the sixteen outcomes is equally probable, then $P(H_1) = k_1/n = 8/16$ and $P(H_2) = k_2/n = 8/16$.

$$
\begin{aligned}
P(H_2|H_1) = r/k_1 = (r/n)/(k_1/n) &= P(H_1H_2)/P(H_1) \\
&= (4/16)/(8/16) \\
&= 1/2
\end{aligned}
$$

We can employ similar reasoning to get the conclusion: $P(H_1|H_2) = P(H_1H_2)/P(H_2)$.

BAYESIAN STATISTICS

We can solve each of the equations for $P(H_1H_2)$, resulting in:

$$P(H_1H_2) \;=\; P(H_2|H_1)P(H_1)$$

and

$$P(H_1H_2) \;=\; P(H_1|H_2)P(H_2),$$

because both are equal to $P(H_1H_2)$,

$$P(H_2|H_1)P(H_1) \;=\; P(H_1|H_2)P(H_2)$$

solving for $P(H_1|H_2)$,

$$P(H_1|H_2) \;=\; P(H_2|H_1)P(H_1)/P(H_2)$$

This last equation is Bayes's formula or rule for the probability of causes. Thomas Bayes in 1763 and Laplace in 1774 calculated it independently. The probability of heads on the first toss given that the second toss was heads is equal to the probability of heads on the second toss given heads on the first toss multiplied by the probability of heads on the first toss. The whole expression is then divided by the probability of heads on the second toss. Here,

$$P(H_1 \,|H_2) = P(H_2|H_1)P(H_1)/P(H_2) = (.5)(.5)\,/\,.5 = .5$$

The chances of heads on the first toss are the same whether or not the second toss has resulted in heads. That is what we expect from a fair coin and independent trials.

Now let us consider a specific example involving presidential ballots in Illinois during the 1982 election. Politicians tend to think that being listed first on a ballot is worth about 5 percent of the vote. In Illinois some politicians filed suit in federal court, charging that county clerks were placing candidates of their own party at the head of the ballot and were, therefore, depriving voters of their constitutional rights to equal protection and a republican form of government. The court agreed and ordered county clerks in Illinois to conduct a lottery before each election to determine whether the Republican or Democratic candidate would get the first ballot position.[14] We have presented the results of those lotteries for ninety of Illinois's 102 counties (the results in twelve counties are unknown) in Table 4.2.

Notice first that Republican county clerks ended up with Republicans in the first ballot position thirty-three times and Democratic county clerks ended up with Republicans in the first ballot position only sixteen times. Coin tosses might also give such results. Another possibility, however, is that some clerks cheated.

There are four possible kinds of clerks: honest Republican clerks (HRC), cheating Republican clerks (CRC), honest Democratic clerks (HDC), and

Table 4.2
Party of County Clerk and Results of Random Process to Determine Ballot Position, Illinois, 1982

First on Ballot	County Clerk's Party		Total	Probability
	Republican	Democratic		
Republican	33	16	49	49/102
Democrat	15	26	41	41/102
Unknown	5	7	12	12/102
Total	53	49	102	
Probability	53/102	49/102		

Source: Authors' calculations from R. Darcy and Ian McAllister, "Ballot Position Effects," *Electoral Studies*, 9 (March 1990), 9.

cheating Democratic clerks (CDC). What are the chances of a coin toss resulting in a Republican first ballot (F_r) for each type of clerk? For the honest Republican clerk and the honest Democratic clerk, the probability is .5. For the cheating Republican clerk, the probability is 1.0; and for the cheating Democratic clerk, it is 0.0. While in actuality there is relevant information we could use here (e.g., there are more Republican than Democratic clerks), for the sake of simplicity we adopted Laplace's principle of insufficient reason (also known as Bayes's Postulate) and set the probability of each of the four types as equal. At this point we have the following probabilities:

$$P(HRC) = P(CRC) = P(HDC) = P(CDC)$$
$$P(F_r|HRC) \quad = \quad .5$$
$$P(F_r|CRC) \quad = \quad 1.0$$
$$P(F_r|HDC) \quad = \quad .5$$
$$P(F_r|CDC) \quad = \quad 0$$

Now we come to the sort of problem Bayes's formula addresses. If we have a Republican listed in the first position and we know the clerk is Republican, what are the chances the clerk was honest?

We start by assuming that half of the Republican clerks are honest and half are not: $P(HRC) = P(CRC) = .5$. From Table 4.2 we know that the probability of a Republican's being first $[P(F_r)]$ when the clerk is a Republican is $33/(33 + 15) = .6875$. We know that the probability of a Republican's being first when the clerk is an honest Republican $[P(F_r|HRC)]$ is .5. Thus,

$$P(HRC) = .5$$
$$P(F_r) = .6875$$
$$P(F_r|HRC) = .5$$

The problem is to use this information to reach an opinion about a particular clerk's honesty given that we have a Republican first ballot and a Republican clerk. Bayes's formula is:

$$P(HRC \mid F_r) = \frac{P(F_r \mid HRC\,)P(HRC\,)}{P(F_r)}$$

substituting

$$P(HRC|F_r) = \frac{.5 X .5}{.6875}$$
$$= .3636$$

The probability of a cheating Republican clerk given a Republican first ballot and a Republican clerk [P(CRC|F_r)] is:

$$P(CRC|F_r) = 1 - P(HRC|F_r)$$
$$= 1 - .3636$$
$$= .6364$$

We can conclude that in this situation, if we have a Republican clerk and a Republican first ballot, the probability that the clerk was cheating is about twice as large as the probability that the clerk was honest. We can make similar calculations about honest and cheating Democratic clerks.

Remember that we have no way of knowing if any particular clerk cheated. Some Republican clerks will legitimately produce a Republican listed in the first ballot position, and some Democratic clerks will legitimately produce a Democrat listed in the first ballot position. Furthermore, all the clerks could be honest, and the laws of chance could produce what we observed—although it is highly unlikely.

In this context, the conditional probabilities are best interpreted as what we believe—a subjective opinion—rather than a frequency. The conditional probability measures our belief that, if the ballot lists the Republican candidate first, it came from a dishonest Republican clerk.

Bayes's formula, as applied here, deals with a reasonable belief as to what a probability is, given the data available. Bayesian probabilities are a logical consequence of the researcher's opinion on the probability of a clerk's being one of several types.

The ideas outlined here are useful in several ways. They provide an introduction to more complex statistical techniques. We also learned that one can gain insight by examining problems from the point of view of probability.

OBSERVED AND EXPECTED PROBABILITIES

Consider another example: the position of African-American women in American politics during the 1980s. A number of researchers have referred to the "double whammy," the disadvantage of African-American women by virtue of both their sex and their color.[15] The double whammy is thought to add an additional disadvantage over and above that of sex and color individually. In 1987, the proportion of women among the 5,515 state legislators (lower house) nationwide was .1590. Likewise, the proportion of African-Americans was .0745. If race and sex were independent in their

influence on election to the state legislatures, we would expect there to be
.1590 X .0745 X 5515—or about sixty-five—African-American female legislators. If the double whammy hypothesis is correct, however, we would
expect less than sixty-five, because of the double whammy's additional
negative influence. In fact, the number of African-American female state
legislators in 1987 was 101—more than 1.5 times that expected if race and
sex were independent.

As women are 52 percent of the over eighteen-year-old population
(men are 48 percent) and African-Americans are 11 percent (non-African-
Americans are 89 percent), we would expect the following if race and sex
were independent of getting elected:

non-African-American women	(.52) (.89) (5,515)	= 2,552
non-African-American men	(.48) (.89) (5,515)	= 2,356
African-American women	(.52) (.11) (5,515)	= 316
African-American men	(.48) (.11) (5,515)	= 291
Total		5,515

In 1987, the actual numbers were as follows:

non-African-American women	776
non-African-American men	4,328
African-American women	101
African-American men	310
Total	5,515

African-American women were half again the proportion of African-
American representatives (101/411 = .246) that non-African-American
women were among non-African-American legislators (776/5,104 = .152).

Although African-American women are clearly underrepresented (there
should have been about 316 in 1987 if our society did not disadvantage race
and sex), being both African-American *and* a woman was an advantage
and was offsetting some of the color and sex disadvantage. African-American
women had a larger share of their "fair" representation (101/316 = .3196)
than non-African-American women (776/2,552 = .3040). Both African-
American (310/291 = 1.065) and non-African-American men (4,328/2,356
= 1.837) had more than their share.

THE BINOMIAL DISTRIBUTION: A SERIES OF INDEPENDENT TRIALS

Historians might consider a discussion of the logic of a series of independent trials unnecessary. Actually, there are some historical applications. The topic is also important to make the connection between the basic notions of probability and the distribution-based statistical significance tests discussed in later chapters.

Once again, we can use the tossing of a fair coin as a model for a series of independent trials. What are the chances of getting exactly three heads in the four tosses? We solved this problem earlier by listing all the possibilities and selecting those outcomes that satisfied that criterion. The probability of getting three heads in four tosses of a fair coin is:

$$P(THHH) + P(HTHH) + P(HHTH) + P(HHHT)$$
$$= (1/16) + (1/16) + (1/16) + (1/16) = 4/16 = .25$$

Another way to solve the problem is with a formula first suggested by Isaac Newton (1642–1727) and applied by Jacob Bernoulli (1654–1705). This is the *binomial formula*. The number of ways to arrange n things taken k at a time is:

$$\frac{n!}{k!\,(n-k)!}$$

Factorial (!) is the symbol for the product of a positive integer and all smaller positive integers [3! = (3)(2)(1) = 6]. Note: 0! equals 1.

Consider this in terms of the coin-tossing problem. Here n is four (four tosses) and k is three (three heads). How many ways can three heads occur in four tosses of a coin?

$$\frac{4!}{3!(4-3)!} = \frac{4 \times 3 \times 2 \times 1}{(3 \times 2 \times 1)1} = \frac{24}{6} = 4$$

There are four ways we can get exactly three heads in four tosses of a coin: THHH, HTHH, HHTH, HHHT. What is the probability of each outcome? Again, we already know that each of the sixteen possibilities is equally likely, so the probability of any one is 1/16 = .0625. But there is another way to figure this. If the probability of heads in a single toss is p (here equal to 1/2) and the probability of tails in a single toss is 1 - p, then the probability of three heads in three tosses (because they are independent events) is p X p X p = p³, and the probability of k heads in k tosses is p^k. Now there are (n - k) tosses remaining—in this case, one toss. It must be tails. The probability of tails in one toss is 1 - p and in (n - k) tosses, $(1 - p)^{(n-k)}$. The probability of getting tails after three heads in four tosses is $p^k(1 - p)^{(n-k)}$. In this instance, it is $.5^3(1 - .5)^{(4-3)} = .0625$—or 1/16—the same probability of any one of sixteen possible outcomes.

Now back to the earlier question. What is the probability of getting three heads in four tosses of a fair coin? If there are four such combinations and each has a probability of $p^k(1 - p)^{(n-k)} = .0625$, then the probability of one of the four mutually exclusive events occurring is the sum of their individual probabilities, or $p^k(1 - p)^{(n-k)}$ taken n!/[k!(n-k)!] times, or

$$\frac{n!}{k!(n-k)!} p^k (1-p)^{(n-k)} = (4)(.0625) = .25$$

This is just what we discover in Table 4.1 when we count the number of outcomes in which exactly three heads occur and then divide by the total number of possible outcomes (4/16 = .25).

There is an obvious advantage of using the formula when dealing with a large number of tosses. In twenty-five tosses there are r^n possible outcomes, where r is the number of possible outcomes in one toss and n is the number of tosses. When r is 2 and n is 25, the number of possible outcomes is $2^{25} = 33,554,432$. This is too many to list and count. With the binomial formula the probability of exactly k = 10 heads in n = 25 tosses of a coin, where the probability of heads in one toss is p = .5, works out to be:

$$P(k) = \frac{n!}{k!(n-k)!} p^k (1-p)^{(n-k)}$$

$$P(10) = \frac{25!}{10!(25-10)!} .5^{10} (1-.5)^{(25-10)} = .09741$$

About 10 percent of the time we expect to get exactly ten heads from twenty-five tosses of a fair coin.

We might now ask a different question. How many heads do we expect to occur in twenty-five tosses of a fair coin? The key word here is *expect*. The probabilities for each outcome, calculated using the binomial formula, are presented in Table 4.3. This is the binomial distribution.

Notice several things about this distribution. First, it is symmetrical, with the probabilities of between zero and twelve heads being the mirror image

Table 4.3
Probabilities of Getting 0–25 Heads in 25 Tosses of a Fair Coin

Number of Heads	Probability	Cumulative Probability
0	.000000030	.000000030
1	.000000745	.000000776
2	.000008941	.000009717
3	.000068545	.000078262
4	.000376999	.000455261
5	.001583397	.002038658
6	.005277991	.007316649
7	.014325976	.021642625
8	.032233447	.053876072
9	.060885400	.114761472
10	.097416639	.212178111
11	.132840872	.345018983
12	.154981017	.500000000
13	.154981017	.654981017
14	.132840872	.787821889
15	.097416639	.885238528
16	.060885400	.946123928
17	.032233447	.978357375
18	.014325976	.992683351
19	.005277991	.997961342
20	.001583397	.999544739
21	.000376999	.999921738
22	.000068545	.999990283
23	.000008941	.999999224
24	.000000745	.999999970
25	.000000030	1.000000000

Source: Authors' calculations.

of the probabilities between thirteen and twenty-five heads. Next, observe that the most probable result is either twelve or thirteen heads. If a histogram is constructed (see Figure 4.1), the results resemble a bell-shaped curve. We can easily calculate the mean and standard deviation of the distribution. The mean, or average number of heads, is simply n X p where n is the number of trials and p is the probability of success in one trial. The standard deviation is $\sqrt{np(1-p)}$. In the case of the twenty-five tosses of a fair coin, the mean number of heads is:

$$(n)(p) = (25)(.5) = 12.5$$

If the mean number of heads is 12.5, the mean proportion of heads is 12.5/ 25 = .5—the true probability of heads in a toss of a fair coin. In Chapter 3,

Figure 4.1
Histogram Representing the Data in Table 4.3

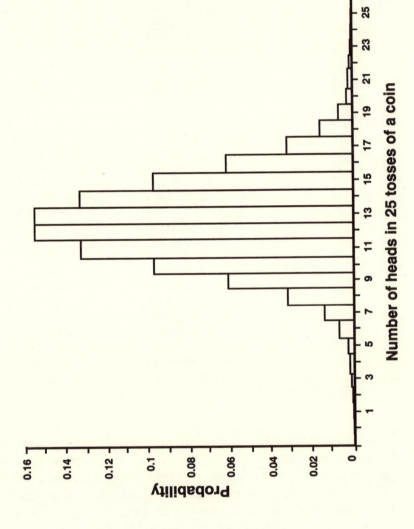

we described the mean of a random sample as most likely to be near the quantity being estimated. Here, the quantity being estimated is the probability of heads (.5). In twenty-five tosses, the ratio of heads to tosses is more likely to be near this true value (.5) than farther away. In this sense, the mean of the binomial distribution is the expected outcome. The variance equals:

$$n\,p(1-p) = 25\,(.5)(1-.5) = 6.25$$

and the standard deviation is:

$$\sqrt{np(1-p)} = \sqrt{6.25} = 2.5$$

The histogram in Figure 4.1 has been drawn in such a way that the base of each bar represents a length of one and the height is proportional to the probability associated with the particular number of heads. The area of a bar—the product of its height and width—is proportional to its probability; and as all the probabilities add up to 1, the sum of the areas of all the bars also equals 1. The probability of any particular outcome or any set of outcomes is proportional to the areas represented by those outcomes.

As the number of possible outcomes increases, the number of vertical bars increase and the resulting figure comes to resemble a curve. If we know the equation for the curve that best approximates the results of the binomial distribution, then we can use calculus to determine the area under the curve. This area will be proportional to the probability of obtaining a value within that defined range. Consider, for example, the probability of getting twelve or fewer heads. The area of the bars represented by 0–12 heads is half of the total area, and the probability of getting twelve or fewer heads is 1/2 or .5.

Now let us review what we have done. We began by thinking about probability in terms of counting among all possible outcomes. That is the "brute force method." Then, we computed probabilities from the binomial formula. Now we are deriving probabilities from the area under a curve. We get the same answers, but each technique has certain advantages. We employed the binomial formula because brute force cannot handle a large number of trials. But the binomial formula also has limitations. Recall that n! needs to be calculated. When n = 25 the value of n! is roughly 15,511,210,040,000,000,000,000,000. The formula becomes impractical after n exceeds 70 or 80.

THE NORMAL DISTRIBUTION

In 1721, these difficulties led Abraham De Moivre (1667–1754), a French mathematician, to develop an approximation formula for binomial probabilities.[16] Later, the German mathematician Karl Friedrich Gauss (1777–1855) independently explored the same question. Today, this approximation is called the "normal distribution" in English—named so by the English statistician Karl Pearson—and the "Gaussian distribution" in other languages. The normal distribution's formula is:

$$f(x) = \frac{1}{\sqrt{2\pi\sigma^2}} e^{-(x-\mu)^2 / 2\sigma^2}$$

In the formula, π and e are mathematical constants, π being approximately 3.141 and e being approximately 2.718. Thus, the only variable parameters for the normal distribution are μ (mu) and σ^2 (sigma squared). The mean is μ, and the standard deviation of the normal distribution is σ. Each possible value of μ and σ defines a different curve. Higher values for σ flatten the curve, and lower values elevate it. Different values for μ pull it to the right or left.

The *standard normal distribution,* or *z-distribution,* is the normal curve with a mean of zero and a standard deviation of one. Before computers and hand calculators, it was useful to publish tabulations of areas under the standard normal distribution. The researcher could convert values under any normal distribution to z–scores by subtracting their mean and dividing the result by their standard deviation. The researcher could then determine the associated area under the curve by looking up the z–score in the tables. Figure 4.2 illustrates several normal curves. Like the binomial distribution it approximates, the normal curve is symmetrical about the mean. If we compute a distance outward from the mean in each direction and measure that distance in terms of standard deviations, we find, through calculus, the areas presented in Table 4.4.

Returning to the case of twenty-five tosses of a fair coin, notice that the probability of getting more than eight but fewer than seventeen heads is .892248—something that can be calculated by just adding the probabilities of 1, 2, . . . 8 heads and the probabilities of 17, 18, . . . 25 heads and subtracting the result from 1 (see Table 4.3). To get the same results from the normal distribution, recall that the mean of the distribution is n X p = 25 X .5 = 12.5, and that the standard deviation is the square root of the variance: $\sqrt{np(1-p)} = \sqrt{25(.5)(1-.5)} = 2.5$. If 90 percent of the out-

Figure 4.2
Several Normal Curves

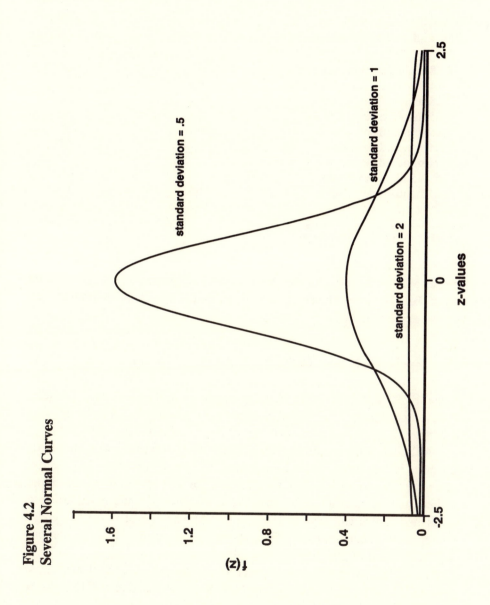

Table 4.4
Areas for Various Standard Deviations

Standard Deviations Plus and Minus the Mean	Area within Range	Area outside Range
0.68 standard deviations	.50	.50
0.84 standard deviations	.60	.40
1.28 standard deviations	.80	.20
1.65 standard deviations	.90	.10
1.96 standard deviations	.95	.05
2.24 standard deviations	.975	.025
2.34 standard deviations	.98	.02
2.58 standard deviations	.99	.01
2.81 standard deviations	.995	.005
3.29 standard deviations	.999	.001

Source: Authors' calculations.

comes are within +/-1.65 standard deviations of the mean (a property of the normal distribution), then only 10 percent should be outside this range. Calculating, we find that

$$12.5 +/- (1.65)(2.5) = 8.375 \text{ and } 16.625$$

Roughly, 90 percent of the outcomes should be in the range of eight heads to seventeen heads. The normal distribution, the binomial formula, and enumerating the probability of each outcome—all produce the same result.

Although it may seem that the normal curve makes things difficult and obscure, it does have certain advantages. It can cope with very large values of n. We can also use it when the outcomes of interest are on a continuum, rather than being discrete values. Using computers, hand calculators, or published tables can resolve the major disadvantage of using the curve: having to do integral calculus. We present a quick hand method for computing these areas in the Appendix.

There are two additional aspects of the normal curve that also prove useful. The first is the Law of Large Numbers, suggested in a 1713 publication by Jacob Bernoulli. The second is the Central Limit Theorem, first presented by Laplace in 1810.

The *Law of Large Numbers* states that the ratio of successes to the total number of trials has a high probability of being closer to the true probability of success as the number of trials increases. In terms of coin tosses, this means that, if we increase the number of tosses—say, from five to twenty-five—chances are that the ratio of heads to the number of tosses will be closer to the actual probability of heads. The *Central Limit Theorem* stipulates that "any sum or mean (not merely the total number of successes in *n* trials) will, if the number of terms is large, be approximately normally distributed."[17] Laplace later expanded the idea: "if each measurement were itself a mean of a large number of more basic observations, the measurements themselves would have the distribution supposed by Gauss."[18] In terms of coin tossing, this means that, if we toss a coin twenty-five times and record the number of heads and then repeat the process many times, the results—the number of heads in each set of tosses—will be distributed approximately normally with a mean and standard deviation that we can calculate from n (the number of tosses in a given set of tosses) and p (the probability of heads in a single toss).

The Law of Large Numbers and the Central Limit Theorem demonstrate that, if there is some random process governing the outcome of events, then certain summary statistics describing those events will be normally distributed. The number of heads repeatedly observed in twenty-five tosses of a coin will be approximately normally distributed. Likewise, the mean chest circumferences of soldiers, as repeatedly observed in sets of ten, will also be approximately normally distributed.

By 1884, statistician Francis Ysidro Edgeworth (1845–1926) used these properties of normal distributions to make statistical inferences. Observing a wasp nest in his hometown in County Longford, Ireland, he recorded the traffic to and from the nest at 8 A.M. and noon. The rate at 8 A.M. was higher than at noon. Because the difference was within what would be expected by chance (as measured by how the rates fluctuated), he concluded that the difference was " 'insignificant.' " This was an early example of using a normal distribution as a test of significance.[19]

In the nineteenth century, the normal and binomial distributions were used to determine whether or not two sets of observations could be said to come from the same population. While these methods were not yet refined to the point they are today, the basic logic of the analysis was there. It focused on the chances of observing something when given certain hypothesized population means (or probabilities) and standard deviations.

Again, consider Edgeworth's wasps. The rates of coming and going varied. From any two sets of observations we would not expect to calculate the same mean. But if we assume the null hypothesis of no difference in wasp comings and goings at 8 A.M. and noon is correct, then we can calculate the probability of finding, from a given number of observations, the difference observed (or greater). If this probability is low, what is observed is evidence against the null hypothesis. Similarly, getting twenty-three (or more) heads in twenty-five tosses of a coin is evidence against the null hypothesis that for the coin toss the probability of getting a head is the same as that of getting a tail. Such an outcome is possible but improbable (see Table 4.3).

$$P(23, 24, \text{ or } 25) = (.000008941 + .000000745 + .000000030)$$
$$= .000009716$$

In examples like coin tossing and others that can be viewed as coin tossing, we can calculate a theoretical mean and variance. The analysis is a simple matter. But what if we had observations like traffic rates about a wasp nest, instead? We can only *estimate* the mean and standard deviation because we have only a small number of observations, not all possible observations.

THE t-DISTRIBUTION

In 1899, William S. Gosset (1876–1937) began work in the St. James's Gate Brewery of Arthur Guinness and Company in Dublin. While employed there, Gosset studied statistics. Ultimately, his job required him to make probability statements based on a relatively small number of observations. As it turned out, this posed special problems.

To examine this point, Richard Lowry suggests we consider New York City. If we observe each resident of the city, we would be able to measure its great ethnic and racial diversity. If we selected only ten residents, we would likely observe less diversity. The larger the number of observations, the closer we will be to the actual diversity of all the city's residents.[20]

There are two variances: the variance of all the cases in the population (or all possible observations), and the variance calculated in a small sample from the population of cases. By 1908, Gosset demonstrated that the variance calculated from a small sample tended to be smaller than the variance calculated from the population of all cases. There were errors when the sample variance was used to determine areas under the normal curve. The solution, reached in 1926, was to define both a sample variance distinct from the population variance and a new distribution—*the t-distribution*—distinct from the z, or standard normal, distribution.

The *population variance* of the variable x is calculated as

$$\sigma_x^2 = [\sum (x_i - \mu_x)^2] / N$$

where N is the number of cases in the population. The *sample variance* is calculated as

$$S_x^2 = [\sum (x_i - \bar{x})^2] / (n - 1)$$

where n is the number of cases in the sample. Notice that, by dividing the sample sum of squares by (n - 1) rather than by N, the value of the variance is increased slightly. The increase is relatively large in small samples but diminishes and becomes negligible as the sample becomes larger.

Gosset found that, when small samples were repeatedly drawn and their means calculated and standardized, they did not quite fit the normal distribution. Instead, the standardized means fit the t-distribution. Gosset's t-distribution had one parameter: the *degrees of freedom*, which, at this point, we can understand to be roughly equal to the sample size. Chapter 6 contains a fuller discussion of degrees of freedom. There is a different t-distribution for each degree of freedom. For very small degrees of freedom —that is, very small sample sizes—the t-distribution has thicker tails than the standard normal distribution. As the degrees of freedom increase, how-ever, the t-distribution more closely approximates the standard normal dis-tribution until the degrees of freedom become infinite and the two distribu-tions are identical. For practical purposes the two distributions are the same when the degrees of freedom reach about thirty.

Before discussing applications of the t-distribution, we must mention two further developments. Before Gosset, there was little discussion of how observations were gathered. Words like "random," "sample," and "ex-periment" were used, but not in the same sense as today. We have dis-cussed samples and sampling in Chapter 2. Here it is only necessary to observe that these are relatively new topics. Most of the work on random-ization and sample selections was done in the twentieth century—after the developments discussed here.

SAMPLES AND POPULATIONS

Statisticians typically frame discussions of inferential statistics in terms of populations and samples—a formulation originating in a 1922 paper by R. A. Fisher.[21] Nonstatisticians think of populations as something a census might enumerate—the population of the United States, for example. They think of a sample as the random selection of cases that survey organizations— like Gallup's poll—investigate. Statisticians, however, assign more meaning to both of these terms.

One can use inferential statistics for more than generalizing from a Gallup-type random sample to a census-type population. In fact, the basis of inferential statistics was developed before modern techniques of random sampling. A random sample was not defined until Charles Sanders Peirce did so in 1896: "A sample is a *random* one, provided it is drawn by such machinery, artificial or psychological, that in the long run any one individual of the whole lot would get taken as often as any other."[22]

Before 1900 there was little systematic attention to how one gathered observations. In his historical survey of sampling, Frederick F. Stephan cites a 1906 study by Arthur Bowley as the earliest example of random sampling. In 1907, Gosset sampled from shuffled cards in a demonstration that small samples followed the t-distribution. In 1926, A. Jensen outlined the characteristics of a modern probability sample[23]: one in which each observation in a wider population has a known probability of selection. In such a sample, the researcher does not exert personal bias in selecting observations, and subjects do not select themselves. According to Stephan, the first use made by a social scientist of random sampling to generalize to populations did not occur until 1931, when Margaret Hogg studied unemployed men in New Haven, Connecticut. The literature on sampling human populations only developed in the 1940s.[24]

SIGNIFICANCE TESTS

In the early 1930s, Jerzy Neyman and Egon Pearson (Karl Pearson's son) published a statistical testing procedure that is widely used in the social and behavioral sciences today.[25] It involves a theory, relevant data, descriptive statistics of the observations, hypotheses, and the probability of observing what was observed if a random process generated the data. Let us look at each of these parts of their procedure.

Start with some theory or explanation. This could involve explaining why infant mortality among African-Americans in the South in 1850 was higher than among whites, or why that same year foreign-born boys in Milwaukee were less likely to attend school than native-born boys.

There must also be some data that we can collect relevant to the theory or explanation—for example, government statistics on infant mortality, or a random sample of boys that includes information on their nativity and whether or not they attended school. The *test statistic* is a number calculated from the observed data and a known distribution under a given set of circumstances. Test statistics commonly used are t, z, chi-square, and the F-ratio.

These are discussed in subsequent chapters.

Next is the hypothesis. With the Neyman and Pearson approach there are two: the null hypothesis and an alternative hypothesis. As used here, both concern the process by which the observed data have been produced. The null hypothesis in most historical research is that one variable (or set of variables) is not causally linked to another. In the case of infant mortality, the null hypothesis might be that race was not a factor in producing Southern infant mortality rates in 1850. In the case of the 1850 school attendance in Milwaukee, the null hypothesis might be that place of birth did not influence whether or not a boy attended school. Under the null hypothesis, any relationship observed in the collected data is attributed to chance; that is, they are *not significant*. If chance is the explanation, then one can determine the probability that the test statistic will have a particular value or a larger value.

The alternative hypothesis is usually that the null hypothesis is incorrect: the observed patterns are not due to chance, but rather to some causal connection; that is, they are *significant*. If the alternative hypothesis is correct, then the expected value of the test statistic will have a greater absolute value than that expected under the chance hypothesis. Generally, the alternative hypothesis will attribute observed relationships to causal forces operating independently of the data-gathering process, while the null hypothesis will attribute any observed relationships to the operation of chance in gathering the data.

Now let us consider how chance might work in this context. It has become conventional to say that the relationship or difference tested is *significant* if we reject the null hypothesis. Yet if the test fails to reject the null hypothesis, the relationship or difference is then *not significant* or *insignificant*.

The Random Sample

If the data are from a random sample of a population (see Chapter 2), then that particular sample is one of many equally likely possible samples. In the case of the Milwaukee boys, some of the foreign-born boys attended school and some worked. Likewise, some of the native-born boys attended school and some worked. Suppose that, in a sample of 400 boys, we find that native-born boys are more likely than foreign-born boys to attend school. The null hypothesis states that in the population there is no difference in the likelihood that native-born and foreign-born boys attended school; the observed difference is due to the chance selection of a sample with a greater proportion of native-born than foreign-born boys attending school. The alternative hypothesis states that, in the population from which the cases were sampled, where a boy was from did indeed affect whether or not he attended school.

An Experiment

Although historians rarely utilize experiments in their research, it may be useful to explore experimental design and its meaning for significance tests. Sir Ronald A. Fisher (1890–1962) made some important contributions to our understanding of experimental designs. Consider a research design to test the effect of medical treatments. The first stage is to divide patients randomly into two groups and randomly assign treatment to one group and not the other. If the two groups are divided randomly, it is probable that they will have the same aggregate characteristics. But it is also possible that chance has packed one group with certain kinds of cases. In this experiment, the null hypothesis is that any difference after treatment is due to the chance assignment of the experimental treatment to a group having characteristics different from the control. The alternative hypothesis is that any difference is due to the treatment.

Additional Interpretations

So far, we have discussed random sampling and experimentation. For historians, there are other interpretations of significance tests that also will be useful. The first is that behavior, like a coin toss, is the result of random forces unrelated to a particular factor of interest. Consider a simple case. There are 100 legislators. Fifty are Republicans, and fifty are Democrats. Suppose that on a particular motion, fifty vote for and fifty against; a breakdown into party shows that thirty-five Republicans voted for and thirty-five Democrats voted against. Is this evidence that party affected the vote?

Here, the null hypothesis could be that the probability of a Democrat voting for the motion is the same as that of a Republican: .5. If each member tossed a coin to decide how to vote, what is the probability such a division could have occurred by chance? We have a hypothesis, on the one hand, that there is no difference in the probability of Republicans or Democrats voting for the bill (i.e., the null hypothesis) and, on the other hand, that party affiliation determined the vote and, hence, the probability of Democrats and of Republicans voting for the bill is different (i.e., the alternative hypothesis). If the observed data had a reasonable probability of being produced under the null hypothesis, then there is not much support for the proposition that party affiliation was important to the vote. Instead, the differences observed can be attributed to random factors unrelated to political party, much like random factors can yield more heads than tails in a series of fair coin tosses. The idea is not to mistake chance differences for a significant pattern.

There are other approaches to interpreting significance tests in the absence of actual sampling or experimentation. First, the historian can conceptualize a hypothetical population and ask if there were such a population, could sampling variation account for the difference between the test statistic expected under the null hypothesis and the observed test statistic. For example, we might have 200 emigrants from Ireland—120 men and 80 women. We could imagine that, instead of having a population of 200, we had a random sample of 200 from an imaginary population. We could then test to determine if there were a significant difference in the chances of a man's emigrating and a woman's emigrating. Second, the historian can assume there are random errors of measurement in the data and can use the significance test to determine the chances that random measurement errors could account for the difference between the observed test statistic and that expected under the null hypothesis.[26]

CONFIDENCE INTERVALS

In the early 1930s Jerzy Neyman, then working in Poland, developed the concept of a confidence interval. Confidence intervals are a method by which sample information is used to make statements about population parameters. The problem is that any particular sample is just one of a large number of possible samples and sample estimates vary from one sample to another. Given this, how can we confidently say anything about the unknown population parameter?

The Law of Large Numbers and the Central Limit Theorem (discussed earlier in this chapter) tell us that if we draw many large random samples of a given sample size (n) from an infinite population and measure the mean of a certain variable in each sample, these sample means will be normally distributed with a mean equal to the population mean (μ_x) and a standard deviation equal to the population standard deviation (σ_x) divided by the square root of the sample size (n). Normally, we would not know the population standard deviation but we can estimate it with the sample standard deviation (S_x). By rule of thumb, a large random sample is a sample of at least thirty observations and an infinite population is one in which the sample is less than 1 percent of the total population.

A property of the normal distribution is that 95 percent of its area is within 1.96 standard deviations of its mean. Thus, 95 percent of all possible sample means will be within 1.96 standard deviations, in this case,

$$1.96 \frac{\sigma_x}{\sqrt{n}}$$

of the population mean (μ_x). As 95 percent of all possible sample means are in the interval

$$\mu_x +/- 1.96 \frac{\sigma_x}{\sqrt{n}}$$

then 95 percent of all such intervals constructed about the sample mean, $\bar{x}$, will contain the population parameter μ_x . We are 95 percent confident, then, that the interval

$$\bar{x} +/- 1.96 \frac{S_x}{\sqrt{n}}$$

will contain the population parameter μ_x.

As an example, consider a random sample of members of three Florentine gilds and their investments in the *Monte*, a public investment scheme discussed in Chapter 7 and presented in Table 7.1. The number of cases sampled (n) is 34, the mean investment ($\bar{x}$) is 1832 florins, and the sample standard deviation (S_x) is calculated to be 4295.266563 by dividing the sum of squares by (n - 1) and taking the square root of the result. Given that sample, what can we say with confidence concerning the mean amount invested by the population of all gild members?

The 95 percent confidence interval (C.I.) about a sample mean is:

$$C.I. = \bar{x} +/- 1.96 \frac{S_x}{\sqrt{n}}$$

Substituting,

$$C.I. = 1832 +/- 1.96 \frac{4295.26656}{\sqrt{34}}$$

$$= 3882.0 - 3275.80$$

We are 95 percent confident that, in the population, the mean contribution to the *Monte* was between 388.20 and 3275.80 florins. This is a wide interval and probably not very useful. A larger sample size would likely give a narrower and more helpful confidence interval.

A confidence interval about a sample proportion can also be calculated. If $\hat{p}$ is the sample proportion and n is the sample size, the 95 percent confidence interval is:

$$C.I. = \hat{p} +/- 1.96 \sqrt{\frac{\hat{p}(1-\hat{p})}{n}}$$

In Chapter 2 we discussed how George Gallup predicted the results of the *Literary Digest* 1936 presidential election survey. The *Literary Digest* mailed out 10,000,000 ballots and received 2,376,523 replies. The results were kept a closely guarded secret until a scheduled release date. Gallup mailed 3,000 postcards to a random sample of the 10,000,000 individuals and received back about 700. Gallup's results from this sample were 44 percent of the two-party vote favoring Franklin D. Roosevelt and 56 percent favoring Alfred Landon. Gallup published his prediction of the *Literary Digest* results in July 1936, before the *Literary Digest* survey was completed. For Gallup's sample $\hat{p}$ was .44 and n was 700. The confidence interval about this proportion is:

$$C.I. = \hat{p} +/- 1.96 \sqrt{\frac{\hat{p}(1-\hat{p})}{n}}$$

substituting,

$$= .44 +/- 1.96 \sqrt{\frac{.44(1-.44)}{700}}$$

$$= .44 +/- .0367$$

$$= .4032 - .4767$$

We could have been 95 percent confident that between 40.32 percent and 47.67 percent of those responding to the *Literary Digest* survey would favor Roosevelt in a two-party vote. The actual *Literary Digest* survey results (at the time the unknown population parameter) was 43 percent favoring Roosevelt.

Here we calculated the 95 percent confidence interval using in our formula the value 1.96, the critical z-value for a .05 two-tail probability (see Table 4.4). If we used 2.24, the critical z-value for a .025 two-tail probability, we would calculate a 97.5 percent confidence interval. While other z-values can be used to calculate any desired confidence interval, 95 percent confidence intervals have become the standard in the social sciences.

5

t-Test

Now we will discuss the t-test as it concerns the significance of the difference between two means or the probability that chance could have produced the differences observed. Chapter 4 discussed the logic of the t-test. We will consider the t-test for both *paired* and *independent* samples. Other uses of the t-test include correlation and regression analysis (discussed in subsequent chapters).

PAIRED CASES

There are many examples that involve the difference between two means calculated from cases paired with one another. They include the ages of mothers at the birth of their first child and last child, and the amount of money that a candidate raised and spent during a campaign, for example. In each instance, the data form pairs of observations from the same person, candidate, or family. Because they form "natural" pairs, one hopes that variation caused by other factors, not being analyzed, is reduced.

Consider the example of the age at which nineteenth-century Irish men and women immigrated to the United States. The 1900 census for Ward 3 of Worcester, Massachusetts, lists twenty-three couples in which the husband and wife both emigrated from Ireland. While three of these people came as small children (we can, therefore, assume that they did not immigrate on their own), there were twenty couples in which both members individually or as a couple came to the United States between the ages of twelve and thirty-one. The mean year of arrival for each group was 1873. The wives arrived at an average age of eighteen, while the husbands came at an average age of twenty (see Table 5.1).

Table 5.1
Age at Time of Arrival in United States of Irish Immigrant Husbands and Wives, Ward 3, Worcester, Massachusetts, 1900 U. S. Census

Couple	Husband Age at Arrival	Wife Age at Arrival	Difference d = (Husand - Wife)	$(d_i - \bar{d})^2$	
Gorman	17	17	0	$(0 - 1.9)^2$ =	3.61
Hill	16	15	1	$(1 - 1.9)^2$ =	0.81
McGrath	25	19	6	$(6 - 1.9)^2$ =	16.81
Ryan	20	18	2	$(2 - 1.9)^2$ =	0.01
Moynihan	16	15	1	$(1 - 1.9)^2$ =	0.81
Sullivan	16	18	-2	$(-2 - 1.9)^2$ =	15.21
Kane	17	18	-1	$(-1 - 1.9)^2$ =	8.41
O'Connor	24	12	12	$(12 - 1.9)^2$ =	102.01
Foley	17	17	0	$(0 - 1.9)^2$ =	3.61
McGourty	20	18	2	$(2 - 1.9)^2$ =	0.01
Powers	24	19	5	$(5 - 1.9)^2$ =	9.61
Cronon	17	19	-2	$(-2 - 1.9)^2$ =	15.21
Barry	18	21	-3	$(-3 - 1.9)^2$ =	24.01
Burke	12	22	-10	$(-10 - 1.9)^2$ =	141.61
McCathy	31	27	4	$(4 - 1.9)^2$ =	4.41
Mulcahy	21	19	2	$(2 - 1.9)^2$ =	0.01
Sullivan	20	16	4	$(4 - 1.9)^2$ =	4.41
Curnan	18	17	1	$(1 - 1.9)^2$ =	0.81
Kane	20	17	3	$(3 - 1.9)^2$ =	1.21
McNamara	29	16	13	$(13 - 1.9)^2$ =	123.21
Total	398	360	38	$\sum(d_i - \bar{d})^2$ =	475.8
n	20	20	20		
mean	19.90	18.00	1.9		
standard deviation(s)	4.678	3.044	5.004208755		

Source: Authors' calculations from Twelfth Census of the United States, 1900. Federal Population Schedules, MSS.

While one might expect that the forces that led to their emigration were unrelated to gender, the social dynamics of the Irish countryside suggest differently. There was considerable pressure to "keep the name" on the land—a responsibility for males in the family. Additionally, older sons were obligated to care for their parents and younger siblings. Sociologists also discuss "male inertia" as a force that kept sons at home. Young women, in contrast—having no familial responsibilities and with an intimate knowledge of the harsh life awaiting them should they stay—were anxious to leave.[1]

This reasoning suggests two hypotheses for the Irish emigration. The first—the null hypothesis—is that the probability of emigration is independent of gender: young men and young women of a given age were equally likely to emigrate. The second—the alternative hypothesis—is that young women were likely to emigrate at an earlier age than young men. If we can assume that the forty emigrants ended up in the Worcester area through a process that worked like a coin toss or random sample, then a test of the significance of the difference between the two mean ages at arrival in the United States is appropriate.

The two elements of a significance test are the test statistic (here, a t-value) and an associated probability. The probability tells us how likely it is that a hypothesized population could have produced the observed test statistic by chance. Here, the population under the null hypothesis is one in which young Irish men and women of the same age had the same probability of emigrating. The alternative hypothesis is a population in which women emigrate at a younger age than men.

Computation of the t-Value for Paired Cases

To obtain a t-value, divide the observed mean difference ($\overline{d} = \overline{x}_1 - \overline{x}_2$) by its estimated standard deviation ($S_{\overline{d}}$). With paired observations, the standard deviation of all possible differences under the null hypothesis of no differences in the population is

$$S_{\overline{d}} = S_d / \sqrt{n} = \frac{\sqrt{\Sigma(d_i - \overline{d})^2 / (n-1)}}{\sqrt{n}}$$

The t-value is

$$t = \overline{d} / S_{\overline{d}}$$

For the Irish immigrants

$$\bar{d} = \bar{x}(Husband) - \bar{x}(Wife)$$

$$= 19.9 - 18$$

$$= +1.9$$

$$S_{\bar{d}} = S_d / \sqrt{n} = \frac{\sqrt{\sum(d_i - \bar{d})^2 / n - 1}}{\sqrt{n}}$$

$$= \frac{\sqrt{475.8 / (20 - 1)}}{\sqrt{20}}$$

$$= 1.1190$$

$$t = \frac{\bar{d}}{S_{\bar{d}}}$$

$$= \frac{1.9}{1.1190}$$

$$= 1.6979$$

The degrees of freedom (DF) can be expressed as n - 1, where n is the number of pairs.

$$DF = n - 1$$
$$= 20 - 1$$
$$= 19$$

If the null hypothesis is correct and there are no differences in the probability of emigration for men and women of the same age, and if we can view the Worcester couples as selected randomly from that population, then we can imagine the process of randomly selecting twenty couples as being repeated many times. If a t- value were computed for each of these occasions, they would be distributed as in Figure 5.1. This is the t-distribution for nineteen degrees of freedom. The figure also shows the standard normal distribution. With nineteen degrees of freedom, the t and standard normal (z) distributions are quite similar.

Figure 5.1
All Possible t_d Values under the Null Hypothesis of No Difference, DF = 19

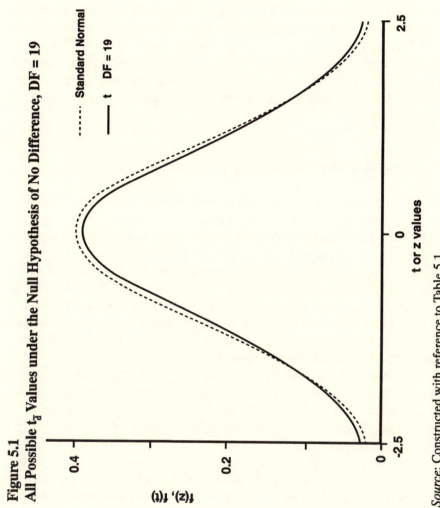

Source: Constructed with reference to Table 5.1.

The Rejection Region

To test the hypothesis that the observed data came from a population in which there were no gender differences in age of emigration, we start with the t-distribution expected with the null hypothesis. We then determine a rejection region such that, if the calculated (observed) t-value falls into the region, this is evidence something has been observed that, while possible under the null hypothesis, is unlikely. In other words, this is evidence supporting the rejection of the null hypothesis and acceptance of the alternative hypothesis. For most social science and historical research, .05 (5 percent) of the total area under the curve has been accepted as appropriate for a rejection region.

One-tailed and Two-tailed Hypotheses

The alternative hypothesis takes three possible forms: the two-tailed and two different one-tailed hypotheses. The *two-tailed hypothesis* involves any theory that predicts the two groups will be different but is uncertain which one will have larger values and which will have smaller values. With the two-tailed hypothesis, the theory does not predict where the difference will be—in the negative region to the left of zero (the center of the distribution under the null hypothesis), or in the positive region to the right of zero. To anticipate both possibilities, the .05 rejection region (or whatever rejection region is selected) is divided into two regions here, of .025 each—one for the left and one for the right tail.

A *one-tailed hypothesis* is used with a theory that predicts which of the two means will be larger—and hence, whether the population difference here $(\bar{d} = \mu_1 - \mu_2)$ will be positive or negative. With a one-tailed hypothesis, the entire .05 rejection region is allocated to the tail in which the t-value is predicted.

The values of t that define the rejection region are determined from a table of critical t-values (see Table A.2 at the end of the Appendix). To locate the appropriate critical t-value for a two-tailed hypothesis, first locate the desired rejection region for two-tailed hypotheses at the top of the table—here, .05—and then the appropriate degrees of freedom: here, 19. The rejection region is defined by a t-value of + or -2.09 (see Figure 5.2).

For a one-tailed hypothesis, the procedure is the same except that the desired rejection region at the top of the table is for the one-tailed hypothesis. For degrees of freedom equal nineteen and a one-tailed .05 positive rejection region, the critical t-value is +1.73. If the one-tailed hypothesis

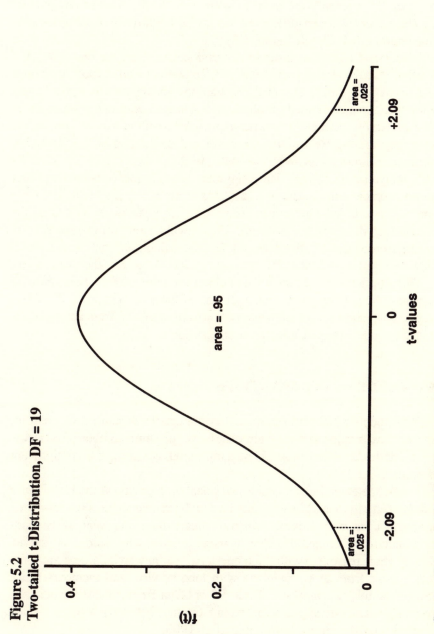

Figure 5.2
Two-tailed t-Distribution, DF = 19

area = .95

area = .025

area = .025

+2.09

0

−2.09

t-values

f(t)

0.4

0.2

0

Source: Constructed with reference to Table 5.1.

were that the women were older than the men at the time of emigration, then the expected mean difference would be negative and the critical t-value would be -1.73 (see Figure 5.3).

Tables and computer programs occasionally report the one-tailed and sometimes the two-tailed probability of t. To convert a one-tailed into a two-tailed probability, simply double the probability. To convert a two-tailed probability of t into a one-tailed probability, divide the two-tailed probability in half. For example, when the two-tailed probability of t is .106, the one-tailed probability is .053. Computer Program A.2 at the end of the Appendix reports both a one-tailed and a two-tailed probability.

Now we return to the Irish emigrants. The alternative hypothesis was that the women came to the United States at an earlier age than their husbands—a one-tailed alternative. The observed mean difference is in the hypothesized direction (+1.9 years). The critical t-value for probability .05 and nineteen degrees of freedom is 1.73. The calculated t-value is 1.6979, which falls just outside the .05 rejection region. We cannot, therefore, reject the null hypothesis. Program A.2 calculates the one-tailed probability to be less than .0529. Thus, more than 5 percent of the time, a group with differences such as those observed could be randomly selected from a population in which gender was not a factor in emigration.

INDEPENDENT OBSERVATIONS

With independent observations, it is impossible to pair cases. Instead, there are two groups that may not even have the same number of observations. The logic of the t-test is the same, although some calculations are different.

In 1968, Nelson Polsby, a political scientist, argued that the U.S. House of Representatives had become institutionalized over time. He contrasted the House in its early period—when members came and went, when leadership came from comparatively new members, and when leadership served for only short periods—with the modern House, in which careers are long, leaders arise from those members with long service, and members finish their public life in Congress.[2] Table 5.2 is taken from Polsby's article and presents the number of years served in Congress before first being elected as Speaker of the House before and after 1900.

The average number of years served before being elected speaker was 7.12 before 1900 and 25.36 after 1900. The theory that speakers were selected from different groups before and after 1900 seems to be supported. But is the difference significant? Could the leaders have been se-

Figure 5.3
One-tailed t-Distribution, DF = 19

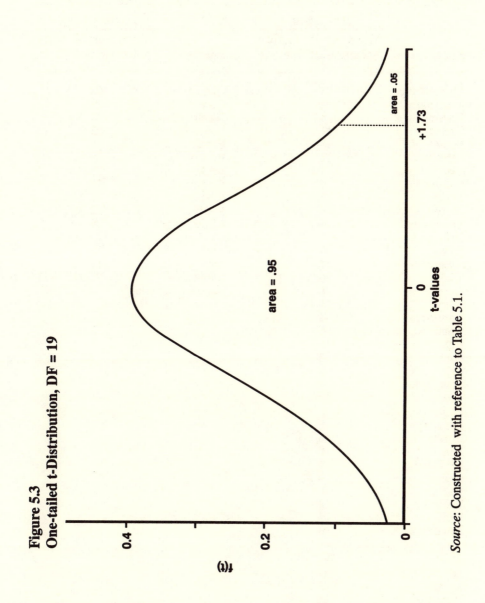

area = .95

area = .05

+1.73

0

t-values

f(t)

0.4

0.2

0

Source: Constructed with reference to Table 5.1.

Table 5.2
Years Served in the U.S. Congress before First Selection as Speaker of the House, 1789–1962

Speaker	1789-1899 Years Served before Selection as Speaker	Speaker	1903-1962 Years Served before Selection as Speaker
Muhlenberg	1	Cannon	28
Trumbull	3	Clark	26
Dayton	4	Gillett	26
Sedgwick	11	Longworth	22
Macon	10	Garner	26
Varnum	12	Rainey	28
Clay	1	Bryns	25
Cheves	5	Bankhead	15
Taylor	7	Rayburn	27
Barbour	6	Martin	22
Stevenson	6	McCormack	34
Bell	7		
Polk	10	Total	279
Hunter	2	(n)	11
White	6	Mean	25.36363636
Jones	8	Variance (sample)	22.25454545
Davis	6		
Winthrop	8		
Cobb	6		
Boyd	14		
Banks	2		
Orr	7		
Pennington	1		
Grow	10		
Colfax	8		
Pomeroy	8		
Blaine	6		
Kerr	8		
Randall	13		
Keifer	4		
Carlisle	6		
Reed	12		
Crisp	8		
Henderson	16		
Total	242		
(n)	34		
Mean	7.117647059		
Variance (sample)	14.16755793		

Source: Authors' calculations from data in Nelson W. Polsby, "The Institutionalization of the U.S. House of Representatives," *American Political Science
Review*, 62 (March 1968), 144–168.

lected from similar groups and the difference observed be due to chance?

The null hypothesis in this case states that there is a population of members from which the speakers have been selected by a random process. Within the population, years of service varies. Some of the members have long service and others less, but the variance and mean years of service for the population before 1900 is the same as for the population after 1900. If the null hypothesis is correct, we can attribute the differences observed to chance—not to a change in the criteria for selecting the speaker, or some other explanation.

The alternative hypothesis is that the population from which speakers are selected by some random process has changed. In the population before 1900, the average number of years served was less than after 1900. This alternative hypothesis is one tailed and has the second mean in the population (after 1900) larger than the first (before 1900).

To decide between the null and alternative hypotheses, a t-value is calculated and its probability determined. The rejection region will be one tailed in the negative tail, the rejection area being .05.

The Pooled Variance Estimate

For the moment, we will assume that the population variances are the same before and after 1900. If this is correct, then, we can combine the two sample variances into a single pooled variance estimate of the common population variance. This is:

$$s^2 = \frac{(n_1 - 1)s_1^2 + (n_2 - 1)s_2^2}{(n_1 - 1) + (n_2 - 1)}$$

$$= \frac{(34 - 1)14.16755793 + (11 - 1)22.2545454}{(34 - 1) + (11 - 1)}$$

$$= 16.0482527$$

The pooled variance estimate of the standard deviation of the distribution of all possible differences under the null hypothesis is:

$$s_{\bar{d}} = \sqrt{(s^2 / n_1 + s^2 / n_2)}$$

$$= \sqrt{(16.0482527 / 34 + 16.0482527 / 11)}$$

$$= 1.38958249$$

From this, we can calculate the t-value

$$t = \frac{\bar{x}_1 - \bar{x}_2}{s_{\bar{d}}}$$

$$= \frac{7.117647059 - 25.3636363}{1.38958249}$$

$$= -13.13055499$$

The degrees of freedom are:

$$DF = (n_1 - 1) + (n_2 - 1)$$
$$= (34 - 1) + (11 - 1)$$
$$= 43$$

From Table A.2 in the Appendix, we determine that the critical t-value for DF = 43 and a one-tailed probability of .05 is -1.68. The observed t-value of -13.13 is well within the rejection region (see Figure 5.4). Using Program A.2, the one-tailed probability is found to be less than .0000023. The null hypothesis is rejected, and the alternative hypothesis—that the population from which speakers were selected changed after 1900—is accepted. In the population, the mean years of service before being elected speaker increased after 1900.

Separate Variance Estimate of t

The assumption made in calculating the t-value in the example above was that the variances about the two means were the same. If the two variances are not equal, then the t-test is approached differently. An example might be helpful. Frederick Mosteller and David L. Wallace studied the authorship of *The Federalist Papers*. Part of their analysis involved counting the number of one-letter words per 1,000 words of text in those of the papers whose authorships were known.[3] The results for the eight Hamilton papers and seven Madison papers are presented in Table 5.3.

Significance of the Difference between Two Variances

The F-ratio (see Chapter 7) is used to test the significance of the differ-

Figure 5.4
All Possible t-Values under the Null Hypothesis of No Difference, DF = 43

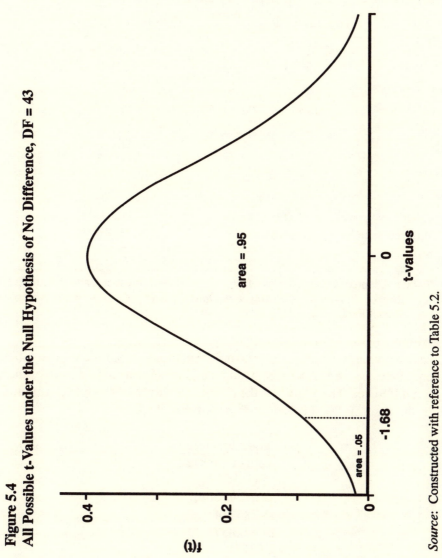

Source: Constructed with reference to Table 5.2.

Table 5.3
Rate of Use of One-letter Words per 1,000 Words of Text in Hamilton and Madison *Federalist Papers*

	Hamilton Papers	Madison Papers
	24	20
	21	27
	23	19
	24	30
	33	11
	28	17
	28	27
	37	
Mean	27.25	21.571428
Variance (sample)	29.642857	45.285714
n	8	7

Source: Adapted from Frederick Mosteller, Stephen E. Fienberg, and Robert E. K. Rourke, *Beginning Statistics with Data Analysis* (Reading, MA: Addison-Wesley Publishing, 1983), 290.

ence between two variances. The null hypothesis is that there is no difference between the two variables, and the alternative hypothesis is that there is a difference. The F -ratio is the ratio of the larger to the smaller variance. In the case of *The Federalist Papers* research,

$$F = \frac{\text{larger variance}}{\text{smaller variance}}$$
$$= \frac{S^2(Madison)}{S^2(Hamilton)}$$
$$= \frac{45.285714}{29.642857}$$
$$= 1.52771$$

Degrees of Freedom $= (n(Madison) - 1)$ and $(n(Hamilton) - 1)$
$= (7 - 1)$ and $(8 - 1)$
$= 6$ and 7

Our alternative hypothesis is that the two variances are simply different—not, for example, that the variance for Hamilton is larger than that for Madison. Thus, a two-tailed F-test is appropriate. Using computer Program A.4 (in the Appendix) we find the one-tailed probability for F = 1.527711 and DF = 6 and 7 to be .2947. The two-tailed probability is twice this, or .5894. The two variances are not significantly different. For the sake of an example, however, we will treat them as if they were.

The null hypothesis is that the same process produced one-letter words and—therefore, with the same frequency—in both Madison's and Hamilton's writings. The alternative hypothesis is that each author had a style that caused him to use a different number of one-letter words in a given amount of text. The alternative hypothesis is a two-tailed hypothesis; the proposition does not predict which author will use more one-letter words. Assuming that the two variances are unequal, we calculated a separate variance estimate of the standard deviation of the distribution of all possible differences between means under the null hypothesis as:

$$
\begin{aligned}
S_{\overline{d}} &= \sqrt{\frac{S^2(Hamilton)}{n(Hamilton)} + \frac{S^2(Madison)}{n(Madison)}} \\
&= \sqrt{\frac{29.642857}{8} + \frac{45.285714}{7}} \\
&= 3.1897874
\end{aligned}
$$

A statistic called t', which approximates t, is calculated as:

$$
\begin{aligned}
t'_{\overline{d}} &= \frac{\overline{x}(Hamilton) - \overline{x}(Madison)}{S_{\overline{d}}} \\
&= \frac{27.25 - 21.571428}{3.1897874} \\
&= 1.7802352
\end{aligned}
$$

As t' and t are not the same, use of the standard tables of t-probabilities or computer programs for calculating probabilities requires adjusting the appropriate degrees of freedom. Statisticians Frederick Mosteller, Stephen Fienberg, and Robert Rourke suggest a conservative approach: use as the degrees of freedom the smaller of the two degrees of freedom—in this case, those associated with Madison.[4]

$$DF(Madison) = n(Madison) - 1$$
$$= 7 - 1$$
$$= 6$$

For six degrees of freedom and a two-tailed significance level of .05, Table A.2 shows that the critical t-value is 2.45. The observed t'-value is smaller than the critical t-value, so the null hypothesis is not rejected. There is no significant difference between Madison's and Hamilton's use of one-letter words in *The Federalist Papers*.

Mosteller, Fienberg, and Rourke's analysis is conservative and increases the risk of accepting the null hypothesis when it is actually incorrect. Hubert Blalock, another statistician, offers a less conservative, but more complicated, calculation of the degrees of freedom.[5]

$$DF = \frac{[\frac{S^2(Hamilton)}{(n(Hamilton)-1)} + \frac{S^2(Madison)}{(n(Madison)-1)}]^2}{[\frac{S^2(Hamilton)}{n(Hamilton)-1}]^2 [\frac{1}{n(Hamilton)+1}] + [\frac{S^2(Madison)}{n(Madison)-1}]^2 [\frac{1}{n(Madison)+1}]} - 2$$

$$= 13.23294331$$
$$\approx 13$$

The two-tailed critical t-value for thirteen (rounding off the degrees of freedom) is 2.16. As the observed t'-value is again less than the critical t-value, the null hypothesis is still not rejected. There is no significant difference between the two means.

If we accept the result of the F-test between the two variances and calculate the ordinary pooled variance estimate of t, we get:

$$S^2 = \frac{[n(Hamilton) - 1]\ S^2(Hamilton) + [n(Madison) - 1]\ S^2(Madison)}{[n(Hamilton) - 1] + [n(Madison) - 1]}$$

$$= \frac{(8 - 1)\ 29.642857 + (7 - 1)\ 45.285714}{(8 - 1) + (7 - 1)}$$

$$= 36.862636$$

$$S_{\bar{d}} = \sqrt{S^2 / n(Hamilton) + S^2 / n(Madison)}$$
$$= 3.14227$$

$$t_{\bar{d}} = \frac{\bar{x}(Hamilton) - \bar{x}(Madison)}{S_{\bar{d}}}$$
$$= \frac{27.25 - 21.571428}{3.14227}$$
$$= 1.80715$$

$$DF = n(Hamilton) - 1 + n(Madison) - 1$$
$$= (8 - 1) + (7 - 1)$$
$$= 13$$

The critical t-value for a two-tailed test and thirteen degrees of freedom at significance level .05 is 2.16. It is still larger than the observed t-value of 1.807. Program A.2 finds the two-tailed probability to be less than .0930. Even with this least conservative approach, there is still no evidence of a significant difference between Hamilton and Madison in their use of one-letter words.

TYPE I AND TYPE II ERRORS

With significance tests there are two possible errors: Type I and Type II. In their original paper on significance tests, J. Neyman and E. S. Pearson recalled Laplace's work on determining the appropriate number of jurors to convict a person accused of a crime. Here also, there are two possible errors: convicting an innocent person, and acquitting a guilty person. If there is a strict criterion for conviction—a unanimous jury, for example—then fewer innocent people will be convicted, but more guilty people will go free. Likewise, if there is a less strict criterion for conviction—the vote of just one juror, say—then more guilty people will be convicted, but more innocent people will be convicted as well.[6] A *Type I error* is to reject the null hypothesis when it is correct. The commonly employed significance level of .05, if used consistently, will result in making this error 5 percent of the time; that is an acceptably low probability.

But what of the Type II error? A *Type II error* is to accept the null hypothesis when it is wrong. Generally, the larger the number of cases and the greater the difference between the population value and the value under the null hypothesis, the less the chances of making a Type II error. In the case of Madison and Hamilton, if we had a larger sample of writings and a bigger difference in their use of one-letter words, there would be less chance of making a Type II error. The probability of a Type II error can be estimated from the available observations if one can hypothesize the true value of the population difference.[7] We will not calculate Type II error probabilities here.

6

Cross-Classification

Cross-classification or cross-tabulation is a procedure used to analyze the relationship between two nominal or ordinal categorical variables. It examines the nature of the relationship between the two variables, whether or not the relationship is significant, and the strength of the relationship. Cross-classification is the most often used method of presenting quantified historical research.

Properly presented cross-classification tables are self-explanatory. For instance, Table 6.1 presents the population of the New England states by race for the year 1790. Table 6.2 presents the same information in a different form; the racial population of each state is now listed in percentages.

Table 6.1
Population of New England States in 1790, by Race

State	White Population	African-American Population	Total
Maine	96,107	536	96,643
New Hampshire	141,112	787	141,899
Vermont	85,072	269	85,341
Massachusetts	373,187	5,369	378,556
Rhode Island	64,670	4,442	69,112
Connecticut	232,236	5,419	237,655
Total	992,384	16,822	1,009,206

Source: Adapted from Lorenzo Johnston Greene, *The Negro in Colonial New England* (New York: Atheneum, 1969), 76.

Table 6.2
Population of New England States in 1790, by Race Given in Percents

State	White Population	African-American Population	Total %	Total n
Maine	99.45	0.55	100.0	96,643
New Hampshire	99.45	0.55	100.0	141,899
Vermont	99.68	0.32	100.0	85,341
Massachusetts	98.58	1.42	100.0	378,556
Rhode Island	93.57	6.43	100.0	69,112
Connecticut	97.72	2.28	100.0	237,655
Total	98.33	1.67	100.0	1,009,206

Source: Authors' calculations from data in Table 6.1.

Both tables tell us different things. Rhode Island, for example, which had only the third highest number of African-American residents, had the highest percentage of African-Americans in its population.

Consider a more intricate example. One of the things investigated by Kathleen Neils Conzen in her study of mid-nineteenth-century Milwaukee was the attitude of native-born and foreign-born residents toward child labor. Table 6.3, adapted from Conzen's research, presents the number of

Table 6.3
School Attendance of Native-born and Foreign-born Five to Seventeen-year-old Boys in Milwaukee, 1850

School Attendance	Nativity Native Born	Nativity Foreign Born[a]	Total
Attended	95	234	329
Did not attend	20	149	169
Total	115	383	498

[a]Children of foreign-born fathers are composed of just three groups: British, Irish, and Germans.

Source: Adapted from Kathleen Neils Conzen, *Immigrant Milwaukee, 1836–1860: Accommodation and Community in a Frontier City* (Cambridge, MA: Harvard University Press, 1976), 91.

native-born and foreign-born boys between the ages of five and seventeen who were attending school. Conzen hypothesized that school attendance was one manifestation of parents' attitudes toward child labor.[1]

Like most statistical procedures, cross-classification involves a certain amount of jargon. Each number within the cross-classification is in a *cell*. The number in the cell is called the *cell frequency*; it is the number of times that result occurred. Using Table 6.3 as an example, ninety-five native-born boys between the ages of five and seventeen attended school, and 149 foreign-born boys did not. *Rows* describe the information presented horizontally across the table—in this case, categories of the boys' school attendance. *Columns* present the data vertically—in this case, categories of the boys' nativity. The last column on the right contains the *row marginal* totals, and the bottom row contains the *column marginal* totals. The sum of the row marginals equals the sum of the column marginals, and both equal the total number of cases.

There are certain things that we can learn simply by examining a table's cell frequencies and its row and column marginals. From Table 6.3, for example, we learn that most of the boys were foreign born and attended school. Different information becomes evident once we convert the cell frequencies to percentages.

There are three ways to calculate percents in a table: by row, column, and cell. To calculate the *row percentages*, divide each cell frequency by the row marginal and multiply the result by 100. Using the data in Table 6.3, divide 95 by 329 and multiply by 100; the results for Conzen's data are shown in Table 6.4. We find that only 28.88 percent of those boys attending school had native-born parents. To calculate *column percentages*, divide each cell frequency by the column marginal and multiply by 100; from Table 6.5 we learn that 82.61 percent of the sons of native-born parents were

Table 6.4
School Attendance of Native-born and Foreign-born Five to Seventeen-Year-old Boys in Milwaukee, 1850, as Percentaged by Row

| School Attendance | Nativity | | Total | n |
	Native Born	Foreign Born		
Attended	28.88	71.12	100.00	(329)
Did not attend	11.83	88.17	100.00	(169)

Source: Authors' calculations from data in Table 6.3.

Table 6.5
School Attendance of Native-born and Foreign-born Five to Seventeen-year-old Boys in Milwaukee, 1850, as Percentaged by Column

School Attendance	Nativity	
	Native Born	Foreign Born
Attended	82.61	61.10
Did not attend	17.39	38.90
Total (n)	100.00 (115)	100.00 (383)

Source: Authors' calculations from data in Table 6.3.

attending school. To calculate *cell percentages*, divide each cell frequency by the total number of cases (the sum of either the row or column marginals) and multiply by 100; from Table 6.6 we learn that 19.07 percent of the male population of Milwaukee between the ages of five and seventeen attended school and had native-born parents. All of these percentages can be easily calculated by hand or with a calculator; computer packages calculate row, column, and other percents in tables, as well.

Which percentage is appropriate? The row percentage tells us what percentage of the row is in each column category. Similarly, the column percentage reports what percentage of the column lies in each row category. Finally, the cell percentage presents what percentage of all the cases are in each cell. The key word is *of*. In Table 6.4 (percentaged by rows), 28.88 percent *of* those attending school were native born. In the table

Table 6.6
School Attendance of Native-born and Foreign-born Five to Seventeen-year-old Boys in Milwaukee, 1850, as Percentaged by Cell

School Attendance	Nativity	
	Native Born	Foreign Born
Attended	19.07	46.99
Did not attend	4.02	29.92
	Total (n) = 100.00 (498)	

Source: Authors' calculations from data in Table 6.3.

percentaged by columns (Table 6.5), 82.61 percent *of* the native-born boys attended school. In the table percentaged by cells (Table 6.6), 19.07 percent *of* all the boys were native born and attending school.

Which is appropriate? To answer this we need to identify the purpose of the table. There are three possibilities: the impact of one variable (the cause or independent variable) on another (the effect or dependent variable); the composition of a group; and finally, the composition of all the cases together.

Let us consider several examples. Is the intent of the research to show the impact of one variable on another? Then percentage by categories of the independent variable—row if the independent variable is the row variable; column if the independent variable is the column variable. Recall Conzen's initial interest: the impact of ethnicity on child labor. The column percentage best answers that question. While 82.61 percent of the sons of native-born parents attended school, only 61.10 percent of the boys with foreign-born parents did. The consequence of being native born, in effect, was to increase school attendance by 21.51 percent.

Or is the purpose to determine the composition of all the cases taken together? Then cell percentages are appropriate. If Conzen intended to show what boys between the ages of five and seventeen were doing in Milwaukee in 1850, she could use cell percentages. The largest group (46.99 percent) was foreign-born boys attending school. The smallest group was native-born boys not attending school (4.02 percent).

Or is the intent to establish the composition of a group? If so, then the researcher would use percentage by categories of that group. Row or column percentages are appropriate depending on whether the row or column variable defines the group. If Conzen were interested in describing the male population of Milwaukee schools in 1850, she could have percentaged by rows to conclude that foreign-born boys outnumbered native-born boys in school by nearly two and a half to one (71.12 percent to 28.88 percent).

TEST OF SIGNIFICANCE: STATISTICAL INDEPENDENCE AND CHI-SQUARE

The next step involves significance. Previously, we defined two events as statistically independent if the occurrence of one had no effect on the occurrence or nonoccurrence of the other. Statistically independent events are not causally connected. Here the same idea applies. If being native born and attending school are independent, then the probability of a boy's being both native born and attending school is the product of his individual probabilities. The probability of a boy's being native born is 115/498; the probability of a boy's attending school is 329/498. If they are independent, we expect the probability of being both to be (115/498)(329/498) = .1526. The actual probability of being both, however, is (95/498) = .1908, which is more than expected. If nativity and attendance were independent, we would expect the number of native-born boys attending school to be:

$$\left(\frac{115}{498}\right)\left(\frac{329}{498}\right)(498) = 75.97$$

The number of native-born boys attending school would be seventy-six, while actually there were ninety-five. This amounts to nineteen boys, or 25 percent more than expected [(19/75.97)(100) = 25.01].

With the probability of attending school calculated to be 329/498 = .6606, and with 115 native-born boys, what is the probability that ninety-five of them attended school? This can be calculated using the binomial formula or the t-distribution, but those calculations would prove tedious. Early in the twentieth century, Karl Pearson developed *chi-square* (x^2)—a method of determining statistical independence in cross-classification. Pearson's chi-square measures the difference between the observed and expected tables. If F_o stands for the *observed frequency* of a particular cell and F_e for the *expected frequency* of that same cell if the variables were independent, then

$$\text{chi-square} = \chi^2 = \sum \frac{(F_o - F_e)^2}{F_e}$$

Chi-square is used to determine whether or not the differences between the observed and expected tables are larger than what would have occurred by sample variation.

To calculate the value of chi-square, we first construct an expected table in which there is no relationship between the two variables. Then we compare it to the observed data. The expected table retains the marginal totals from the observed table (Table 6.3). We calculate the frequencies for each cell of the expected table by multiplying either the row proportion by the column totals or the column proportion by the row totals (because each method gives the same result). We calculated Table 6.7, the expected table, using the row proportions and the column totals.

The value of chi-square in this example is 18.26. If there were no difference between the observed and expected frequencies, then the value of chi-square would equal zero. Notice that, in calculating chi-square, it is important to retain as many decimals as possible in intermediate calculations, although chi-square itself need only be reported to two decimal places. We rounded the table of expected values only to simplify comparison. Note also that the chi-square statistic is calculated from the raw cell frequencies, and not from cell percentages.

Table 6.7
Expected Cell Frequencies Derived from Data on School Attendance of Native-born and Foreign-born Five to Seventeen-year-old Boys in Milwaukee, 1850

| School Attendance | Nativity | | Total | Row Proportion |
	Native Born	Foreign Born		
Attended	75.9739 (329/498)115	253.0261 (329/498)383	329	329/498
Did not Attend	39.0261 (169/498)115	129.9739 (169/498)383	169	169/498
Total	115	383	498	
Column proportion	115 / 498	383 / 498		

chi − square = $\chi^2 = \Sigma (F_o - F_e)^2 / F_e$

F_o	F_e	$\dfrac{(F_o - F_e)^2}{F_e}$		
95	(329/498)115	$\dfrac{[95-(329/498)115]^2}{(329/498)115}$	=	4.76469775
234	(329/498)383	$\dfrac{[234-(329/498)383]^2}{(329/498)383}$	=	1.43065337
20	(169/498)115	$\dfrac{[20-(169/498)115]^2}{(169/498)115}$	=	9.27565420
149	(169/498)383	$\dfrac{[149-(169/498)383]^2}{(169/498)383}$	=	2.78511810
Total 498	498		χ^2 =	18.25612342

Source: Authors' calculations from data in Table 6.3.

How can the χ^2 statistic be evaluated? What does a χ^2 value of 18.26 mean? If there is no relationship between the two variables—that is, if attending school and nativity are independent—then any combination of school attendance and nativity is *possible*, but not all possibilities are equally likely. The χ^2 distribution indicates the probability of getting a particular χ^2 value through sample variation given the fact that the two variables are independent.

If the value of χ^2 is greater than or equal to the critical value of chi-square, then we can reject the null hypothesis and conclude that the relationship is significant. (See the discussion of significance in Chapter 4.) If the value of chi-square is less than the critical chi-square, then we cannot reject the null hypothesis and we conclude instead that there is no significant relationship between the two variables.

The χ^2 distribution has one parameter: *degrees of freedom* (DF). The degrees of freedom are the number of independent values possible when assigning expected cell frequencies with fixed marginals. That notion is not quite as intimidating as it seems. If the null hypothesis is correct—that is, if the two variables are statistically independent—then the expected cell frequencies can be calculated from the row and column marginals. But as these expected frequencies must total the row and column marginals, we can calculate only a certain number before we can determine the remainder by subtracting from the known expected cell frequencies and marginals. The number of expected cell frequencies that *must* be calculated and from which the rest can be calculated is what constitutes the degrees of freedom for the cross-tabulation.[2] In a two by two table, once you calculate one cell frequency, it determines the values of all the other cell frequencies. See the example illustrated in Table 6.8. If you were to calculate an expected cell

Table 6.8
Setup for Finding Degrees of Freedom in a Two by Two Table, with Reference to Tables 6.3 and 6.7

School Attendance	Nativity		
	Native Born	Foreign Born	Total
Attended	a	c	329
Did not attend	b	d	169
Total	115	383	498

frequency of 75.97 for cell a, you would no longer have the freedom to assign any other cell frequencies, as the marginals are fixed. If a is 75.97, then b must be 115 - 75.97, and c must be 329 - 75.97. And if b is 115 - 75.97 = 39.03, then d must equal 169 - 39.03. There is, therefore, one degree of freedom in a two by two table.

Fortunately, it is unnecessary to do all this to determine the degrees of freedom. There is a convenient formula: multiply the number of rows (r) minus one (r - 1) by the number of columns (c) minus one (c - 1)

$$degrees\ of\ freedom = (r - 1)(c - 1)$$

In a two by two table the number of degrees of freedom equals:

$$(2 - 1)(2 - 1) = 1$$

Now let us complete the significance test. Recall the observed results presented in Table 6.3. The degrees of freedom in a two by two table are (2 - 1)(2 - 1) = 1. Earlier, we calculated chi-square to be 18.25612342. Now consult Table A.3 at the end of the Appendix to determine the value of the critical chi-square. In this case, the critical chi-square for one degree of freedom at a 95 percent significance level is 3.84. Program A.3 finds this probability to be less than .001. As the chi-square value is equal to or greater than the critical chi-square, we can conclude that there is a significant relationship between school attendance and nativity—see Figure 6.1. This conclusion can be generalized from Conzen's sample to the entire population with confidence. As the degrees of freedom increase, the χ^2 distribution shifts to the right, as in Figure 6.2.

Consider another example, using a table of a different size. Melvyn Hammarberg studied the election behavior of rural Americans in the late nineteenth century. He composed a sample of more than 1,000 residents of Indiana in the early 1870s. One finding, presented in Table 6.9, was that the Republican and Democratic parties attracted nearly equal affiliation in the open countryside, but the Republicans attracted a majority of the voters in small towns.[3]

Table 6.10 presents the expected cell frequencies had party affiliation and place of residence been independent (i.e., no relationship), and then calculates chi-square. As the critical chi-square value for DF = 2 (in this three by two table) and probability = .05 (see Table A.3 at the end of the Appendix) is 5.99—(smaller than our calculated chi-square value)—we can be confident that there is a significant difference between the party affiliations of small-town and open countryside voters. Program A.3 calcu-

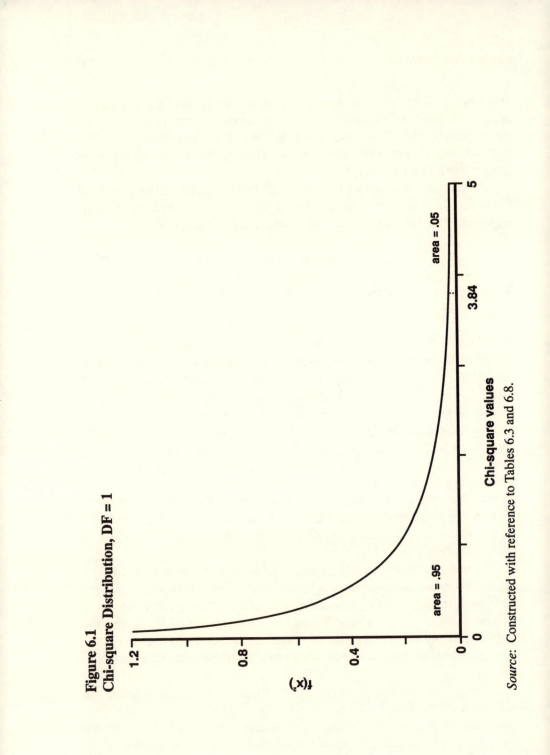

Figure 6.1
Chi-square Distribution, DF = 1

f(x²)

area = .95

area = .05

0   3.84   5

Chi-square values

Source: Constructed with reference to Tables 6.3 and 6.8.

118

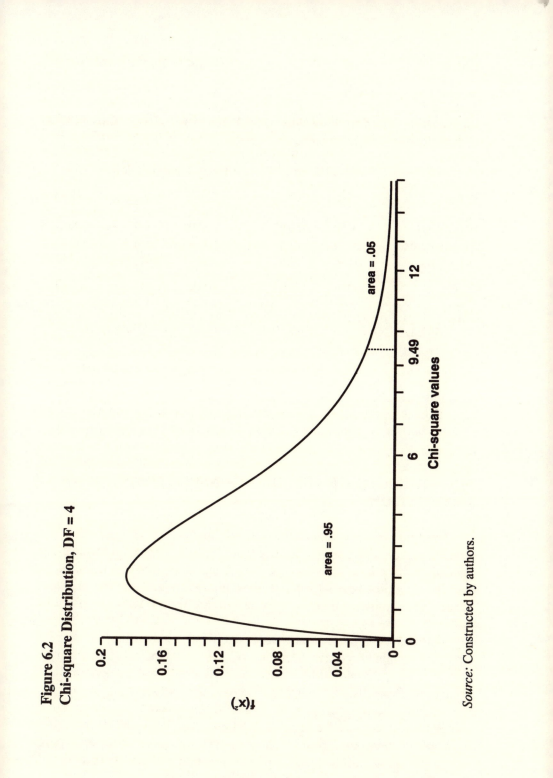

Figure 6.2
Chi-square Distribution, DF = 4

Source: Constructed by authors.

119

Table 6.9
Party Affiliation of Indiana Voters, by Place of Residence, Early 1870s

	Place of Residence				
	Small Towns		Open Countryside		
Party	%	(n)	%	(n)	Total
Republicans	66.00	(526)	43.06	(149)	(675)
Independents	12.04	(96)	17.05	(59)	(155)
Democrats	21.96	(175)	39.89	(138)	(313)
Total	100.00	(797)	100.00	(346)	(1143)

Source: Adapted from Melvyn Hammarberg, "Indiana Farmers and the Group Basis of the Late Nineteenth-century Political Parties," *Journal of American History*, 61 (June 1974), 109.

lates this probability to be less than .001. Small-town voters were more likely to be Republicans (66.00 percent); open countryside voters were more likely to be Democrats or independents (17.05 + 39.89 = 56.94 percent).[4]

THE STRENGTH OF THE RELATIONSHIP: MEASURES OF ASSOCIATION

Thus far we have concentrated on whether or not two variables are related; we can, however, learn more than that. We also can determine the strength of that relationship. Using Conzen's example given earlier, we might want to determine how strong a relationship exists between school attendance and nativity. Is that relationship strong? Weak? How much is explained?

Significance is not central here; a significant relationship may not be strong or explain very much. Measures of association indicate how strongly the variables are related. Most measures of association share certain characteristics. Typically, they range from zero to one; zero denotes no association, and one the strongest possible or a perfect association. By convention, values from 0 to .30 indicate a *weak* relationship, between .30 and .70 a *moderate* relationship, and .70 and above a *strong* relationship. These ranges refer to absolute values. Thus, with a measure of association that ranged from -1 to +1, a value of -.4 would also be moderate.

Table 6.10

Expected Cell Frequencies Derived from Data on Party Affiliation of Indiana Voters, by Place of Residence, Early 1870s

Party	Place of Residence		Total
	Small Towns	Open Countryside	
Republicans	470.6692913 (675/1143)797	204.3307087 (675/1143)346	675
Independents	108.0796151 (155/1143)797	46.9203849 (155/1143)346	155
Democrats	218.2510936 (313/1143)797	94.7489064 (313/1143)346	313
Total	797	346	1143

$$\text{chi} - \text{square} = \chi^2 = \sum (F_o - F_e)^2 / F_e$$

F_o	F_e	$\dfrac{(F_o - F_e)^2}{F_e}$		
526	(675/1143)797	$\dfrac{[526 - (675/1143)797]^2}{(675/1143)797}$	=	6.50454020
149	(675/1143)346	$\dfrac{[149 - (675/1143)346]^2}{(675/1143)346}$	=	14.98300155
96	(155/1143)797	$\dfrac{[96 - (155/1143)797]^2}{(155/1143)797}$	=	1.35008901
59	(155/1143)346	$\dfrac{[59 - (155/1143)346]^2}{(155/1143)346}$	=	3.10988710
175	(313/1143)797	$\dfrac{[175 - (313/1143)797]^2}{(313/1143)797}$	=	8.57112360
138	(313/1143)346	$\dfrac{[138 - (313/1143)346]^2}{(313/1143)346}$	=	19.74331071
Total 1143	1143	χ^2	=	54.26195217

Source: Authors' calculations from data in Table 6.9.

Chi-square-based Measures of Association

The magnitude of chi-square depends on three things: the number of cases, the size of the table, and the strength of the relationship between the two variables. First let us consider the effect of the *number of cases*. In Table 6.11 we have a sample of twenty and a chi-square value of twenty. If you increase the sample size ten times while holding the relationship the same, as we did in Table 6.12, the value of chi-square also increases ten times.

Chi-square is also a function of the *size of the table*; all things being equal, the larger the table, the larger the value of chi-square. If L equals the lesser of the number of rows or columns, then the maximum value of chi-square is (L - 1) n, where n equals the number of cases.

In the middle of the twentieth century, Harald Cramér, a Swedish statistician, introduced Cramér's V^2 as a measure of association. Cramér's V^2 is a chi-square-based measure of association that divides chi-square by the size of the table (L - 1) and the number of cases (n) to isolate the *strength of the relationship*. Cramér's V^2 measures the extent to which the observed table departs from statistical independence (the expected table). A great departure produces a large Cramér's V^2; a small departure produces a small Cramér's V^2.

$$\text{Cramér's } V^2 = \chi^2/(L - 1)n$$

If chi-square is equal to zero (i.e., the observed and the expected are identical), then the strength of the relationship between the two variables will also equal zero. If chi-square equals its maximum value, then the strength of the relationship between the two variables will equal one. Cramér's V^2 is

Table 6.11
Chi-square Value with Sample Size of 20

Observed Results		Expected Frequencies		$(F_o - F_e)^2/F_e$	
10	0	5	5	$(10-5)^2/5$	= 5
0	10	5	5	$(0-5)^2/5$	= 5
				$(0-5)^2/5$	= 5
				$(10-5)^2/5$	= 5
				chi-square	= 20

Table 6.12
Chi-square Value with Sample Size of 200

Observed Results		Expected Frequencies		$(F_o - F_e)^2/F_e$	
100	0	50	50	$(100 - 50)^2/50$	$= 50$
0	100	50	50	$(0 - 50)^2/50$	$= 50$
				$(0 - 50)^2/50$	$= 50$
				$(100 - 50)^2/50$	$= 50$
				chi-square	$= 200$

appropriate for tables of any size.

Using Hammarberg's data provided above (see Table 6.9), the value of Cramer's V² is .0474732.

$$\chi^2 / (L - 1)n = 54.261952 / (1)1143 = .0474732$$

This demonstrates that there was only a weak relationship between the place of residency and the political affiliation of Indiana voters.

Another measure of association based on chi-square is phi-square (ϕ^2). Karl Pearson originated this measure during the 1920s. It is used only with two by two tables. Calculate ϕ^2 by dividing the value of chi-square by n. As L - 1 in a two by two table is always equal to one, then

$$\phi^2 = V^2 = \chi^2 / (L-1)n = \chi^2 / n$$

Consider Conzen's data presented in Table 6.3. In that instance,

$$\phi^2 = \chi^2 / n = 18.256123 / 498 = .0366588$$

This is also a weak relationship.

Some researchers and prepackaged statistical programs report the square root of Cramér's V² and ϕ^2. The effect of using the square root, of course, is to increase the value of the results and, therefore, inflate the strength of the relationship. Remember that the square root of any number between zero and one is larger than the original number. Consider the following example. If a researcher gets a Cramér's V² value of .25 (a weak relationship), it might be tempting to portray the results as the square root of Cramér's V², or as Cramér's V. That value is .50—indicative of a moderate relationship.

Chi-square measures of association have several weaknesses. First, they refer to an entire table. The strength of the relationship for one part of a table, however, may be different from other parts of the table (see Table 6.13). It is important, therefore, to analyze each cell. If there is a stronger relationship in one section of the table or with the table collapsed, you may wish to refocus the analysis. Collapsing the table and then comparing the expected and observed cells can achieve that (see Table 6.14). Table 6.14 presents the same ethnicity data as in Table 6.13, but in a collapsed form. The strength of the relationship also changes. Table 6.14 shows that distinguishing the ethnicity of the spouse beyond German-born or not achieves little gain in explanatory power.

Second, another problem with chi-squared-based measures of association is that, even when properly calculated, Cramér's V^2 or ϕ^2 may not reach their maximum value because of the distribution of the marginals. If the marginals are not equally distributed among the categories, then neither Cramér's V^2 nor ϕ^2 can reach one (their maximum value) even when the strongest possible relationship exists. Consider the example in Table 6.15 of two roll calls. There is almost a perfect relationship between them. In other words, most legislators voted for the first motion and against the second, or vice versa. Yet, given the marginals, the value of ϕ^2 is .7655677. There are no cell frequencies consistent with these marginals that will yield the maximum value of ϕ^2.

Third, chi-square-based measures of association have no practical interpretation. One might find it more useful to compare the observed and expected cells. For example, consider the data presented in Tables 6.9 and 6.10. Although the V^2 value indicates only a weak relationship, comparison of the observed and expected tables provides interesting results. There were considerably more Republicans in the small towns than expected, and considerably more Democrats in the open countryside than expected. Independents, in contrast, were distributed more or less as expected.

Fourth and finally, there are other things that can be measured besides departures from statistical independence. Some of these are discussed below.

Proportional Reduction in Error Measures of Association

In 1954, Leo A. Goodman and William H. Kruskal published the first of several papers advocating *proportional reduction in error* (PRE) measures of association.[5] Their idea was to measure the degree to which cells

Table 6.13
Ethnicity of Spouse of German-born and German-American
Residents of Kingfisher County, Oklahoma Territory, 1890-1900

Ethnicity of Spouse	Ethnicity				Totals
	German Born		German-American[a]		
	%	(n)	%	(n)	
German born	61.66	(156)	16.06	(40)	196
American	10.67	(27)	46.19	(115)	142
German-American[a]	15.02	(38)	20.88	(52)	90
Hyphenated-American[b]	5.53	(14)	11.25	(28)	42
Other foreign born	7.12	(18)	5.62	(14)	32
Total	100.00	(253)	100.00	(249)	502

F_o	F_e	$(F_o - F_e)^2 / F_e$	
156	(196/502)253	$[156 - (196/502)253]^2$ / (196/502)253	= 33.1443515
40	(196/502)249	$[40 - (196/502)249]^2$ / (196/502)249	= 33.6767909
27	(142/502)253	$[27 - (142/502)253]^2$ / (142/502)253	= 27.7521759
115	(142/502)249	$[115 - (142/502)249]^2$ / (142/502)249	= 28.1979939
38	(90/502)253	$[38 - (90/502)253]^2$ / (90/502)253	= 1.1937875
52	(90/502)249	$[52 - (90/502)249]^2$ / (90/502)249	= 1.2129648
14	(42/502)253	$[14 - (42/502)253]^2$ / (42/502)253	= 2.4268827
28	(42/502)249	$[28 - (42/502)249]^2$ / (42/502)249	= 2.4658688
18	(32/502)253	$[18 - (32/502)253]^2$ / (32/502)253	= 0.2174110
14	(32/502)249	$[14 - (32/502)249]^2$ / (32/502)249	= 0.2209035

Total 502 502 chi-square = 130.5091305
DF = 4 Critical Chi-square = 9.49
Cramér's $V^2 = \chi^2 / (L - 1)n = 130.5091305/502 = .2599783$

[a]German-American is defined as native born with at least one parent born in Germany.
[b]Hyphenated-American is defined as native born with at least one parent born in any foreign country but Germany.

Source: Eleventh Census of the United States, 1890. Federal Population Schedules, MSS; Twelfth Census of the United States, 1900. Federal Population Schedules, MSS.

in cross-classification could be correctly filled, given knowledge of the marginals and the nature of the relationship. This approach has several advantages over chi-square-based measures of association. First, there is an external referent to the measure. It represents, in classifying a case, the proportion of error that can be reduced from knowing both the nature of the relationship and the marginals, instead of knowing only the marginals.

Table 6.14
Collapsed Version of Table Showing the Ethnicity of Spouse of German-born and German-American Residents of Kingfisher County, Oklahoma Territory, 1890-1900

	Ethnicity				
	German Born		German-American		
Ethnicity of Spouse	%	(n)	%	(n)	Totals
German born	61.66	(156)	16.06	(40)	196
All Others	38.34	(97)	83.94	(209)	306
Total	100.00	(253)	100.00	(249)	502

F_o	F_e	$\dfrac{(F_o - F_e)^2}{F_e}$	
156	(196/502)253	$\dfrac{[156 - (196/502)253]^2}{(196/502)253}$ =	33.1443515
40	(196/502)249	$\dfrac{[4 0 - (196/502)249]^2}{(196/502)249}$ =	33.6767909
97	(306/502)253	$\dfrac{[97 - (306/502)253]^2}{(306/502)253}$ =	21.2297153
209	(306/502)249	$\dfrac{[209 - (306/502)249]^2}{(306/502)249}$ =	21.5707550

| Total | 502 | 502 | chi-square = | 109.6216127 |

DF = 1   Critical Chi-square =   3.84

$\varnothing^2 = \chi^2/n = 109.6216127/502 = .218369$

Source: Data presented in Table 6.13.

Table 6.15
Roll Call Example Illustrating a Problem Associated with ϕ^2

Roll Call 2	Roll Call 1		
	Yea	Nay	Total
Yea	0	11	11
Nay	19	2	21
Total	19	13	32

	F_o	F_e	$\dfrac{(F_o - F_e)^2}{F_e}$		
	0	(11/32)19	$\dfrac{[0 - (11/32)19]^2}{(11/32)19}$	=	6.5312500
	11	(11/32)13	$\dfrac{[11 - (11/32)13]^2}{(11/32)13}$	=	9.5456731
	19	(21/32)19	$\dfrac{[19 - (21/32)19]^2}{(21/32)19}$	=	3.4211309
	2	(21/32)13	$\dfrac{[2 - (21/32)13]^2}{(21/32)13}$	=	5.0001145
Total	32	32	chi-square	=	24.4981685

DF = 1   Critical chi-square = 3.84

$\phi^2 = 24.4981685/32 = .7655677$

Goodman and Kruskal's approach also allows for the specification of several possible relationships to be measured. Second, this procedure measures the extent to which the observed table fits a specific hypothetical model, rather than the degree to which it departs from statistical independence. Third and finally, new statistical tests have been developed to test the significance of specific models, rather than just statistical independence. PRE measures of association can, therefore, be more powerful than the more general chi-square tests.

Calculating PRE Measures for Historians

The two most useful PRE measures of association for historians are tau-b and γ. The choice of tau-b (τ_b) or gamma (γ) is based on the intent of the research. Tau-b is an index that measures agreement or disagreement between two variables. It is used when the number of categories of each variable is the same, and is easiest to interpret when the categories of each variable are the same. Gamma is a good measure of causal effect. To calculate tau-b or gamma, we must first define some terms:

P = positive trend—the sum of the products of each cell frequency and the cell frequencies below and to the right in the table.

Q = negative trend—the sum of the products of each cell frequency and the cell frequencies above and to the right in the table.

T_{row} = ties on the row variable—the sum of the products of each cell frequency and those of the cells on the same row in the table.

T_{column} = ties on the column variable—the sum of the products of each cell frequency and those of the cells on the same column in the table.

We can look at ties this way: if two cases are in the same category for one variable but are in different categories for the other variable, they are tied on the first variable.

Tau-b is calculated using the formula:

$$\tau_b = \frac{P - Q}{\sqrt{(P + Q + T_{row})(P + Q + T_{column})}}$$

Gamma is calculated using the formula:

$$\gamma = \frac{P - Q}{P + Q}$$

Notice that when there are no ties (i.e., $T_{row} = T_{column} = 0$), tau-b equals gamma. If there are ties, gamma is larger than tau-b.

One of the advantages of using the proportional reduction in error measures of association is the opportunity to test how far one's observed results vary from specific models of relationships between two variables. One of these models is a monotonic relationship, in which either any case that is higher than another case on one variable is as high or higher on the other variable (*positive monotonic*), or else, if a case is higher than another case on one variable, it is as high or lower on the other variable (*negative mono-tonic*). In a table in which both the row and column variables are ordered from low to high, those cells in a positive monotonic relation will be those below and to the right of the cell. Those in a negative monotonic relation will be those above and to the right of a particular cell.

We use γ and a monotonic model to measure the *impact* of one variable upon another. Consider Stephan Thernstrom's analysis in *The Other Bostonians*, as portrayed in Table 6.16. Thernstrom hypothesized that "family origins determined the career patterns of Boston residents."[6] Both variables are ordinal, in that the categories suggest progression.

We can transfer the positive monotonic relationship onto a cross-classification table where X represents some value and 0 represents no value; we then have Table 6.17. Notice that this "perfect" table does not limit data to cells showing perfect agreement or disagreement (i.e., low manual–low manual, skilled–skilled, etc.). With a perfect positive monotonic relationship, the gamma value is +1; with a perfect negative monotonic relationship, the gamma value equals -1.

Now let us work through the specific example in Table 6.17, using Thernstrom's data in Table 6.16. Here, the monotonic model seems most appropriate. One would anticipate that the son's occupational status would be the same or better than the father's occupational status. The proper

Table 6.16
Sons' Occupation by Fathers' Occupation, Boston, 1860–1879

	Sons' Occupation			
Fathers' Occupation	Low Manual	Skilled	Low White Collar	High White Collar
Low Manual	104	52	89	13
Skilled	63	91	96	22
Low White Collar	18	12	74	24
High White Collar	2	10	37	72
Total	187	165	296	131

Source: Adapted from Stephan Thernstrom, *The Other Bostonians: Poverty and Progress in the American Metropolis, 1880–1970* (Cambridge, MA: Harvard University Press, 1973), 89. Slight differences between our marginals and Thernstrom's are due to rounding.

Table 6.17
One Possible Perfect Monotonic Relationship that Could Have Been Observed in Sons' Occupation Relative to Fathers' Occupation, Boston, 1860–1879

	Sons' Occupation			
Fathers' Occupation	Low Manual	Skilled	Low White Collar	High White Collar
Low Manual	X	X	0	0
Skilled	0	X	0	0
Low White Collar	0	X	X	X
High White Collar	0	0	0	X

Source: Derived from data in Table 6.16.

statistic is γ. Its calculation is worked through below:

$$P = (104X91) + (104X12) + (104X10) + (104X96)$$
$$+ (104X74) + (104X37) + (104X22) + (104X24) + (104X72)$$
$$+ (52X96) + (52X74) + (52X37) + (52X22) + (52X24)$$
$$+ (52X72) + (89X22) + (89X24) + (89X72) + (63X12)$$
$$+ (63X10) + (63X74) + (63X37) + (63X24) + (63X72)$$
$$+ (91X74) + (91X37) + (91X24) + (91X72) + (96X24)$$
$$+ (96X72) + (18X10) + (18X37) + (18X72) + (12X37)$$
$$+ (12X72) + (74X72)$$
$$= 124212$$

$$Q = (2X12) + (2X91) + (2X52) + (2X74) + (2X96) + (2X89)$$
$$+ (2X24) + (2X22) + (2X13) + (18X91) + (18X52) + (18X96)$$
$$+ (18X89) + (18X22) + (18X13) + (63X52) + (63X89)$$
$$+ (63X13) + (10X74) + (10X96) + (10X89) + (10X24)$$
$$+ (10X22) + (10X13) + (12X96) + (12X89) + (12X22)$$
$$+ (12X13) + (91X89) + (91X31) + (37X24) + (37X22)$$
$$+ (37X13) + (74X22) + (74X13) + (96X13)$$
$$= 39943$$

$$\gamma = \frac{P - Q}{P + Q}$$

$$= \frac{124212 - 39943}{124212 + 39943}$$

$$= +.5133501$$

There is, therefore, a moderate positive monotonic relationship between fathers' and sons' occupations.

Some older sources refer to Yule's Q. Yule's Q is simply gamma calculated on a two by two table. Today, historians can use the statistic gamma, whatever the table size.

A second useful model takes shape as the agreement/positive main diagonal or the disagreement/negative main diagonal. These diagonals are actually special cases of a monotonic relationship. Both assume that, if the categories of each variable are the same and are listed in the same order on a cross-classification table, then each case will have the same category for both variables. The PRE measure of association used here is tau-b—an index that measures agreement or disagreement between two variables. Consider Table 6.18, which presents data from a study of miscegenation among various racial groups in Parral, a parish in Northern Mexico. If there is a perfect fit, all the cases will be on the agreement/positive main diagonal. Departures from that will reduce the perfect fit.

Table 6.18
Marriage in Parral, Mexico, 1767–1805, by Race of Bride and Groom

Race of Groom	Race of Bride			
	Spanish	Mestizo	Pardo	Indian
Spanish	589	127	13	7
Mestizo	129	959	59	30
Pardo	12	114	134	15
Indian	7	46	14	113
Total n	737	1246	220	165

Source: Adapted from David J. Robinson, "Population Patterns in a Northern Mexican Mining Region: Parral in the Late Eighteenth Century," *Geoscience and Man*, 21 (March 17, 1980), 91.

$$\tau_b = \frac{P - Q}{\sqrt{(P + Q + T_{row})(P + Q + T_{column})}}$$

$$P = (589X959) + (589X59) + (589X30) + (589X114)$$
$$+ (589X134) + (589X15) + (589X46) + (589X14)$$
$$+ (589X113) + (129X114) + (129X134) + (129X15)$$
$$+ (129X46) + (129X14) + (129X113) + (12X46) + (12X14)$$
$$+ (12X113) + (127X59) + (127X30) + (127X134) + (127X15)$$
$$+ (127X14) + (127X113) + (959X134) + (959X15)$$
$$+ (959X14) + (959X113) + (114X14) + (114X113) + (13X30)$$
$$+ (13X15) + (13X113) + (59X15) + (59X113) + (134X113)$$
$$= 1282661$$

$$Q = (7X114) + (7X959) + (7X127) + (7X134) + (7X59)$$
$$+ (7X13) + (7X15) + (7X30) + (7X7) + (12X959) + (12X127)$$
$$+ (12X59) + (12X13) + (12X30) + (12X7) + (129X127)$$
$$+ (129X13) + (129X7) + (46X134) + (46X59) + (46X13)$$
$$+ (46X15) + (46X30) + (46X7) + (114X59) + (114X13)$$
$$+ (114X30) + (114X7) + (959X13) + (959X7) + (14X15)$$
$$+ (14X30) + (14X7) + (134X30) + (134X7) + (59X7) = 93082$$

$$T_{row} = (589X127) + (589X13) + (589X7) + (127X13)$$
$$+ (127X7) + (13X7) + (129X959) + (129X59) + (129X30)$$
$$+ (959X59) + (959X30) + (59X30) + (12X114) + (12X134)$$
$$+ (12X15) + (114X134) + (114X15) + (134X15) + (7X46)$$
$$+ (7X14) + (7X113) + (46X14) + (46X113) + (14X113)$$
$$= 342314$$

$$T_{column} = (589X129) + (589X12) + (589X7) + (129X12)$$
$$+ (129X7) + (12X7) + (127X959) + (127X114) + (127X46)$$
$$+ (959X114) + (959X46) + (114X46) + (13X59) + (13X134)$$
$$+ (13X14) + (59X134) + (59X14) + (134X14) + (7X30)$$
$$+ (7X15) + (7X113) + (30X15) + (30X113) + (15X113)$$
$$= 410444$$

$$\tau_b = \frac{1282661 - 93082}{\sqrt{(1282661 + 93082 + 342314)(1282661 + 93082 + 410444)}}$$

$$= .679065$$

This is indicative of a moderate main diagonal relationship. Marriages in Parral tended to occur within racial groups, rather than across them.

The order of the categories vertically and horizontally is important. You will get different values for tau-b depending on the order. Thus, tau-b—like γ—is used with ordinal data.

Another example of a disagreement/negative main diagonal would be when two roll calls reflect opposite approaches to the same question, as was used as an example in Table 6.15 and shown again in Table 6.19. In fact, these two roll calls were recorded during the U.S. Senate debate over whether or not to declare war against Great Britain in June 1812. The first vote was on a motion to delay further consideration of the declaration of war, and the second was on a motion to declare war. We would expect people voting yea on the first motion to vote nay on the second, and vice versa. Here a perfect relationship would have all the cases on the disagreement/negative main diagonal. The extent to which data vary from the diagonal is the extent to which the data fail to fit the model.

$$\tau_b = \frac{P-Q}{\sqrt{(P+Q+T_{row})(P+Q+T_{column})}}$$

$$
\begin{aligned}
P &= 0 \times 2 \\
&= 0 \\
Q &= 19 \times 11 \\
&= 209 \\
T_{row} &= (0 \times 11) + (19 \times 2) \\
&= 38 \\
T_{column} &= (0 \times 19) + (11 \times 2) \\
&= 22
\end{aligned}
$$

$$\tau_b = \frac{0 - 209}{\sqrt{(0 + 209 + 38)(0 + 209 + 22)}}$$

$$= -.8749672$$

This indicates a strong disagreement or negative main diagonal relationship.

Table 6.19
Roll Call Example Illustrating a Disagreement or Negative Main Diagonal

| | Roll Call 2[b] | | |
Roll Call 1[a]	Yea	Nay	Total
Yea	0	11	11
Nay	19	2	21
Total	19	13	32 = n

[a]Motion to postpone further consideration of a declaration of war against England, June 16, 1812. Defeated 11–21.
[b]Motion to declare war against England, June 17, 1812. Passed 19–13.

Source: Adapted from *Annals of Congress*, 12th Congress, 1st Session, 1812, 296–297.

Significance Test

In 1963, Goodman and Kruskal also developed a significance test for both tau-b and gamma.[7] The test statistic is z from the standard normal distribution.

$$z = P - Q / \sigma_{P-Q}$$

and

$$\sigma_{P-Q} = \sqrt{[n^3 / 9][1 - (\sum r_i^3)/n^3][1 - (\sum c_i^3)/n^3]}$$

where n is the number of cases
    r_i is the number of cases in the ith row
    c_i is the number of cases in the ith column

Using the data in Table 6.19,

$$P - Q = -209$$

$$n^3 = 32^3 = 32768$$

$$\Sigma r_i^3 = 11^3 + 21^3$$
$$= 10592$$

$$\Sigma c_i^3 = 19^3 + 13^3$$
$$= 9056$$

$$\sigma_{P-Q} = \sqrt{[32768/9][1-(10592/32768)][1-(9056/32768)]}$$
$$= 42.2259$$

$$z = P - Q / \sigma_{P-Q}$$
$$= -209 / 42.2259$$
$$= -4.9496$$

From Table A.1 in the Appendix, we find that, if the null hypothesis of no relationship is correct, the probability of -4.9496 (one tail) is less than .0005. Tau-b for Table 6.19 is significant: p < .0005. Using Program A.1, the one-tailed probability is found to be less than .0000011. Notice that chi-square calculated from the same table (see Table 6.15) is also significant: $X^2 = 24.498$ when DF = 1 and p < .05. Using Program A.3, the probability is found to be less than .001.

7

Analysis of Variance

Analysis of variance examines the relationship between an interval-level variable and one (or more) categorical variables. It is also possible to include an interval-level covariate in the analysis. Ronald A. Fisher (1890–1962) developed the analysis of variance procedure in the first half of the twentieth century for agricultural and eugenics experimentation, first at the Rothamsted Agricultural Experimental Station in England, later at University College, and finally as a Professor of Genetics at Cambridge University. Two of his books, *Statistical Methods for Research Workers* and *The Design of Experiments*,[1] have had a profound influence on several generations of statisticians.

As with other techniques, analysis of variance addresses three questions: the effect of one (or more) variables on each other; the significance of that effect; and the strength of the relationship. We assess the nature of the effect by comparing means, examining the significance with the F-ratio, and determining the strength of the relationship with E^2, a measure of association.[2]

ONE-WAY ANALYSIS OF VARIANCE

One-way analysis of variance examines the relationship between one categorical variable and one interval-level variable. Consider an example generated from the *Catasto*, a register of persons and property that was conducted in Florence in 1427. The *Catasto* provides historians a rich source of information about fifteenth-century Florentine society. David Herlihy and Christiane Klapisch-Zuber used this data in their book *Tuscans and Their Families: A Study of the Florentine* Catasto *in 1427*.[3]

Table 7.1 presents the amount of public investment in the *Monte* (a scheme similar to bonds by which the city financed its activities and citizens

Table 7.1
Value of Public Investments of a Random Sample of Individuals in Three Florentine Gilds, 1427 (in florins)

Silk Merchants and Weavers	Wool Merchants and Manufacturers	Money Changers
0	0	1132
517	2184	8825
20586	24	
0	369	
1181	954	
0	0	
48	0	
2536	0	
627	0	
150	0	
	79	
	0	
	507	
	4082	
	1437	
	0	
	604	
	13485	
	207	
	1938	
	0	
	816	

Within categories:

n_j 10	22	2
$\bar{x}_j$ 2564.5	1213	4978.5
SS_j 366528072.5	179112164	29591124.5

All cases ignoring categories:

n: 34;   Grand mean: 1832;   SS(total): 608827390

Source: Authors' random sample of data from Florentine *Catasto*; Census and Property Survey of Florentine Domains in the Province of Tuscany, 1427-1480. Data set compiled by David Herlihy and Christiane Klapisch-Zuber; see their *Tuscans and Their Families: A Study of the Florentine* Catasto *of 1427* (New Haven, CT: Yale University Press, 1985).

profited through generous interest rates) on the part of a sample of Florentines from three gilds. Investment in the *Monte* was an indication of wealth, influence, and power in Florence.

In the original data set prepared by Herlihy and Klapisch-Zuber, there were 100 silk merchants and weavers, 229 wool merchants and manufacturers, and twenty-two money changers. Our random sample consists of ten silk merchants and weavers, twenty-two wool merchants and manufacturers, and two money changers. We used a sample here to simplify the presentation of our example.

Nature of the Relationship

Describing the relationship between gild membership and public investment involves a comparison of means. There are two types of means: category means, calculated from values within each category; and a grand mean, calculated from all the cases. If j is used to indicate a category and i a case within that category, then x_{ij} is the ith case in the jth category, n_j is the number of cases in the jth category, and N is the total number of cases—($N = \sum n_j$). The mean for the jth category is:

$$\bar{x}_j = \sum (x_{ij}) / n_j$$

The sum of squares about this mean is:

$$SS_j = \sum (x_{ij} - \bar{x}_j)^2$$

The grand mean (GM) is the mean of all values, that is,

$$GM = \sum (x_{ij}) / N$$

The total sum of squares (SS) about the grand mean is:

$$SS(total) = \sum (x_{ij} - GM)^2$$

These values have been calculated and appear at the bottom of Table 7.1.

The Model

The model for analysis of variance assumes a certain way of viewing a case's value on a variable. It examines an individual score as consisting of three components: the grand mean; the effect of being in a particular category; and an individual effect that represents all other influences.

Consider the first money changer. He invested 1,132 florins into the *Monte*. The grand mean—the average of all thirty-four investments—is 1,832 florins. The category mean for money changers, $\bar{x}$ (money changer), is 4,978.5 florins. Thus, the average person invested 1,832 florins, while the average money changer invested 4,978.5 florins.

$$\bar{x} \text{ (money changer) - } GM = 4,978.5 - 1,832$$
$$= 3,146.5 \text{ florins}$$

The difference between the category mean and the grand mean (here, 3,146.5 florins) represents the effect of being a money changer on investment in the *Monte*. Money changers, on average, invested 3,146.5 florins more than the overall average. For the other groups, the effects are:

$$\bar{x} \text{ (silk merchants) - } GM = 2,564.5 - 1,832$$
$$= 732.5 \text{ florins,}$$

$$\bar{x} \text{ (wool merchants) - } GM = 1,213 - 1,832$$
$$= -619 \text{ florins}$$

The wool merchants contributed below the average; and silk merchants, above it.

The difference between the category mean and the grand mean is the effect of the category on the dependent variable—here, the effect of being in a particular category on the amount invested. The nature of the relationship between the two variables is described in terms of category effects.

$$\text{category effect} = \bar{x}_j - GM$$

The next part of the model is the individual effect. This is the difference between an individual's score and the category mean for that individual's group. It represents what the analysis cannot explain, that is, differences among individuals in the same group.

$$\text{individual effect} = x_{ij} - \bar{x}_j$$

For the first money changer,

$$\text{individual effect} = 1,132 - 4,978.5$$
$$= -3,846.5$$

He invested 3,846.5 fewer florins than the average investment for money changers. This leads to the following way to describe the observed data:

$$x_{ij} = GM + \text{category effect} + \text{individual effect}$$
$$= GM + (\overline{x}_j - GM) + (x_{ij} - \overline{x}_j)$$

For the first money changer,

$$x_{ij} = 1,132$$
$$= 1,832 + 3,146.5 - 3,846.5$$
$$= 1,132$$

Analysis of variance does more than simply describe a set of observations. If some random process produces the observations, the concern is to make inferences to the parameters of that process. The analysis of variance model is:

$$x_{ij} = \mu + \alpha_j + e_{ij}$$

where x_{ij} is the value on the dependent (x) variable for the ith case in the jth category of the independent variable

μ (mu) is the population grand mean

α_j (alpha) is the population effect of being in the jth category of the independent variable—the difference between the category mean and the grand mean in the population

e_{ij} is the net effect of all other influences on the ith case in the jth category

In the example of gild members, each individual's investment in the *Monte* (i.e., x_{ij}) is composed of three parts: the population overall mean (μ); the effect due to membership in gild j (α); and a random element unique to a particular individual and not associated with gild membership (e_{ij}).

Significance: The F-Test

The null hypothesis is that there is no relationship between gild membership and personal investment in the *Monte*—and therefore that, in the total population, the mean personal investment in the *Monte* is the same for each gild. The alternative hypothesis is that, in the population (the 351 original cases), members of certain gilds invested more or less than members of other gilds.

In this context, the null hypothesis can refer to the population of 351 Florentines from which we have a sample of thirty-four. The null hypothesis is that, in the population, the three means are the same and the sample differences are due to the chance selection of cases. If the null hypothesis is correct, chance selected wool merchants, who invested less than the average, or money changers, who invested more.

There is variation in the amount invested within each gild. This is a reflection of the variation in investment rates of individuals in the population. Likewise, there is variation among the gilds' means. Under the null hypothesis, the means vary from one random sample to another due to the chance selection of cases. The amount of variation among sample means is a function of the variation of the variable in the population as well as the sample size, if the null hypothesis of no difference among population means is correct.

If the null hypothesis is true, we can use differences among the gild means to estimate the variance of investment in the population, σ^2. Likewise, the variation in investment within the same gild is also a function of the variance of the variable in the population and can also be used to estimate σ^2. Thus, if the null hypothesis is true, the ratio of these two estimates should be about one. If the population means are different from one another, then there is an additional source of variation among the sample means. As a result, the ratio of the population variance estimate from the means, to the estimate from within categories, should be greater than one.

The F-ratio—named and tabulated by American George Snedecor[4]— is the test statistic. It is calculated in several steps.

Total Sum of Squares

The total sum of squares, SS(total), is the variation of all cases about the grand mean. We discussed it earlier in the chapter. In the case of our Florentine gild sample,

$$SS(total) = \sum (x_{ij} - GM)^2$$
$$= (0-1832)^2 + (517-1832)^2 + (20586-1832)^2 + (0-1832)^2 + (1181-1832)^2 + (0-1832)^2 + (48-1832)^2 + (2536-1832)^2 + (627-1832)^2 + (150-1832)^2 + (0-1832)^2 + (2184-1832)^2 + (24-1832)^2 + (369-1832)^2 + (954-1832)^2 + (0-1832)^2 + (0-1832)^2 + (0-1832)^2 + (0-1832)^2 + (0-1832)^2 + (79-1832)^2 + (0-1832)^2 + (507-1832)^2 + (4082-1832)^2 + (1437-1832)^2 + (0-1832)^2 + (604-1832)^2 + (13485-1832)^2 + (207-1832)^2 + (1938-1832)^2 + (0-1832)^2 + (816-1832)^2 + (1132-1832)^2 + (8825-1832)^2 = 608,827,390$$

Unexplained Sum of Squares. The *unexplained sum of squares* (also called the "error," "within," or "residual" sum of squares) is the variation not explained by the categorical variable. It is the variation among cases in the same category. In terms of the model discussed above, it is the variation about the category mean summed across the several categories. If the variation within category j is:

$$SS_j = \Sigma(x_{ij} - \bar{x}_j)^2$$

then

$$SS(\text{unexplained}) = \Sigma SS_j$$

In the case of the Florentine gilds,

$$
\begin{aligned}
SS(\text{silk merchant}) &= 366{,}528{,}072.5 \\
SS(\text{wool merchant}) &= 179{,}112{,}164.0 \\
SS(\text{money changer}) &= 29{,}591{,}124.5 \\
SS(\text{unexplained}) &= 575{,}231{,}361.0
\end{aligned}
$$

The unexplained sum of squares is the total of the variation about the category means.

Explained Sum of Squares. The *explained sum of squares* (or "between" sum of squares) is the variation of the category means about the grand mean weighted by the number of cases in each category. In terms of the model discussed above, it is the category component squared and summed across all cases.

$$SS(\text{explained}) = \Sigma n_j(\bar{x}_j - GM)^2$$

For the Florentine data, the explained sum of squares is:

$$
\begin{aligned}
10(2{,}564.5 - 1{,}832)^2 &= 5{,}365{,}562.5 \\
22(1{,}213 - 1{,}832)^2 &= 8{,}429{,}542.0 \\
2(4{,}978.5 - 1{,}832)^2 &= 19{,}800{,}924.5 \\
SS(\text{explained}) &= 33{,}596{,}029.0
\end{aligned}
$$

Notice that SS(total) = SS(explained) + SS(unexplained):

$$608{,}827{,}390 = 33{,}596{,}029 + 575{,}231{,}361$$

Degrees of Freedom

Each of the sums of squares has an associated degrees of freedom that is equal to the number of values the researcher can freely assign before being constrained by the number of cases and the mean.

In the case of the SS(total), there are thirty-four cases and one mean—the grand mean.

$$DF(total) = N - 1 = 34 - 1 = 33$$

In the case of the SS(unexplained), there are ten cases and one mean, plus twenty-two cases and one mean, plus two cases and one mean. The DF(unexplained) = n - k, where k is the number of categories (means).

$$DF(unexplained) = n - k = 34 - 3 = 31$$

In the case of the SS(explained), there are three means (categories, k) and one grand mean. The degrees of freedom are:

$$DF(explained) = k - 1 = 3 - 1 = 2$$

The Mean Square

The mean square, calculated by dividing the appropriate sum of squares by the appropriate degrees of freedom, estimates the population variance. We are interested here in the mean square both explained and unexplained.

$$\begin{aligned}
\text{mean square} \\
\text{(explained)} &= SS(explained)/DF(explained) \\
&= 33{,}596{,}029/2 \\
&= 16{,}798{,}014.5
\end{aligned}$$

$$\begin{aligned}
\text{mean square} \\
\text{(unexplained)} &= SS(unexplained)/DF(unexplained) \\
&= 575{,}231{,}361/31 \\
&= 18{,}555{,}850.35
\end{aligned}$$

The F-Ratio

The F-ratio is the ratio of the mean square explained to the mean square unexplained. If the null hypothesis is correct, the two values should be similar. But if the alternative hypothesis of differences in the population means is correct, then the mean square explained should be larger than the mean square unexplained.

$$F = \frac{mean\ square\ (explained)}{mean\ square\ (unexplained)}$$
$$= 16,798,014.5/18,555,850.35$$
$$= .9053$$

The F-Distribution

If the null hypothesis is correct, all sample F-values form a distribution for the particular degrees of freedom. There are two degrees of freedom: the DF(explained) and the DF(unexplained). These define the relevant F-distribution. Here, the degrees of freedom are two and thirty-one. In Table A.4 at the end of the Appendix, the DF(explained) are read horizontally and the DF(unexplained) are read vertically. The critical F-value for probability .05 and DF = 2 and 31 is 3.32. As the calculated F-value is less than the critical F- value, the differences among the means are not significant at .05. Program A.4 calculates this probability to be <.415. This is illustrated in Figure 7.1.

In the sample, there are differences among the various gilds in amount invested, but the differences are not significant. We cannot generalize, then, to the population from which the sample was taken.

As the degrees of freedom increase, the F-distribution—like the chi-square—pulls to the right. Compare Figure 7.1 with Figure 7.2, which illustrates the F-distribution for DF = 4 and 31.

Strength of Association

E^2 measures the strength of association between a categorical and an interval-level variable. E^2 is the ratio of the explained sum of squares to the total sum of squares.

$$E^2 = SS(explained)\ /\ SS(total)$$

E^2 has a minimum value of zero (i.e., there are no differences among the means) and a maximum value of one (i.e., there are no differences within the categories, although there are differences between the means). When E^2 equals one, the categorical variable explains all the variation in the interval variable. For the Florentine example,

Figure 7.1
The F-Distribution for All Possible Sample F-Values for DF = 2 and 31 under
the Null Hypothesis

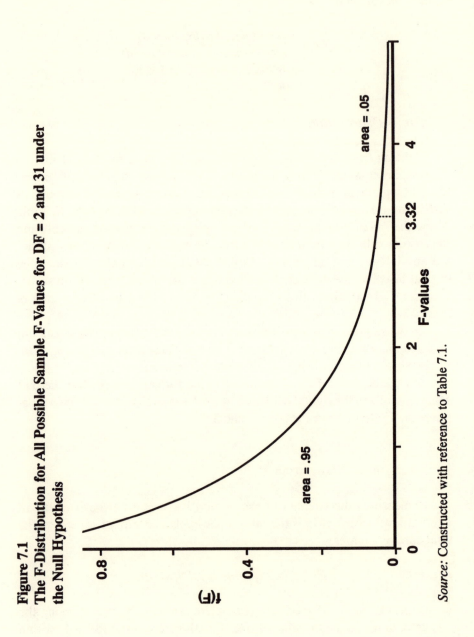

Source: Constructed with reference to Table 7.1.

Figure 7.2
The F-Distribution for All Possible Sample F-Values for DF = 4 and 31 under the Null Hypothesis

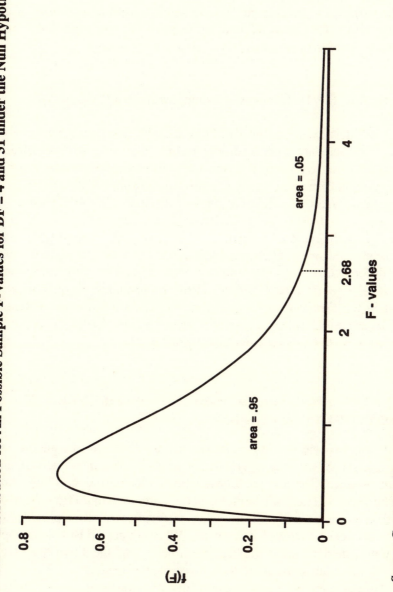

Source: Constructed by authors.

$$E^2 = 33,596,029 / 608,827,390$$
$$= .05518$$

We can interpret this as meaning that gild membership explains 5.5 percent of the variation in investment in the *Monte*. As with all measures of association, 0 to +.3 is a weak relationship, +.3 to +.7 is moderate, and +.7 to +1 is strong. Here the relationship is weak and insignificant.

Testing the Differences between Individual Means

The F-test examines the significance of differences among the several means. If there are more than two means, this test can be misleading. Consider some hypothetical case in which there are five categories and three of the means are virtually identical to one another while the other two are quite different. Dividing the degrees of freedom for the explained sum of squares (k - 1 = 5 - 1 = 4) into the explained sum of squares reduces the overall F-ratio. In cases like that, it will prove useful to use a t-test to evaluate the significance of differences between the two distinct category means. The difference may prove significant even though the differences among all means together are not. A second problem is the reverse of the first: this is when the F-ratio proves significant, but each mean is not necessarily significantly different from each of the other means. A solution, again, is to use the t-test to examine pairs of category means.

TWO-WAY ANALYSIS OF VARIANCE WITH UNRELATED INDEPENDENT VARIABLES

When two independent variables are unrelated to one another, two-way analysis of variance is a relatively simple extension of one-way analysis of variance. Consider the following example. During the 1760s, American northern and middle colonies generally imported more from Great Britain than they exported, while the southern colonies usually exported more to the mother country than they imported. What impact did British attempts to regulate American trade with the West Indies, and the Townshend Duties, have on the trade patterns of these two colonial regions?

This question can be examined with a two-way analysis of variance — the two independent variables being region and time period, and the dependent variable being trade balance. We have presented relevant data for examining the question, drawn from Carl Becker's *The History of Politi-*

Table 7.2
Balance of American Trade with Great Britain by Year and Region, 1760–1770, in Thousands of Pounds

Year	Northern & Middle	(Total)	Southern	(Total)	Period Total
	Colonial Region				
1760	-1706		-145		
1761	-694		-110		
1762	-604		-32		
1763	-615		89		
1764	-1232		93		
1765	-972		178		
1766	-832	(-6655)	72	(145)	-6510
1767	-968		163		
1768	-1039		136		
1769	-260		-32		
1770	-758	(-3025)	-151	(116)	-2909
Total	-9680		261		-9419

Source: Authors' calculations from Carl Lotus Becker, *The History of Political Parties in the Province of New York, 1760–1776* (Madison: University of Wisconsin Press, 1968), 68–69. Figures are the difference between the total exports and the total imports for the region.

cal Parties in the Province of New York, 1760-1776, in Table 7.2. Notice that region and time period (the two independent variables) are not related to one another. Table 7.3 shows that 64 percent of the northern and middle cases were in the early time period, exactly the same as for the southern cases.

As with one-way analysis of variance, we calculated category means for each category of time period and region, and a grand mean for all the cases. In addition, we calculated cell means for each combination of the two independent variables. A total sum of squares is calculated for the grand mean and for each cell mean. If x_{ijk} is the kth observation in the cell defined by the ith category of the row variable (period) and the jth category of the column variable (region), then the cell mean for cell ij is:

$$\bar{x}_{ij} = \Sigma (x_{ijk}) / n_{ij}$$

Table 7.3
Relationship between Region and Time Period in Trade Balance
Data of Table 7.2, in Percentage

	Colonial Region	
Time Period	Northern & Middle	Southern
1760-1766	63.64	63.64
1767-1770	36.36	36.36
Total (n)	100.00 (11)	100.00 (11)

For the four cases in the cell defined by the southern colonies during the period 1767–1770, the cell mean is:

$$\bar{x}(cell) = \frac{163 + 136 + (-32) + (-151)}{4}$$
$$= 29$$

The sum of squares for cell ij is:

$$SS_{ij} = \Sigma[x_{ijk} - \bar{x}(cell)]^2$$

For the four cases in the cell defined by southern colonies in the period 1767–1770, the cell sum of squares is:

$$
\begin{aligned}
SS(cell) &= (163 - 29)^2 + (136 - 29)^2 + [(-32) - 29]^2 + \\
&\quad [(-151) - 29]^2 \\
&= 65,526
\end{aligned}
$$

We then calculated the grand mean (GM) and the SS(total) for all cases, as in the one-way analysis of variance. Likewise, we calculated the category means for the regions and the time periods and the sum of squares within each of the categories as they were in one-way analysis of variance. These are presented (calculations not shown) in Table 7.4.

The variation explained by period is calculated the same way as the one-way analysis of variance

$$
\begin{aligned}
SS(period) &= \Sigma n_i(\bar{x}_i - GM)^2 \\
&= 14[(-465) - (-428.136)]^2 + 8[(-363.625) \\
&\quad - (-428.136)]^2 \\
&= 52,318.716
\end{aligned}
$$

Table 7.4
Analysis of Variance of Differences in America's Colonial Exports to Great Britain and Imports from Great Britain, in Thousands of Pounds, by Time Period and Region

	Colonial Region		Mean, n, and SS for Period
Time Period	Northern & Middle	Southern	
1760–1766			
$\bar{x}$(cell)	-£950.714	+£20.714	-£465.000
n (cell)	7	7	14
SS (cell)	962941.4284	84583.42858	4350382.000
1767–1770			
$\bar{x}$(cell)	-£756.250	+£29.000	-£363.625
n (cell)	4	4	8
SS (cell)	371052.7501	65526.000	1669813.875
Region			
$\bar{x}$(region)	-£880.000	£23.727	
n(region)	11	11	
SS(region)	1430254.000	150284.181	

Change in Trade Balance [$\bar{x}$(1767–1770) - $\bar{x}$(1760–1766)]1000

£194,464	£8,286	£101,375

All data:
n = 22; GM = -£428.136; SS(total) = 6072514.591

Source: Authors' calculations from data in Table 7.2.

So is the variation explained by region

$$SS(region) = \sum n_j (\bar{x}_j - GM)^2$$
$$= 11[(-880) - (-428.1363636)]^2 + 11[23.72727273$$
$$- (-428.1363636)]^2$$
$$= 4,491,976.409$$

The main effects are the additive effects of the several independent variables. Here,

$$SS(main\ effects) = SS(period) + SS(region)$$
$$= 52,318.716 + 4,491,976.409$$
$$= 4,544,295.125$$

The total explained variation is the variation of the several cell means about the grand mean weighted by the number of cases in the cell; it can also be called the "sum of squares" (cells).

$$SS(explained) = \Sigma n_{ij}(\bar{x}_{ij} - GM)^2$$
$$= 7[(-950.7142857) - (-428.1363636)]^2$$
$$+ 7[20.71428517 - (-428.1363636)]^2$$
$$+ 4[(-756.25) - (-428.1363636)]^2$$
$$+ 4[29 - (-428.1363636)]^2$$
$$= 4,588,410.984$$

Interaction

When we examine the joint effects of two categorical independent variables (here, period and region) upon a third, interval-level variable (here, trade balances), it is often found that the effect of one independent variable varies from one level of the second categorical variable to another. This is *interaction*. Substantively, interaction requires that the effect of a variable be interpreted individually for each category of a third variable.

Becker's discussion of the reaction of the colonies to British legislation suggests that northern merchants moved to halt the importation of goods from Great Britain. The net effect was to reduce the trade imbalance with England by an average of £101,375 per year (see Table 7.4). In the northern and middle colonies, the trade imbalance dropped an average of £194,464 annually—a rather substantial sum. The southern colonies exported more to England and imported less. Here, a positive trade imbalance increased in a favorable direction an average of £8,286 per year. Did these events have a different effect on the trade balances of the two regions?

Consider an additive model of the observed trade-balance cell means:

$$\bar{x} \; (cell) = GM + (effects \; of \; period) + (effects \; of \; region)$$

where, if $\bar{x}$ (1760–1766) is the mean for the early period category, the effect of the early period is $\bar{x}$ (1760–1766) - GM and the effect of being a northern or middle colony is $\bar{x}$ (northern) - GM. Thus, for the first cell (1760–1766, northern or middle colonies), if the effects of the two variables are additive, the cell means should be:

$$\bar{x}(cell) = GM + (\textit{effects of period}) + (\textit{effects of region})$$
$$= GM + [\bar{x}(1760\text{-}1766) - GM] + [\bar{x}(\textit{northern}) - GM]$$
$$= \text{-}428.136 + [(\text{-}465) - (\text{-}428.136)]$$
$$+ [(\text{-}880) - (\text{-}428.136)]$$
$$= \text{-}916.864$$

The actual cell mean, -£950.714, is more (in absolute value) than expected from the additive effects of the two variables. This difference between what we expect from the additive effects of the two main variables and the actual cell mean is the interaction. In this case, the combination of early period and northern or middle region join together to produce a trade imbalance in excess of the additive effects of region and period. The interactive effect for the first cell is:

$$\bar{x} \ (cell) - [GM + (\textit{effects of period}) + (\textit{effects of region})]$$
$$= \text{-}950.714 - [(\text{-}428.136) + [(\text{-}465) - (\text{-}428.136)]$$
$$+ [(\text{-}880) - (\text{-}428.136)]]$$
$$= \text{-}33.850$$

The various additive and interactive effects observed are shown in Table 7.5.

Notice that we can calculate the SS(main effects) from the additive effects

$$SS(\textit{main effects}) = \Sigma \ n(cell)(\textit{cell additive effect})^2$$
$$= 7(\text{-}488.7272728)^2 + 7(415)^2$$
$$+ 4(\text{-}387.3522728)^2 + 4(516.3749999)^2$$
$$= 4{,}544{,}295.125$$

We calculate the interaction sum of squares in a similar way from the interaction effects

$$SS(\textit{interaction}) = \Sigma \ n(cell)(\textit{cell interaction effects})^2$$
$$= 7(\text{-}33.85064935)^2 + 7(33.85064935)^2$$
$$+ 4(59.2386363)^2 + 4(\text{-}59.2386363)^2$$
$$= 44{,}115.859.$$

The interaction sum of squares can also be calculated from the explained and the main-effects sum of squares

Table 7.5
Additive and Interactive Effects of Region and Period on America's Colonial Trade Balance with Great Britain, 1760-1770, in Thousands of Pounds

Period	Colonial Region		Category Effect
	Northern & Middle	Southern	
1760–1766 (n)	(7)	(7)	(14)
Additive	-488.727	414.999	-36.864
Interactive	-33.851	33.851	
Grand mean	-428.136	-428.136	-428.136
Observed mean	-950.714	+20.714	-465.000
1767–1770 (n)	(4)	(4)	(8)
Additive	-387.352	516.375	64.511
Interactive	59.239	-59.239	
Grand mean	-428.136	-428.136	-428.136
Observed mean	-756.250	+29.000	-363.625
Category effect (n)	(11)	(11)	(22)
Additive	-451.864	451.863	
Grand mean	-428.136	-428.136	-428.136
Observed	-880.000	23.727	

Note: We have done calculations to more decimal places than shown here. Consequently, if you use the values presented in the table in your calculations, your results may not correspond exactly with ours.

Source: Authors' calculations from data in Table 7.4.

$$SS(interaction) = SS(explained) - SS(main\ effects)$$
$$= 4,588,410.984 - 4,544,295.125$$
$$= 44,115.859$$

The unexplained sum of squares is the variation within the several cells, as presented in Table 7.4.

$$SS(unexplained) = \sum (SS(cell))$$
$$= \sum [\bar{x} \ (cell) - GM]^2$$
$$= 962,941.4284 + 84,583.42858 + 371,052.7501$$
$$+ 65,526$$
$$= 1,484,103.607$$

The various sum of squares total to the SS(total)

$$SS(total) = SS(period) + SS(region) + SS(interaction)$$
$$+ SS(unexplained)$$
$$6,072,514.591 = 52,318.716 + 4,491,976.409 + 44,115.859 +$$
$$1,484,103.607$$
$$= 6,072,514.591.$$

An examination of the several effects in Table 7.5 demonstrates that the greatest effect is region: northern and middle colonies have an average trade balance £451,864 below that of all the colonies together, while that of the southern colonies is £451,863 above the average of all the colonies. Time period has a smaller effect: the average trade balance between 1760 and 1766 is £36,864 below the average for all years and that for 1767–1770 is £64,511 above that average. The interaction effect is also relatively small: the southern colonies between 1767 and 1770, for example, have a mean trade balance £59,239 below what we would expect from the additive effects of region and time period. The northern and middle colonies in that same period are £59,239 above the additive effects of region and period.

Significance: The F-Test

As with one-way analysis of variance, we calculate the significance of each effect, and the overall explained variation, with the F-ratio. F is the mean sum of squares for an effect divided by the mean sum of squares for the unexplained variation.

Degrees of Freedom

The degrees of freedom for each main effect equal the number of categories for the variable minus one. Thus, if the number of categories in the categorical variable is k, the degrees of freedom are calculated as k - 1. For the additive effects of the independent variables

$$DF(period) = 2 - 1$$
$$= 1$$

$$DF(region) = 2 - 1$$
$$= 1$$

The degrees of freedom for the main effects are the sum of the degrees of freedom for the additive effects of the two independent variables

$$DF(main\ effects) = DF(period) + DF(region)$$
$$= 1 + 1$$
$$= 2$$

The interaction degrees of freedom are the product of the two main-effects degrees of freedom

$$DF(interaction) = DF(period)\ X\ DF(region)$$
$$= 1\ X\ 1$$
$$= 1$$

The degrees of freedom for the explained variation are the sum of the degrees of freedom for each of the components

$$DF(explained) = DF(period) + DF(region) + DF(interaction)$$
$$= 1 + 1 + 1$$
$$= 3$$

The unexplained degrees of freedom are the number of cases (n) less the product of the number of categories in each of the categorical variables. As there are two categories in period and two in region, this is $2\ X\ 2 = 4$. Thus,

$$DF(unexplained) = n - k(period)\ X\ k(region)$$
$$= 22 - 2\ X\ 2$$
$$= 18$$

The total degrees of freedom are the number of cases minus one. Thus,

$$DF(total) = n - 1$$
$$= 22 - 1$$
$$= 21$$

Notice:

$$DF(total) = DF(explained) + DF(unexplained)$$
$$21 = 3 + 18$$

Calculating the F-Ratio

The F-test involves dividing the mean square for a variety of sources by the mean square unexplained. We can determine the associated probability for the degrees of freedom either by computing the associated probability directly with a computer or by locating the critical F-ratio for the appropriate set of degrees of freedom.

The Mean Square. We calculated the mean squares (MS) for the colonial trade data as follows:

$$
\begin{aligned}
MS(period) &= SS(period)/DF(period) \\
&= 52,318.716/1 \\
&= 52,318.716
\end{aligned}
$$

$$
\begin{aligned}
MS(region) &= SS(region)/DF(region) \\
&= 4,491,976.409/1 \\
&= 4,491,976.409
\end{aligned}
$$

$$
\begin{aligned}
MS(main\ effects) &= SS(main\ effects)/DF(main\ effects) \\
&= 4,544,295.125/2 \\
&= 2,272,147.563
\end{aligned}
$$

$$
\begin{aligned}
MS(interaction) &= SS(interaction)/DF(interaction) \\
&= 44,115.859/1 \\
&= 44,115.859
\end{aligned}
$$

$$
\begin{aligned}
MS(explained) &= SS(explained)/DF(explained) \\
&= 4,588,410.984/3 \\
&= 1,529,470.328
\end{aligned}
$$

$$
\begin{aligned}
MS(unexplained) &= SS(unexplained)/DF(unexplained) \\
&= 1,484,103.607/18 \\
&= 82,450.200
\end{aligned}
$$

The various F-tests are presented in Table 7.6. The F-ratio is simply the mean square from a source divided by the unexplained mean square. For example, the F-ratio for period is:

$$
\begin{aligned}
MS(period)/\ MS(unexplained) &= 52,318.716/82,450.200 \\
&= .635
\end{aligned}
$$

We can evaluate the significance of the F-ratio either by comparing the observed F-ratio with the critical F-ratio for a probability of .05 obtained

Table 7.6
F-Tests for Various Effects: America's Colonial Trade Balance with Great Britain, 1760-1770

Effect	F – Ratio	DF	.05 Critical F–Ratio	Significant at .05	Probability
Period	0.635	1, 18	4.41	no	.436
Region	54.481	1, 18	4.41	yes	.0000097
Main effects	27.558	2, 18	3.57	yes	.005
Interaction	0.535	1, 18	4.41	no	.474
Explained	18.550	3, 18	3.16	yes	.005

Source: Authors' calculations from data in Table 7.4.

from Table A.4 in the Appendix (significant observed F-ratios are larger than the critical F- ratio), or by obtaining the actual probability from a computer (actual probabilities less than .05 are significant).

In this example, there are significant regional effects (and, hence, significant main and explained effects), but the interaction and period effects are not significant.

Strength of Association

As with one-way analysis of variance, E^2 measures the strength of association in two-way analysis of variance. E^2 is the ratio of the explained sum of squares from some source to the total sum of squares. For example, for region,

$$E^2 = SS(region)/SS(total)$$
$$= 4,491,976.409/6,072,514.591$$
$$= .7397$$

Region has a strong association with trade balance. It accounts for more than 73 percent in the variation of trade balances. As already determined by the F-test, this explained variation is significant. Period has a weak relation and an insignificant relationship to trade balances. In Table 7.7, we have presented explained variations for the various sources.

Table 7.7
Explained Variation in America's Colonial Trade Balance with Great Britain, 1760-1770, by Source

Source	Explained Variation: E^2
Period	.0086
Region	.7397
Main effects	.7483
Interaction	.0073
Explained	.7556
Unexplained	.2444
Total	1.0000

Source: Authors' calculations from data in Table 7.4.

TWO-WAY ANALYSIS OF VARIANCE WITH RELATED INDEPENDENT VARIABLES

Historians will often be confronted with two or more explanatory variables that are related to one another as well as to the dependent variable. Then, two-way analysis of variance requires some adjustments. Consider, for instance, the rate at which U.S. presidents have vetoed legislation. Before Andrew Jackson, presidents rarely used the veto, while after him it was used more often as a source of executive power. However, one could argue that it was not Jackson who produced the change, but instead conflict between the legislative and executive branches.

Table 7.8 shows the number of vetoes executed by each president from George Washington to James Buchanan (excluding William Henry Harrison and Zachary Taylor, who died soon after entering office) by time period (before Jackson, and after) and by whether or not the political party or faction aligned with the president was in control of at least one house of Congress.

As we can see in Table 7.9, the two independent variables are related. There was a tendency toward same-party control of the presidency and Congress during the early period, while different parties tended to control the two branches of government during the later period. To a certain extent, some of the effect of the early period is due to same-party control and some

Table 7.8
Presidential Vetoes for Thirteen U.S. Presidents, 1789-1861, by Time Period and Party/Faction Control of Congress

Period(early & late):	Washington-J. Q. Adams		Jackson-Buchanan	
Congressional Control:	Same[a]	Opposition[b]	Same[a]	Opposition[b]
No. of	0	2	12	10
Vetoes per	0	0	1	3
Administration	7			0
	1			9
				7
n (cell)	4	2	2	5
$\bar{x}$ (cell)	2	1	6.5	5.8
SS (cell)	34	2	60.5	70.8

All data:
   $n = 13$; $GM = 4$; SS (total) $= 230$

Congress:
   same: $n = 6$; $\bar{x} = 3.5$; SS $= 121.5$
   different: $n = 7$; $\bar{x} = 4.428$; SS $= 105.714$

Period:
   early: $n = 6$; $\bar{x} = 1.6667$; SS $= 37.333$
   late: $n = 7$; $\bar{x} = 6$; SS $= 132$

[a]president and at least one house of Congress were of same party.
[b]president and both houses of Congress were of different parties at some point in the administration.

Source: U.S. Department of Commerce, Bureau of the Census, *Historical Statistics of the United States: Colonial Times to 1970*, pt. 2 (Washington, DC: Government Printing Office, 1975), 1082–1084.

of the effect of the later period is due to opposite-party control. The effects of the independent variables overlap. Besides overlap, there is also the effect of any possible interaction. The analysis of variance needs to take this overlapping explanatory power into account.

The first step is to calculate the total sum of squares in the usual way:

$$
\begin{aligned}
SS(total) &= \sum (x_i - GM)^2 \\
&= (0 - 4)^2 + (0 - 4)^2 + (7 - 4)^2 + (1 - 4)^2 + (2 - 4)^2 + \\
&\quad (0 - 4)^2 + (12 - 4)^2 + (1 - 4)^2 + (10 - 4)^2 + (3 - 4)^2 + \\
&\quad (0 - 4)^2 + (9 - 4)^2 + (7 - 4)^2 \\
&= 230
\end{aligned}
$$

The next step is to calculate the unexplained variation—the variation within the four categories of period and congressional control. Again, this is the variation that the variables cannot explain—the variation among administrations that is the same on all the variables being analyzed. The unexplained sum of squares is the variation about the cell means summed across all four cells. If $\bar{x}$ (cell) is the mean in any particular cell and x_i is the ith case in that cell, then

$$
SS(cells) = \sum [x_i - \bar{x}(cell)]^2
$$

Calculating the sum of squares for each cell individually and totally across all cells we get

$(0 - 2)^2 + (0 - 2)^2 + (7 - 2)^2 + (1 - 2)^2$	=	34.0
$(2 - 1)^2 + (0 - 1)^2$	=	2.0
$(12 - 6.5)^2 + (1 - 6.5)^2$	=	60.5
$(10 - 5.8)^2 + (3 - 5.8)^2 + (0 - 5.8)^2 + (9 - 5.8)^2 + (7 - 5.8)^2$	=	70.8
Total	=	167.3

Table 7.9
Relationship between Time Period and U.S. Presidents' Party Control of Congress Shown in Percentage

Time Period	Party Control of Presidency and Congress	
	Same	Opposition
Washington-J. Q. Adams	66.7	28.6
Jackson-Buchanan	33.3	71.4
Total (n)	100.0 (6)	100.0 (7)

Source: Authors' calculations from data in Table 7.8.

If SS(cell) is the variation of cases in each cell about its cell mean, then the sum of these for all the cells is the unexplained sum of squares. The total sum of squares (cells) is the unexplained sum of squares. Thus,

$$SS(unexplained) = 34 + 2 + 60.5 + 70.8$$
$$= 167.3$$

Finally, we also calculate the explained sum of squares. As before, it is the variation of the several cell means about the grand mean, weighted by the number of cases in the cell.

$$SS(explained) = \sum n(cell)\ [\bar{x}\ (cell) - GM)^2]$$
$$= 4(2 - 4)^2 + 2(1 - 4)^2 + 2(6.5 - 4)^2 + 5(5.8 - 4)^2$$
$$= 62.7$$

At this point, the analysis has proceeded as it did with the unrelated independent variables discussed in the previous section, and the total variation has been partitioned into two sources: explained by the variables, and unexplained. Thus,

$$SS(total) = SS(explained) + SS(unexplained)$$
$$230 = 62.7 + 167.3$$

Analysis of variance with related independent variables differs from the analysis with unrelated independent variables in assessing the contribution of the two variables to this explanatory power. If we compute the sum of squares associated with period and congressional control in the usual way, it is the variation of the two category means about the grand mean, weighted by the number of cases in the category, and summed across the categories, as follows:

$$SS(period) = \sum n_j (\bar{x}_j - GM)^2$$
$$= 6(1.6667 - 4)^2 + 7(6 - 4)^2$$
$$= 60.666$$

and

$$SS(Congress) = \sum n_j (\bar{x}_j - GM)^2$$
$$= 6(3.5 - 4)^2 + 7(4.428 - 4)^2$$
$$= 2.786$$

But the SS(explained) is smaller than the SS(period) added to the

SS(Congress).

$$62.7 < 60.666 + 2.786$$
$$62.7 < 63.452$$

Interaction

If we calculate the interaction sum of squares as we did with unrelated independent variables, the results would be a meaningless negative explanatory power:

$$SS(interaction) = SS(explained) - [SS(period) + SS(Congress)]$$
$$= 62.7 - (60.666 + 2.786)$$
$$= -0.752.$$

The Venn diagram in Figure 7.3 might help us demonstrate the nature of the problem. Each circle represents one of the variables in the analysis, as well as the interaction effect itself. The circles overlap, producing seven areas in the circle representing the variation in vetoes. Thus, A is the unexplained variation, SS(unexplained) = A; BCDEFG is the explained variation, SS(explained) = BCDEFG; and ABCDEFG is the total variation in vetoes, SS(total) = ABCDEFG.

The sum of squares for the individual effects together can exceed the explained sum of squares when the areas overlap, as is the case here, and some areas are counted twice. Thus,

$$SS(explained) < SS(period) + SS(Congress) + SS(interaction)$$
$$BCDEFG < DEF + BCD + CDEG$$

The problem is to decide where to attribute the shared variation. There are several approaches to the problem. Here, we will develop a hierarchical analysis of variance by first calculating the total sum of squares, the unexplained sum of squares, and the explained sum of squares as the difference between the two. Next, we calculate the maximum explanatory effect of each independent variable—the sum of squares due to Congress, and the sum of squares due to period. All these have been calculated above. The following areas of the Venn diagram are thus determined:

$$SS(total) = ABCDEFG = 230$$
$$SS(unexplained) = A = 167.3$$
$$SS(explained) = BCDEFG = 62.7$$
$$SS(Congress) = BCD = 2.786$$
$$SS(period) = DEF = 60.666.$$

Figure 7.3
Venn Diagram of Shared Variation among Three Variables and an Interactive Effect

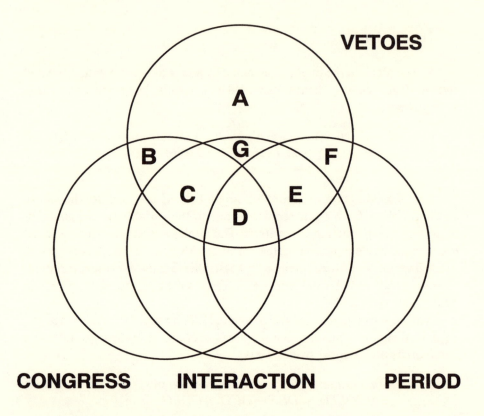

Source: Constructed with reference to Table 7.8.

What remains is the interaction (G). Once we determine the interaction sum of squares, we can calculate the main-effects sum of squares (BCDEF) by subtracting the interaction (G) from the explained sum of squares (BCDEFG). The unique effects of Congress (BC) can be calculated by subtracting the effects of period (DEF) from the main effects (BCDEF). Similarly, we can calculate the unique effects of period (EF) by subtracting the effects of Congress (BCD) from the main effects (BCDEF). Thus, determining the effects of interaction (G) permits calculation of the other effects by subtraction from sums of squares.

Calculation of Interaction Sum of Squares

The method used here for calculating the interaction sum of squares— when the independent variables are related (unequal and unproportional cell frequencies)—is suitable when at least one of the independent variables has only two categories. (When both independent variables have more than two categories, we must use other methods.)[5] Table 7.10 illustrates the calculations.

Recall, earlier we calculated the interaction sum of squares for the colonial trade to be 44,115.859 by determining the interaction effects of each cell. Notice that we get the same results for the colonial trade data (see Table 7.11) when we calculate the interaction sum of squares by the method described above.

Table 7.10
Calculation of Interaction Sum of Squares for Presidential Veto Data from Table 7.8

Congress	Period Early		Late		$W =$	$D=$		
Control	n_1	$\bar{x}_1$	n_2	$\bar{x}_2$	$n_1 n_2/n_1 + n_2$	$\bar{x}_1 - \bar{x}_2$	WD	WD²
Same	4	2	2	6.5	1.333333	-4.5	-6.0	27.00
Opposite	2	1	5	5.8	1.428571	-4.8	-6.8571	32.9142
Total					2.761904		-12.8571	59.9142

$SS(interaction)$ $= \sum WD^2 - (\sum WD)^2 / \sum W$
$= 59.9142 - (-12.8571)^2 / 2.761904$
$= 0.062$

Table 7.11
Calculation of Interaction Sum of Squares for Colonial Trade Balances Data from Table 7.2

Period	Colonial Region North n_1	$\bar{x}_1$	South n_2	$\bar{x}_2$	W= $\dfrac{n_1 n_2}{n_1 + n_2}$	D= $\bar{x}_1 - \bar{x}_2$	WD	WD^2
1760–1766	7	-6655/7	7	145/7	3.5	-6655/7 -145/7	-3400	3302857.143
1767–1770	4	-3025/4	4	116/4	2	-3025/4 -116/4	-1570.5	1233235.125
Total					5.5		-4970.5	4536092.268

$$SS(interaction) = \Sigma WD^2 - (\Sigma WD)^2 / \Sigma W$$
$$= 4536092.268 - (-4970.5)^2 / 5.5$$
$$= 44115.859$$

Note: We used the ratio from which the mean is calculated, rather than the means themselves, because of the larger number of digits that would be required with the means to get accurate results.

Hierarchical Attribution of Variation

We can now complete the partitioning of explained variation to the several sources. We calculate the main effects sum of squares (BCDEF) by subtracting the interaction (G) from the explained sum of squares (BCDEFG)

$$SS(main\ effects) = SS(explained) - SS(interaction)$$
$$= 62.7 - 0.06206$$
$$= 62.6379$$

We calculate the unique effects of period (EF) by subtracting the effects of Congress (BCD) from the main effects (BCDEF)

$$unique\ SS(period) = SS(main\ effects) - SS(Congress)$$
$$= 62.6379 - 2.786$$
$$= 59.85$$

And the unique effects of Congress (BC) are calculated by subtracting the effects of period (DEF) from the main effects (BCDEF)

$$unique\ SS(Congress) = SS(main\ effects) - SS(period)$$
$$= 62.6379 - 60.6666$$
$$= 1.9713$$

At this point, the total variation in presidential vetoes has been partitioned in two ways, as indicated in Table 7.12. Which of the two analyses is best suited to the problem? The hypothesis is that the increase in vetoes after John Quincy Adams's administration was due to opposition-party control of Congress. Period is not a causal variable; instead, it is a surrogate for a set of causal factors we wish to identify. Party control of Congress is hypothesized to be one of these factors. In this case, then, we should allow party control of Congress to explain what it can, period being assigned the remaining variation. The second analysis of variance is appropriate.

The hypothesis that opposition-party control of Congress was one of the factors causing the increase in presidential vetoes is not substantiated. At best, it accounts for 2.786 of the total variation of 230, or 1.2 percent. Some factor other than opposition-party control of Congress must account for the increase in vetoes.

Table 7.12

Two Hierarchical Attributions of Variance Used in Analyzing Presidential Vetoes by Time Period and Party Control of Congress, 1789-1861

Priority to Time Period		Priority to Party Control of Congress	
Source	Sum of Squares	Source	Sum of Squares
Main effects	62.6379	Main effects	62.6379
Period	60.6666	Congress	2.7820
Congress	1.9713	Period	59.8558
Interaction	0.0620	Interaction	0.0620
Explained	62.7000	Explained	62.7000
Unexplained	167.3000	Unexplained	167.3000
Total	230.0000	Total	230.0000

Note: We have done calculations to more decimal places than shown here. Consequently, if you use the values presented in the table in your calculations, your results may not correspond exactly with ours.

Source: Authors' calculations from data in Tables 7.8 and 7.10; also see calculations in the text.

Nature of Effect

How to show the nature of the effect, when the independent variables are related, depends on the presence of interaction.

Interaction Present

When there is interaction—either significant interaction or substantial interaction—the nature of the effect is best shown by comparing the cell means with the grand mean. While there is very little interaction present in the presidential veto data, we can use it to demonstrate the process. In Table 7.13, the grand mean is subtracted from each cell mean to show the interactive effect. Thus, for the early period the effect is:

$$\bar{x}\ (cell) - GM\ =\ 2 - 4$$
$$=\ -2$$

During both periods, there were fewer vetoes when the opposition party or faction controlled Congress. Although the effect was weaker in the later period, there were more vetoes when the same party or faction controlled both Congress and the presidency. This interaction, however, is small and insignificant. The effects of period and congressional control are better understood individually as part of an additive model.

Interaction Not Present

When the independent variables are not related, we can calculate the effect of each category by subtracting the grand mean from the category

Table 7.13
Interaction Effects of Period and Congressional Control on Use of Presidential Veto

Period:	Washington-J. Q. Adams		Jackson-Buchanan	
Congressional Control:	Same	Opposition	Same	Opposition
Effect on vetoes ($\bar{x}$(cell) - GM)	-2	-3	+2.5	+1.8

Source: Authors' calculations from data in Table 7.8.

mean. When the independent variables are related, however, the category means reflect the effects of both independent variables. To isolate the effects of one variable, we must control the other. Let us look again at the various means for the veto data, as shown in Table 7.14.

We can calculate the observed category mean for the Washington–John Quincy Adams period from the two cell means (same-party and opposite-party control) weighted by the number of cases in each cell. Thus,

$$observed\ mean = \sum (n(cell)\bar{x}(cell)\ /\ n(category))$$
$$= [(4 \text{X} 2) + (2 \text{X} 1)]\ /\ 6$$
$$= 1.666$$

Among all the cases, the portion of administrations with the same party controlling both Congress and the presidency is 6/13, or 46 percent; but in the early period, this occurs in 4/6 of the administrations, or 67 percent. Same-party control is overrepresented, and opposite-party control is underrepresented in computing the observed mean for the early period. The

Table 7.14
Mean Presidential Vetoes by Period and Party Control of Congress

| Period | Party Control of Congress | | Mean | |
	Same	Opposite		
Washington–J. Q. Adams	$\bar{x} = 2$ n = 4 e = (6/13)6	$\bar{x} = 1$ n = 2 e = (6/13)7	Observed: Adjusted: n:	1.6666 1.4615 6
Jackson–Buchanan	$\bar{x} = 6.5$ n = 2 e = (7/13)6	$\bar{x} = 5.8$ n = 5 e = (7/13)7	Observed: Adjusted: n:	6 6.1230 7

Mean
  Observed:
  Adjusted:
  n:
	3.5
	4.4230
	6
		4.428
		3.584
		7		

Grand mean
  Observed:
  Adjusted:
  n:
	4
	3.9716
	13			

Source: Authors' calculations from data in Table 7.8.

opposite is true for the later period. One way to remove the effects of the other variable in computing a category mean is to adjust the number of cases in each cell to that expected if there were no relationship between the two independent variables. This is the expected cell frequency used in the calculation of chi-square (see Chapter 6). The expected cell frequency, e, for the first cell is calculated by taking the proportion of cases in the first row (6/13) and multiplying it by the number of cases in the first column (6). Thus, for the first cell,

$$e = (6/13)6$$
$$= 2.7692$$

Table 7.14 presents the expected cell frequency for each cell. The adjusted category mean weights each cell mean by the expected cell frequency, rather than the observed cell frequency. Thus, for the early period,

$$adjusted\ category\ mean\ = [\sum e(cell)X\bar{x}(cell)]/n(category\ )$$
$$= ([(6/13)X6X2] + [(6/13)X7X1])/6$$
$$= 1.4615$$

We have presented the adjusted category means for each category in Table 7.14.

We calculated the adjusted grand mean in a similar manner across all cells:

$$adjusted\ grand\ mean\ = [\sum e(cell)X\bar{x}(cell)]/n$$
$$= ([(6/13)X6X2] + [(6/13)X7X1]$$
$$+ [(7/13)X6X6.5] + [(7/13)X7X5.8])/13$$
$$= 3.9716$$

We can now compute the unadjusted and adjusted additive effects for each category in the usual way by subtracting the unadjusted grand mean from each unadjusted category mean and the adjusted grand mean from each adjusted category mean. These are presented in Table 7.15.

Once the effects of party control are removed, the differences in average vetoes between the earlier and later periods increase somewhat. When the effects of period are removed, the effects of party control diminish (i.e., the difference between same-party and opposite-party control becomes less) and reverse direction. Same-party control produces more rather than less vetoes than opposite-party control.

Table 7.15
Unadjusted and Adjusted Additive Effects of Period and Party
Control of Congress on Presidential Vetoes, 1789-1861

Variable	Category	Unadjusted Effect	Adjusted Effect
Period	Early	-2.3333	-2.5101
	Late	+2.0000	+2.1514
Congress	Same	-0.5000	+0.4515
	Opposition	+0.4286	-0.3869

Source: Authors' calculations from data in Table 7.14.

The adjusting of category means is the essence of MCA (Multiple Classification Analysis) available in some statistical packages.[6]

Significance: The F-Test

We calculate significance of each effect and the overall explained variation with the F-ratio, which takes the mean square for an effect and divides it by the mean square for the unexplained variation.

Degrees of Freedom

The degrees of freedom for each main effect are the number of categories in the variable minus one. Thus, if the number of categories in the categorical variable is k, the degrees of freedom are k - 1. For the main effects,

$$DF\ (period) = 2 - 1 = 1$$
$$DF(Congress) = 2 - 1 = 1$$
$$DF(main\ effects) = DF(period) + DF(Congress) = 1 + 1 = 2$$

The interaction degrees of freedom are the product of the two main-effect degrees of freedom

$$DF(interaction) = DF(period) \times DF(Congress)$$
$$= 1 \times 1$$
$$= 1$$

The degrees of freedom for the explained variation are the sum of the degrees of freedom for each of the components

$$DF(explained) = DF(period) + DF(Congress) + DF(interaction)$$
$$= 1 + 1 + 1$$
$$= 3$$

The unexplained degrees of freedom are the number of cases (n) less the product of the number of categories in each of the categorical variables. As there are two categories in period and two categories in congressional control, this is $2 \times 2 = 4$. Thus

$$DF(unexplained) = n - [k(period) \times k(Congress)]$$
$$= 13 - (2 \times 2)$$
$$= 9$$

The total degrees of freedom are the number of cases minus one. Thus,

$$DF(total) = n - 1$$
$$= 13 - 1$$
$$= 12$$

Notice that

$$DF(total) = DF(explained) + DF(unexplained)$$
$$12 = 3 + 9$$

Calculating the F-Ratio

As noted earlier in the chapter, the F-ratio involves dividing the mean square for a variety of sources by the mean square unexplained. We can determine the associated probability for the degrees of freedom either by computing the associated probability directly with a computer or by locating the critical F-ratio for the appropriate set of degrees of freedom.

Because there are several ways to allocate the explained sums of squares among the different sources when independent variables are related, several F-ratios can be computed. For example, if we allocate period the maximum explanatory variation, its sum of squares is 60.6666. But if we allow party control of Congress to explain a maximum amount of variation, the period sum of squares is 59.85 (see Table 7.12). Here, the F-test will follow the latter alternative approach; the analysis gives priority to party control of Congress in Table 7.16.

Table 7.16
F-Tests for Various Effects, Using Hierarchical Model: Priority Given to Party Control of Congress in Presidential Vetoes, 1789-1861

Effect	Mean Sums of Squares	F = Ratio	DF	.05 Critical F-Ratio	Significant at .05
Period	59.855/18.5888	= 3.2199	1, 9	5.12	no
Congress	2.782/18.5888	= 0.1496	1, 9	5.12	no
Main effects	31.319/18.5888	= 1.6848	2, 9	4.29	no
Interaction	0.062/18.5888	= 0.0033	1, 9	5.12	no
Explained	20.900/18.5888	= 1.1243	3, 9	3.86	no

Source: Authors' calculations from data in Table 7.12; see text, where calculations are shown.

The Mean Square. We calculated the mean square for the presidential veto data as follows:

$$MS(period) = SS(period) / DF(period)$$
$$= 59.85/1$$
$$= 59.85$$

$$MS(Congress) = SS(Congress) / DF(Congress)$$
$$= 2.786/1$$
$$= 2.786$$

$$MS(main\ effects) = SS(main\ effects) / DF(main\ effects)$$
$$= 62.6379 / 2$$
$$= 31.319$$

$$MS(interaction) = SS(interaction) / DF(interaction)$$
$$= .06206 / 1$$
$$= .06206$$

$$MS(explained) = SS(explained) / DF(explained)$$
$$= 62.7 / 3$$
$$= 20.9$$

$$MS(unexplained) = SS(unexplained) / DF(unexplained)$$
$$= 167.3 / 9$$
$$= 18.5888$$

We presented the various F-tests in Table 7.16. There are no significant effects, either individually or collectively, with regard to the variation in vetoes by presidents. There is nothing present in the data that we could not attribute to a chance assignment of veto rates.

Strength of Association

As with one-way analysis of variance, E^2 measures the strength of association in two-way analysis of variance. E^2 is the ratio of the explained sum of squares from some source to the total sum of squares. As with the F-ratios, the calculated E^2 value depends on how one allocates the explained variation among the several explanatory sources. Here, we calculated the various E^2 values presented in Table 7.17 by giving the maximum explanatory power to party control of Congress.

Notice that when we allocate the explanatory sum of squares according to the hierarchical method, the various E^2 values for the sources add up to the explained E^2. The various effects, taken together or individually, have a weak relationship with the presidential use of the veto. What explanatory power there is—insignificant though it be—lies with the period effect.

Table 7.17

Strength of Association for the Several Effects in a Two-way Analysis of Variance: Giving Party Control of Congress the Maximum Explanatory Power in Presidential Vetoes, 1789-1861

Effect	Ratio of Sums of Squares	=	E^2
Period	59.855/230	=	.260
Congress	2.782/230	=	.012
Interaction	0.062/230	=	.000
Explained	62.700/230	=	.272

Source: Authors' calculations from data in Table 7.12.

8

Regression Analysis

An Englishman, Francis Galton, developed regression analysis in the second half of the nineteenth century. His work was focused on heredity—an interest stimulated in part by his first cousin, Charles Darwin. The term *regression* derives from Galton's finding that individuals with some extreme characteristic—height, for example—tended to have offspring who were less extreme. Thus, people who were unusually short tended to have taller offspring, and people who were unusually tall tended to have shorter offspring—a regression toward the mean.

As developed by Galton between 1865 and 1885, and by others later, regression analysis involves four parts:

1. A graphical display of the relationship between two interval-level variables

2. A mathematical description of the relationship between two variables in terms of the "best-fitting" straight line

3. Significance tests for relationships between two interval-level variables

4. A measure of the strength of association between two interval-level variables

Regression analysis can also accommodate several variables for multivariate analysis and has techniques for including categorical variables and examining nonlinear (i.e., other than straight-line) relationships.

THE SCATTERPLOT

Regression analysis begins with a scatterplot. Using a technique originally devised by René Descartes (1596–1650) in 1635, Galton represented

data geometrically. He used the famous Cartesian coordinates of two per-
pendicular axes: the vertical (or y) axis to represent the dependent (or effect) variable; and the horizontal (or x) axis to represent the independent (or
causal) variable. Each axis is divided into intervals to represent the appropriate variable, and cases are plotted individually according to their values
on the two variables.

The relationship between Antimasonic voting and church organization
will be used to illustrate the scatterplot technique. Kathleen Smith Kutolowski
has demonstrated that, while particular religious denominations were not
associated with Antimasonic voting in Genesee County, New York, in the
period between 1828 and 1832, religious activity—as measured by number
of church buildings—was (see Table 8.1). As Kutolowski concluded,

> In predicting a positive response to Antimasonry, the
> specific denominational makeup in that relatively ho-
> mogeneous religious environment mattered less than
> the number of organized church bodies, the number of
> church buildings (an indicator of religious zeal, given
> the economics operative), and the degree of revival ac-
> tivity.[1]

Kutolowski suggested that church organization produced Antimasonic
voting: the more church organization, the greater percentage of votes for
Antimasonic candidates. Her independent or causal variable was the number of church buildings in the township, and her dependent or effect variable was the average Antimasonic vote in the 1828, 1830, and 1832 elections. We assigned the number of churches to the x or horizontal axis, and
the average Antimasonic vote to the y or vertical axis.

We then plotted the two variables on a scatterplot (see Figure 8.1). To
illustrate the process, consider Alabama Township. There were two churches
there and the average Antimasonic vote was 60 percent. As indicated on
the scatterplot, Alabama Township is placed at a point to correspond to 2 on
the x axis and 60 on the y axis.

Visual observation of the scatterplot suggests two things. First, there is
a tendency for townships with fewer churches to have lower percentages
of Antimasonic voting, and for townships with more churches to have higher
percentages of Antimasonic voting. Second, all the townships have high
Antimasonic vote averages—the minimum is Alexander with an average of
53.1 percent and four churches; the maximum is Elba with 88.3 percent and
seven churches.

Table 8.1
Antimasonic Voting and Number of Churches in Townships of Genesee County, New York, 1828–1832

Township	Number of Churches	Antimasonic Vote in 1828, 1830, and 1832 (%)
Alabama	2	60.0
Alexander	4	53.1
Attica	4	65.0
Batavia	4	70.6
Bennington	2	59.1
Bergen	4	63.9
Bethany	7	71.6
Byron	6	84.2
Castile	3	62.9
China	3	57.4
Covington	6	81.7
Elba	7	88.3
Gainesville	4	55.6
LeRoy	6	78.4
Middlebury	6	63.5
Orangeville	5	80.6
Pembroke	3	59.6
Perry	6	86.2
Sheldon	5	57.1
Stafford	5	74.0
Warsaw	4	61.6
Wethersfield	4	71.5

Total

$$\sum x_i = 100 \qquad \sum y_i = 1505.9$$

n = 22

$$\bar{x} = \frac{\sum x_i}{n} \qquad \bar{y} = \frac{\sum y_i}{n}$$

$$= \frac{100}{22} \qquad = \frac{1505.9}{22}$$

$$= 4.5454 \qquad = 68.45$$

Source: Adapted with additional calculations from Kathleen Smith Kutolowski, "Antimasonry Reexamined: Social Bases of the Grass-roots Party," *Journal of American History,* 71 (September 1984), 273.

Figure 8.1
Scatterplot of Average Antimasonic Vote Percentages for 1828, 1830, and 1832 and
the Number of Churches in Genesee County, New York

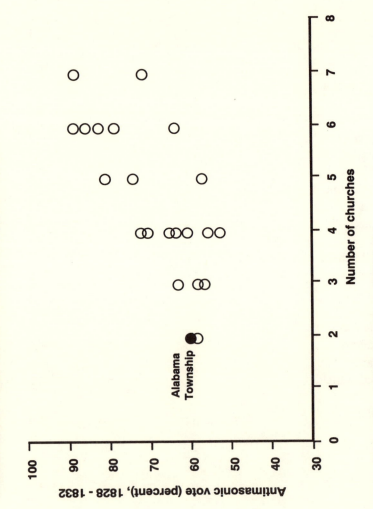

Source: Constructed from data shown in Table 8.1.

THE REGRESSION EQUATION

Although a careful examination of the scatterplot can be suggestive, it is also useful to construct a more precise statement of the relationship between the two variables. While not all relationships can be represented this way, the simplest relationship between most interval-level variables is a straight line. Using the scatterplot in Figure 8.1, we can characterize the relationship between the two variables in terms of a straight line that "best fits" all the data points. This is what Galton did.

What constitutes the single "best-fitting" straight line? Is there more than one such line? Figure 8.2 is a simplified version of Figure 8.1. It shows Alexander Township and a line that, for the moment, will be considered "best" in terms of all twenty-two townships. We want the best-fitting straight line to minimize the "error" between the value of y predicted by the line and the actual value in the data. The best-fitting line should be the straight line that makes the smallest errors in prediction. The goal is to minimize the total error of all twenty-two townships. Notice we have only drawn the line within the actual range of the x variable (number of churches) and extends to the y axis only by inference. There are no townships with zero or one churches.

Actually, Galton never solved the problem of the best-fitting straight line. Francis Ysidro Edgeworth, from Ireland, and George Udny Yule (1871–1951), from Scotland, resolved it in the 1890s.[2] Their solution was that the best-fitting straight line was the one that minimized the sum of the total squared error. There is only one such line. At this point, it is useful to introduce some mathematical notations.

x_i—The value of the ith case on the x variable. The ith can be any particular case. If the ith case is Alexander Township and the x variable is number of churches, then $x_i = x_{\text{Alexander}} = 4$.

y_i—The value of the ith case on the y variable. If the ith case is Alexander Township and the y variable is the average Antimasonic vote, then $y_i = y_{\text{Alexander}} = 53.1$.

$\hat{y}_i$—The value of the ith case on the y variable predicted from the x_i value and the best–fitting line. Here that predicted value is 65.57.

The best-fitting straight line minimizes the value

$$\Sigma (y_i - \hat{y}_i)^2$$

This is the least squares criterion.

Figure 8.2
Plotting the "Best-Fitting" Straight Line to Characterize the Relationship between the
Average Antimasonic Vote Percentages for 1828, 1830, and 1832 and the Number of Churches
in Genesee County, New York

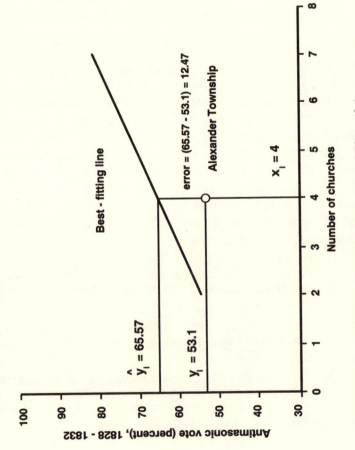

Source: Constructed with reference to Table 8.1 and Figure 8.1.

In modern notation, the *regression equation* for a straight line is:

$$\hat{y}_i = a + bx_i$$

The equation can be viewed as a machine into which we can put any possible number replacing x_i; this number is converted to a y_i value by being multiplied by b and added to a.

Again, in modern notation, the solution is in two steps (see Table 8.2). First, the slope of the line, b, is:

$$b = \frac{\Sigma(x_i - \bar{x})(y_i - \bar{y})}{\Sigma(x_i - \bar{x})^2}$$

We can calculate this directly from the available information, although it is a tedious process without a computer or hand calculator with statistical functions. For the Genesee data,

$$b = \frac{239.9}{45.4545}$$
$$= 5.2778$$

The best-fitting straight line will pass through the point represented by the means of the two variables. The means of the two variables best represent each variable. In this case, the mean number of churches is 4.5454 and the mean Antimasonic vote is 68.45 percent. As the line passes through this point, we can substitute the two means into the equation for the values x_i and $\hat{y}_i$. Now, the equation has only one remaining unknown value, a. To find a, simply substitute b, $\bar{x}$, and $\bar{y}$ and then solve the equation. Thus,

$$\hat{y}_i = a + bx_i$$
$$\bar{y} = a + b\bar{x}$$
$$68.45 = a + 5.2778(4.5454)$$
$$a = 44.46$$

The equation is:

$$\hat{y}_i = 44.46 + 5.2778x_i$$

predicted Antimasonic vote = 44.46 + 5.2778(number of churches)

Table 8.2
Calculation of Regression Equation to Describe the Relationship between Antimasonic Voting and Number of Churches in Townships of Genesee County, New York, 1828–1832

x_i	y_i	$(x_i - \bar{x})(y_i - \bar{y})$		$(x_i - \bar{x})^2$
2	60.0	(-2.5454)	(-8.45)	$(-2.5454)^2$
4	53.1	(-0.5454)	(-15.35)	$(-0.5454)^2$
4	65.0	(-0.5454)	(-3.45)	$(-0.5454)^2$
4	70.6	(-0.5454)	(2.15)	$(-0.5454)^2$
2	59.1	(-2.5454)	(-9.35)	$(-2.5454)^2$
4	63.9	(-0.5454)	(-4.55)	$(-0.5454)^2$
7	71.6	(2.4546)	(3.15)	$(2.4545)^2$
6	84.2	(1.4546)	(15.75)	$(1.4545)^2$
3	62.9	(-1.5454)	(-5.55)	$(-1.5454)^2$
3	57.4	(-1.5454)	(-11.05)	$(-1.5454)^2$
6	81.7	(1.4546)	(13.25)	$(1.4545)^2$
7	88.3	(2.4546)	(19.85)	$(2.4545)^2$
4	55.6	(-0.5454)	(-12.85)	$(-0.5454)^2$
6	78.4	(1.4546)	(9.95)	$(1.4545)^2$
6	63.5	(1.4546)	(-4.95)	$(1.4545)^2$
5	80.6	(0.4546)	(12.15)	$(0.4545)^2$
3	59.6	(-1.5454)	(-8.85)	$(-1.5454)^2$
6	86.2	(1.4546)	(17.75)	$(1.4545)^2$
5	57.1	(0.4546)	(-11.35)	$(0.4545)^2$
5	74.0	(0.4546)	(5.55)	$(0.4545)^2$
4	61.6	(-0.5454)	(-6.85)	$(-0.5454)^2$
4	71.5	(-0.5454)	(3.05)	$(-0.5454)^2$

$\Sigma x_i = 100 \qquad \Sigma y_i = 1505.9 \qquad \Sigma(x_i - \bar{x})(y_i - \bar{y}) = 239.9 \qquad \Sigma(x_i - \bar{x})^2 = 45.4545$

$$b = \frac{\Sigma(x_i - \bar{x})(y_i - \bar{y})}{\Sigma(x_i - \bar{x})^2} = \frac{239.9}{45.4545} = 5.2778$$

$$a = \bar{y} - b\bar{x} = 68.45 - (5.2778)(4.5454) = 44.46$$

$$\hat{y}_i = 44.46 + 5.2778(x_i)$$

Note: We have done the calculations to more decimal places than shown here. Consequently, if you use the values presented in the table in your calculations, your results may not correspond exactly with ours.

Source: Authors' calculations from data in Table 8.1.

Plotting the Line

While it is only necessary to calculate two values of $\hat{y}_i$ to plot the line, calculating a third value as a check is a good practice. When plotting the regression line, it is best to use extreme points on the x axis. If we use points close to one another, the drawn line is likely to diverge from the correct line at one extreme. We suggest using the maximum and minimum value of x and the middle value. Examining the x axis, the minimum value is zero and the maximum is eight. (This accommodates all the observed number of churches.) The middle value on the axis is four. Substituting each of these for x_i in the equation,

$$\hat{y}_i = 44.46 + 5.2778x_i$$
$$= 44.46 + 5.2778(0)$$
$$= 44.46$$

$$\hat{y} = 44.46 + 5.2778(4)$$
$$= 65.57$$

$$\hat{y} = 44.46 + 5.2778(8)$$
$$= 86.68$$

When x is 0, $\hat{y}$ is 44.46. When x is 4, $\hat{y}$ is 65.57. When x is 8, $\hat{y}$ is 86.68. We plotted the points in Figure 8.3. The regression line passes through all three of them.

Interpretation of the Regression Equation

By examining Figure 8.3 we can determine several things. First, as the number of churches in a township increases, so does the Antimasonic vote. The value of a in the regression equation is called the *y intercept*. It is the value for $\hat{y}_i$ when x_i is zero and, therefore, the point where the line intersects the y axis. In the present analysis, if there are no churches ($x_i = 0$), the percent of Antimasonic vote is projected to be 44.46. But recall that this is a projection beyond the available data; no township had less than two churches.

The b term in the equation is the *slope*. The slope is either positive (increasing) or negative (decreasing). With a positive slope, as one variable increases, the other increases. This is the case with our data in Figure 8.3. With a negative slope, as one variable increases, the other decreases. A

Figure 8.3
Construction of Regression Line from Extreme Values on the x Axis, Corresponding to Regression Equation for Genesee County Data on Antimasonic Voting and Number of Churches

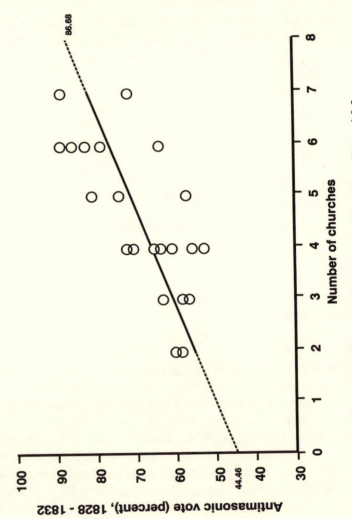

Source: Constructed with reference to Table 8.2; see also Figures 8.1 and 8.2.

slope of 1.0 means that, as the x variable increases by a given amount, the y variable increases by the same amount (assuming the two variables are measured on the same scale). If the slope is 0.0, the regression line is a horizontal line that indicates there is no relationship between the two variables. In that case, the prediction $\hat{y}_i$ is exactly the same for every value of x. The slope can also be interpreted as the impact or influence of the x variable on the y variable. In the case of the Antimasonic vote, the slope is 5.2778. For each church in the township, the average Antimasonic vote increases by 5.2778 percent (over the zero-base value of 44.46 percent).

The regression equation is asymmetric. If we switched the x and y variables, the equation will usually be different. In fact, if we make the number of churches the dependent (y) variable and the average Antimasonic vote the independent (x) variable, the equation becomes:

$$\hat{y}_i = a + bx_i$$
$$\hat{y}_i = -2.1362 + .0976x_i$$

predicted number of churches = −2.1362
+ .0976 (Antimasonic vote percentage)

While this is a valid equation for predicting or estimating the number of churches from the Antimasonic vote, causal interpretations are inappropriate. It is difficult to imagine an increase in support for a political party producing more church buildings.

A word of caution is necessary. While we can substitute any value for x_i to predict a value of y, the regression equation is based on data within a certain range. Outside that range, predictions can be misleading. In the case of the Genesee County elections, for example, the number of churches in the townships ranged from two to seven. If, for example, one church was substituted for x_i, it would result in the prediction ($\hat{y}_i$) of 49.74 as the Antimasonic vote percentage. Similarly, fifteen churches would predict the Antimasonic vote to be 123.63 percent—an impossible value. Generally, the predicted values in a regression equation are most accurate when calculated from values close to the mean of the independent variable. Projections beyond the range of the observed independent variable—here, the number of churches—should be done with caution.

Significance

The significance of the slope should be tested. A number of quantities are involved. First, there is the residual or error sum of squares. This is the variation of the actual y_i values about the $\hat{y}_i$ values that the regression line and x_i predict.

Residual Sum of Squares

The residual sum of squares, or sum of squares error (SSE), is the total of the squared differences between the actual value on the y variable and the value predicted from the regression equation and the x variable.

$$SSE = \Sigma (y_i - \hat{y}_i)^2$$

This is the value that is minimized by the regression equation. The calculation of SSE involves using the regression equation to calculate the predicted $\hat{y}_i$ value for each x_i value, subtracting $\hat{y}_i$ from the actual y_i value, and squaring the result. All the results are then added together (see Table 8.3). In the example of the Genesee County data,

$$SSE = \Sigma (y_i - \hat{y}_i)^2$$
$$= 1,191.4908$$

Standard Deviation of the Residuals. The residuals are the difference between the predicted ($\hat{y}_i$) and actual y_i values for y: residuals $= (y_i - \hat{y}_i)^2$. As with other standard deviations, we calculate the standard deviation of the residuals as the square root of the sum of squares divided by their degrees of freedom. Here, the degrees of freedom are (n - 2)—the number of cases (n) less the two parameters used to estimate the predicted values (the slope and the intercept of the regression equation). The standard deviation is:

$$S(residuals) = \sqrt{\frac{SSE}{(n-2)}}$$
$$= \sqrt{\frac{\Sigma (y_i - \hat{y}_i)^2}{(n-2)}}$$

Table 8.3
Calculation of Residuals (Error or Unexplained Variation) and Explained Variation in Genesee County Data on Antimasonic Voting and Number of Churches

x_i	y_i	$\hat{y}_i$	$(y_i - \hat{y}_i)^2$	$(\hat{y}_i - \bar{y})^2$	$(y_i - \bar{y})^2$
2	60.0	55.0156	24.8442	180.4831	71.4025
4	53.1	65.5712	155.5308	8.2875	235.6225
4	65.0	65.5712	.3263	8.2875	11.9025
4	70.6	65.5712	25.2888	8.2875	4.6225
2	59.1	55.0156	16.6823	180.4831	87.4225
4	63.9	65.5712	2.7929	8.2875	20.7025
7	71.6	81.4046	96.1302	167.8217	9.9225
6	84.2	76.1268	65.1766	58.9333	248.0625
3	62.9	60.2934	6.7944	66.5301	30.8025
3	57.4	60.2934	8.3718	66.5301	122.1025
6	81.7	76.1268	31.0606	58.9333	175.5625
7	88.3	81.4046	47.5465	167.8217	394.0225
4	55.6	65.5712	99.4248	8.2875	165.1225
6	78.4	76.1268	5.1674	58.9333	99.0025
6	63.5	76.1268	159.4361	58.9333	24.5025
5	80.6	70.8490	95.0820	5.7552	147.6225
3	59.6	60.2934	.4808	66.5301	78.3225
6	86.2	76.1268	101.4694	58.9333	315.0625
5	57.1	70.8490	189.0350	5.7552	128.8225
5	74.0	70.8490	9.9288	5.7552	30.8025
4	61.6	65.5712	15.7704	8.2875	46.9225
4	71.5	65.5712	35.1507	8.2875	9.3025
100	1505.9		1191.4908	1266.1445	2457.6350

$\hat{y}_i = 44.46 + 5.2778(x_i)$

Sum of squares error (SSE) $\Sigma(y_i - \hat{y}_i)^2 = 1191.4908$

Sum of squares explained: $\Sigma(\hat{y}_i - \bar{y})^2 = 1266.1445$

Sum of squares total: $\Sigma(y_i - \bar{y})^2 = 2457.635$

Note: We have done the calculations to more decimal places than shown here. Consequently, if you use the values presented in the table in your calculations, your results may not correspond exactly with ours.

Source: Authors' calculations from data in Table 8.1; see also Table 8.2.

For the Genesee County data this is:

$$S(residuals) = \sqrt{\frac{SSE}{(n-2)}}$$

$$= \sqrt{\frac{1191.4908}{(22-2)}}$$

$$= 7.7185$$

The average predicted Antimasonic vote is roughly 7.7 percent away from the actual vote.

Standard Error of the Slope. There are situations in which the calculated slope b may be regarded as a sample estimate of some population slope. If some random process involving variables unrelated to the number of churches produced Antimasonic voting, then we can view the observed Antimasonic vote in the twenty-two townships as a random sample of the results of the process. We might ask if chance or accident from such a process could have produced the observed slope. The null hypothesis is that the process producing Antimasonic voting was independent of the number of churches (i.e., slope = 0). The alternative hypothesis, suggested by Kutolowski, is that, in the random process by which Antimasonic voting was produced, the number of churches was positively related to Antimasonic voting. In random sampling, the slope has a standard error estimated by:

$$S_b = \frac{S(residuals)}{\sqrt{\Sigma(x_i - \bar{x})^2}}$$

$\Sigma(x_i - \bar{x})^2$ is the sum of squares for the x variable.

For the Genesee County data,

$$S_b = \frac{S(residuals)}{\sqrt{\Sigma(x_i - \bar{x})^2}}$$

$$= \frac{7.7185}{\sqrt{45.4545}}$$

$$= 1.1448$$

A Test for the Significance of the Slope b

To test the hypothesis that the slope is different from zero (the null hypothesis being that ß, the population slope, = 0), we calculate a t-value from the observed slope and its standard error.

$$t = b / S_b$$

For the Genesee County data

$$t = b / S_b$$
$$= 5.2778 / 1.1448$$
$$= 4.61$$

The degrees of freedom are n - 2. Here, n equals twenty-two and the degrees of freedom are, therefore, twenty.

If the null hypothesis is correct, the expected slope and the expected t-value amount to zero. The alternative hypothesis, from Kutolowski's theory, is that the slope is positive or greater than zero. We can determine the chances of observing a slope as large or larger than what we observed here (5.2778), if the null hypothesis that in the population the slope is zero is correct, by consulting a table of t-values. The critical one-tailed value for t at probability of .05 and DF = 20 is 1.73 (see Table A.2 at the end of the Appendix). As the observed t-value exceeds this, we reject the null hypothesis and accept the alternative hypothesis. Program A.2 in the Appendix calculates the one-tailed probability to be less than .000087. Kutolowski's theory incorporates a variable—number of churches—with a better predictive or explanatory power for Antimasonic voting than is likely by chance.

Notice that this is a one-tailed t-test. The hypothesis was that churches would be related to increases in Antimasonic voting. If the hypothesis had not specified the nature of the relationship (whether a positive or negative slope), a two-tailed t-test would have been appropriate. For the Genesee County data, the slope is significant at less than .000087 (one tailed). If the hypothesis were two tailed, the probability would be less than .000174 (double the one-tailed probability).

MEASURE OF ASSOCIATION: CORRELATION

There are two measures of association used with regression analysis that determine the strength of the relationship between two variables. They are R^2 and Pearson's product-moment correlation coefficient (r). Curiously, Karl Pearson developed correlation in the 1890s, before regression analysis took its present form.[3]

R^2

For historians, the simplest measure of association to interpret is R^2. It is the proportion of the total variation in the dependent variable, y, that the independent variable, x, explains. Recalling Kutolowski's example, we can determine how much variation in voting for Antimasonic candidates is explained by the extent of religiosity.

total variation
(or the sum of squares total) in y $= \Sigma (y_i - \bar{y})^2$

explained variation
(or sum of squares explained) in y $= \Sigma (\hat{y}_i - \bar{y})^2$

unexplained variation
(or residual, or SSE) in y $= \Sigma (y_i - \hat{y}_i)^2$

$$R^2 = \frac{\text{explained variation}}{\text{total variation}}$$

Recall that we measure the variation of a variable as the total of the squared differences between each case's score and the mean of all the cases. The explained variation is the variation of the predicted values, $\hat{y}_i$, about the mean. These are the values determined by the x_i values and the regression equation—and, hence, explained by them. The unexplained variation is the error—the total of the squared differences between the actual (y_i) and the predicted values ($\hat{y}_i$) for the y variable. The x_i values and the regression equation do not explain this difference. For the Genesee County data (see Table 8.3),

total variation in y $= \Sigma (y_i - \bar{y})^2$

$= 2457.63$

explained variation in y $= \Sigma (\hat{y}_i - \bar{y})^2$

$= 1266.14$

unexplained (or residual) variation in y $= \Sigma (y_i - \hat{y}_i)^2$

$= 1191.49$

Notice that the explained variation plus the unexplained variation equals the total variation.

R^2 varies from zero to one. A maximum value of one occurs when all the observed points on the scatterplot lie on the regression line. There is no error of prediction and the equation and x_i completely account for the dependent variable. The minimum value of R^2 is zero. In this case, the slope of the regression line is zero, and the line and the x variable do not explain any of the variation in the dependent variable. For the Genesee County data,

$$R^2 = \frac{\text{explained variation}}{\text{total variation}}$$

$$= \frac{1,266.14}{2,457.63}$$

$$= .5151$$

The interpretation of this is that the number of churches in a township explains (or is associated with) 51.51 percent of the variation in Antimasonic voting. Left unexplained is 48.49 percent ($1 - .5151 = .4849$) of the variation. Generally, a measure of association between 0 and .3 is weak, .3 to .7 moderate, and .7 to 1 strong. In this case, the association is moderate. Unlike the regression equation, R^2 is symmetrical. It does not matter which variable we consider independent (x) and which variable dependent (y); R^2 will be the same either way.

Pearson's r

Pearson's correlation coefficient (r) is the square root of R^2 with the sign of the slope (b).

$$r = \sqrt{R^2} \text{ , having the sign of the slope (b)}$$

For the Antimasonic data,

$$r = \sqrt{R^2}$$

$$= \sqrt{.5151}$$

$$= +.7177$$

The correlation coefficient varies between -1 and +1. A value of -1 indicates a perfect negative association, with all the points of the scatterplot on a negatively sloping regression line. A value of +1 indicates a perfect positive association, with all the points of a scatterplot on a positively sloping regression line. A value of zero indicates the two variables are linearly independent of one another.

In accord with the general rule for evaluating a measure of association, between 0 and +/-.3 is weak, +/-.3 to +/-.7 is moderate, and +/-.7 to +/-1 is strong. The relationship here is strong. Pearson's r will give larger absolute values than R^2 (except when R^2 is zero or +/- 1). As with R^2, Pearson's r is symmetrical; it has the same value regardless of which is the x and which is the y variable.

Significance of r

The significance of r is the same as the significance of the slope of the regression equation. It is easier to calculate the t-value for r than the significance of the slope, if the value of r is known.

$$t = b / S_b$$

$$= \frac{5.2778}{1.1448}$$

$$= 4.61$$

$$t = \frac{r\sqrt{(n-2)}}{\sqrt{(1-R)^2}}$$

$$= \frac{.7177\sqrt{22-2}}{\sqrt{1-.5151}}$$

$$= 4.61$$

The degrees of freedom are 22 - 2 = 20. As was the case with the slope, the one-tailed significance is less than .000087.

SOME ADDITIONAL CONSIDERATIONS

Typically, regression is understood to indicate the extent to which one variable can explain the variation in another. That implies that three possible factors caused the unexplained (or residual, or error) variation. First, the unexplained variation can be seen as the effect of all other variables. Thus, the number of churches explains 52 percent of the Antimasonic vote; economic conditions, social factors, the varying appeal of the candidates, and everything else accounts for the remaining 48 percent of the Antimasonic vote. Variables not included in the analysis are called *exogenous variables*. Second, the unexplained variation can be attributed to the random or probabilistic nature of people and society. There is unexplained variation because there is a limit to how much we can explain about people. They exercise free will. Third, we work with imperfect data that are crude and have errors. In the case of the Genesee County elections, the number of churches measured church organization. Yet churches varied in size and zeal. The Antimasonic vote was a composite of the 1828, 1830, and 1832 votes—again, a crude index. Errors in the original observations and the indirect nature of our measured concepts will also reduce the explanatory power of the regression equation.

There are two additional sources of error that we must also consider. Both involve misspecification of the model. The first problem is that the model is linear. That means that the regression equation accounts for the linear (straight-line) relationship between the independent and dependent variables. What if the relationship is not linear? That may be the case with the Kutolowski data. A visual inspection of the scatterplot (Figure 8.1) suggests that there is little increase in Antimasonic voting as the number of churches increases from two to four, but that, as the number of churches increases from four to seven, the Antimasonic vote increases sharply. We calculated the regression equations and found that this was, in fact, the case. When we use only the townships with two to four churches, the regression line is:

$$\text{predicted Antimasonic vote} = 54.90 + 1.99(\text{churches})$$

And when we use only townships with four to seven churches, the regression line is:

$$\text{predicted Antimasonic vote} = 37.20 + 6.60(\text{churches})$$

The impact of churches on Antimasonic voting in the townships with four or more churches is more than three times what it is in townships with four or less churches. Any nonlinear relationship will not be included in the simple linear model and, if present, will result in erroneous conclusions. The remedy for nonlinear relationships is to detect them with scatterplots and adjust the analysis to accommodate them.

A second problem involves the relationship between the variables included in the analysis and those excluded—the exogenous variables. In society, things are complex. In the case of the Genesee County elections, we have the Antimasonic vote and the number of churches. How are these related to each other and the exogenous variables? The remedy for omitting other variables is to include them in a multivariate analysis that includes all appropriate variables. This is done with multiple regression analysis.

9

Multiple Regression

Not long after its development, the regression model was expanded to include more than one independent variable. The first application, by George Yule, was an analysis of the distribution of aid to the poor in England.[1] The earliest use of multiple regression by political scientists was William F. Ogburn and Inez Goltra's 1919 study of referendums in Portland, Oregon. Women were allowed to vote for some contests but not others. Because the results were tabulated by precinct by sex, it was possible to answer the question, Do women vote differently than men? The problem was to control for class; a greater percentage of upper-class women voted than did those of the lower class. The solution was multiple regression. Ogburn and Goltra discovered that, once they controlled for class, women were more supportive of Prohibition than men were, and less supportive of an eight-hour day for female workers. On some issues, at least, women and men did vote differently.[2]

AN EXAMPLE OF MULTIPLE REGRESSION

For an example of multiple regression, let us again consider Kathleen Smith Kutolowski's study of Antimasonic voting in Genesee County, New York, from 1828 to 1832. In Chapter 8, we explored the relationship between church organization (as indicated by the number of churches) and Antimasonic voting. The relationship was significant, with the number of churches accounting for about one-half of the variation in Antimasonic voting. The evangelical churches in Genesee County were sympathetic to Antimasonic calls for moral reform.

Antimasonic candidates also supported economic reforms that appealed to the upwardly mobile residents of the county, who were interested in expanded economic opportunities. This suggests a second explanation for Antimasonic voting: voters in the economically more mature and prosperous areas would be more supportive of Antimasonic candidates.[3]

Does religious affiliation explain Antimasonic voting? Does the economic factor explain Antimasonic voting? Are both necessary to explain Antimasonic support? Or do neither account for this? We have diagrammed several possible explanatory models in Figure 9.1. The arrows represent causal influence and spurious (non-causal) associations.

In each model, we assumed that religious and economic factors were related—the religious factor influencing the economic, and not the other way around. Further, we assumed that other factors not explicitly included affected each factor in the model. These excluded (or exogenous) factors are not causally linked with one another. Let us also assume that all the relationships are linear; that is, a regression equation can properly represent them. Model 1 suggests that, if we remove (or control) the effects of economic factors, there is no relationship between Antimasonic voting and the religious factor. The effect it had on Antimasonic voting was through the economic factor. Model 2 suggests that controlling for economic factors will not eliminate the relationship between the religious factor and Antimasonic voting. Nor will controlling for religious factors eliminate the relationship between economic factors and Antimasonic voting. Each has an independent impact on Antimasonic voting. Model 3 suggests that controlling for religious factors will eliminate the relationship between economic factors and Antimasonic voting, because any relationship is an artifact of the religious factors affecting them.

There are several ways to measure the economic maturity of a township; Kutolowski explores several. Here, we will use the value of land per acre in 1836. This satisfies the requirement for an overall measure of economic development without being hampered by the missing or suspect data present in other alternatives. The relevant data, taken from Kutolowski, are presented in Table 9.1.

Which model, if any, is appropriate to the Genesee County situation? We need a method of controlling for a variable or removing its effects. Given the assumptions we have made previously, we can accomplish this with multiple regression. It measures the *partial* effect of each independent variable upon a dependent variable by controlling the effects of each of the other independent variables.[4]

Recall that the regression equation—Antimasonic vote = 44.46 + 5.2778 X (number of churches)—predicted the Antimasonic vote from the number of churches in a township. Subtracting the predicted value from the actual value resulted in the residual error. The residual, in this case, is the

Figure 9.1
Three Explanatory Models that Link Religious and Economic Factors with Antimasonic Voting in Genesee County, New York, 1828–1832

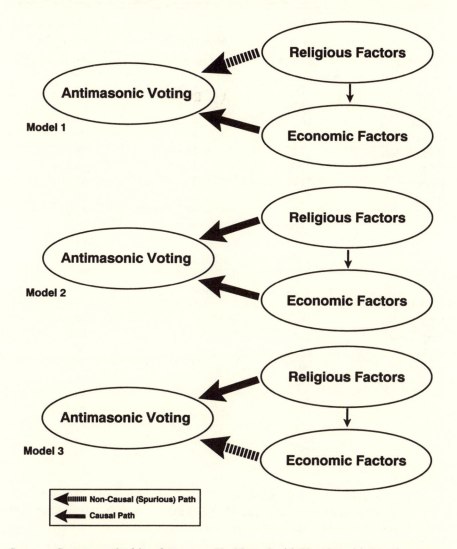

Source: Constructed with reference to Kathleen Smith Kutolowski, "Antimasonry Reexamined: Social Bases of the Grass-roots Party," *Journal of American History*, 71 (September 1984).

Table 9.1
Value of Land per Acre, Number of Churches, and Antimasonic Voting in Genesee County, New York, 1828-1832

Township	Value Per Acre, 1836 ($)	Number of Churches	Antimasonic Vote in 1828, 1830, and 1832 (%)
Alabama	7.66	2	60.0
Alexander	18.38	4	53.1
Attica	19.23	4	65.0
Batavia	29.20	4	70.6
Bennington	7.23	2	59.1
Bergen	21.06	4	63.9
Bethany	21.47	7	71.6
Byron	22.30	6	84.2
Castile	15.71	3	62.9
China	5.00	3	57.4
Covington	22.35	6	81.7
Elba	19.79	7	88.3
Gainesville	10.91	4	55.6
LeRoy	30.81	6	78.4
Middlebury	16.49	6	63.5
Orangeville	8.47	5	80.6
Pembroke	12.65	3	59.6
Perry	22.03	6	86.2
Sheldon	6.29	5	57.1
Stafford	21.72	5	74.0
Warsaw	16.42	4	61.6
Wethersfield	6.16	4	71.5
Total	361.33	100	1,505.9
n	22	22	22
Mean	16.424	4.545	68.45

Source: Authors' calculations from data in Kathleen Smith Kutolowski, "Antimasonry Reexamined: Social Bases of the Grass-roots Party," *Journal of American History*, 71 (September 1984), 273.

Antimasonic vote with the effects of churches controlled. For Alabama Township, the actual Antimasonic vote was 60.0 percent and the predicted vote (from number of churches) was $+44.46 + 5.2778(2) = 55.02$. The residual, then, for Alabama Township was +4.98 (actual - predicted = 60 - 55.02 = +4.98). There was actually more support for the Antimasons than that predicted from the number of churches in the township.

Our approach to multiple regression analysis requires the calculation of four sets of residuals. We outlined the equation for calculating the first set in Chapter 8. We now calculate three more equations in the same way from the data in Table 9.1. We will not show the steps necessary to calculate each equation, but only the final results.

$$\text{Antimasonic vote} = 44.46 + 5.2778 \text{ (number of churches)}$$
$$\text{Antimasonic vote} = 56.2640 + 0.7420 \text{ (value of land per acre)}$$
$$\text{number of churches} = 2.7604 + 0.1087 \text{ (value of land per acre)}$$
$$\text{value of land per acre} = 3.625 + 2.8158 \text{ (number of churches)}$$

In each case, the predicted value for each township can be calculated from the equation and then subtracted from the actual value observed—which will give us the residuals. We earlier calculated as +4.98 the residual Antimasonic vote when removing the effects of the churches in Alabama Township. We now calculate the remaining residuals for Alabama Township from the equations and the data presented in Table 9.1.

$$
\begin{aligned}
\text{predicted Antimasonic vote} &= 56.2640 + 0.7420 \text{ (value of land per acre)} \\
&= 56.2640 + 0.7420 \,(7.66) \\
&= 61.947
\end{aligned}
$$

$$
\begin{aligned}
\text{residual} &= \text{actual - predicted} \\
&= 60.0 - 61.947 \\
&= -1.947
\end{aligned}
$$

$$
\begin{aligned}
\text{predicted number} \\
\text{of churches} &= 2.7604 + 0.1087 \text{ (value of land per acre)} \\
&= 2.7604 + 0.1087 \,(7.66) \\
&= 3.5930
\end{aligned}
$$

$$
\begin{aligned}
\text{residual} &= \text{actual - predicted} \\
&= 2 - 3.593 \\
&= -1.593
\end{aligned}
$$

$$
\begin{aligned}
\text{predicted value of} \\
\text{land per acre} &= 3.625 + 2.8158 \text{ (number of churches)} \\
&= 3.625 + 2.8158 \,(2) \\
&= 9.2566
\end{aligned}
$$

$$
\begin{aligned}
\text{residual} &= \text{actual - predicted} \\
&= 7.66 - 9.2566 \\
&= -1.5966
\end{aligned}
$$

We have shown here the calculations for only Alabama Township. The residuals for all the townships are presented in Table 9.2.

If we treat the residuals as variables, we can calculate new regression equations showing the relationship between two variables while a third is held constant or controlled. Here, two such equations concern us: one predicting vote from churches with value per acre held constant; and the other predicting vote from value per acre with number of churches controlled. The first is a simple two-variable regression using the residuals in the first column of Table 9.2 as the dependent variable and the residuals in the third column as the independent variable. The second equation uses the residuals in the second column as the dependent variable and the residuals in the fourth column as the independent variable.

The regression equation using residuals as independent and dependent variables will have partial slopes—that is, slopes showing the effects of one variable on another with the effects of a third variable held constant. The calculations for the two partial slopes are the same as that of the simple slope shown in Chapter 8, with the exception that we now use residuals and not the original variables. The relevant calculations are shown in Tables 9.3 and 9.4. We have simplified the notation somewhat, but the calculations for the partial slopes are the same as for the simple slopes discussed earlier, except that we used the residuals from Table 9.2 instead of the original values.

Recall that the formula for the simple slope is:

$$b = \frac{\sum (x_i - \bar{x})(y_i - \bar{y})}{\sum (x_i - \bar{x})^2}$$

In Tables 9.3 and 9.4, $(x_i - \bar{x})(y_i - \bar{y})$ is represented as $(l)(m)$, and $(x_i - \bar{x})^2$ as m^2. Thus, in the notation used in Tables 9.3 and 9.4, the slope equation becomes

$$\text{partial } b = \frac{\sum (l)(m)}{\sum m^2}$$

The interpretation of the partial slope is similar to that of the simple slope. In Table 9.4, we have calculated the partial slope to be 4.5947. We interpret this as follows: for every church in a township, the Antimasonic vote increases by 4.5947 percent when we hold the value per acre constant. In Table 9.3, we calculated the partial slope to be .2426. We interpret this as follows: for every dollar of value per acre, the Antimasonic vote increases

Table 9.2
Residuals Pertaining to Antimasonic Voting in 1828-1832, Number of Churches, and Land Value per Acre in 1836, Calculated for Townships of Genesee County, New York

Township	Antimasonic Vote, with Effects of Land Value Removed	Antimasonic Vote, with Effects of Number of Churches Removed	Number of Churches, with Effects of Land Value Removed	Land Value, with Effects of Number of Churches Removed
Alabama	-1.95	4.98	-1.59	-1.59
Alexander	-16.80	-12.47	-0.76	3.49
Attica	-5.53	-0.57	-0.85	4.34
Batavia	-7.33	5.03	-1.93	14.31
Bennington	-2.53	4.08	-1.55	-2.02
Bergen	-7.99	-1.67	-1.05	6.17
Bethany	-0.59	-9.80	1.91	-1.86
Byron	11.39	8.07	0.82	1.79
Castile	-5.02	2.61	-1.47	3.64
China	-2.57	-2.89	-0.30	-7.07
Covington	8.85	5.57	0.81	1.84
Elba	17.35	6.90	2.09	-3.54
Gainesville	-8.76	-9.97	0.05	-3.97
LeRoy	-0.72	2.27	-0.11	10.30
Middlebury	-5.00	-12.63	1.45	-4.02
Orangeville	18.05	9.75	1.32	-9.23
Pembroke	-6.05	-0.69	-1.14	0.58
Perry	13.59	10.07	0.85	1.52
Sheldon	-3.83	-13.75	1.56	-11.41
Stafford	1.62	3.15	-0.12	4.02
Warsaw	-6.85	-3.97	-0.55	1.53
Wethersfield	10.67	5.93	0.57	-8.72
Total residuals	0.00	0.00	0.01	0.1
Mean of residual	0.00	0.00	0.0005	0.005

Note: We have done calculations to more decimal places than shown here. Consequently, if you use the values presented in the table in your calculations, your results may not correspond exactly with ours.

Source: Authors' calculations from data in Table 9.1.

Table 9.3
Calculation of Partial Slope: Effect of Value per Acre on Antimasonic Vote, Controlling for Number of Churches, Genesee County Data

Township	(Residuals - Mean of Residual)		(l) (m)	m^2
	Antimasonic Vote, with Effects of Number of Churches Removed (l)	Land Value, with Effects of Number of Churches Removed (m)		
Alabama	4.98440	-1.59864	-7.96824	2.55564
Alexander	-12.47120	3.49136	-43.54149	12.18962
Attica	-0.57120	4.34136	-2.47979	18.84744
Batavia	5.02880	14.31136	71.96899	204.81513
Bennington	4.08440	-2.02864	-8.28576	4.11537
Bergen	-1.67120	6.17136	-10.31358	38.08573
Bethany	-9.80460	-1.86364	18.27221	3.47314
Byron	8.07320	1.78136	14.38130	3.17326
Castile	2.60660	3.63636	9.47855	13.22314
China	-2.89340	-7.07364	20.46686	50.03633
Covington	5.57320	1.83136	10.20656	3.35389
Elba	6.89540	-3.54364	-24.43479	12.55736
Gainesville	-9.97120	-3.97864	39.67178	15.82955
LeRoy	2.27320	10.29136	23.39433	105.91217
Middlebury	-12.62680	-4.02864	50.86879	16.22991
Orangeville	9.75100	-9.23364	-90.03719	85.26004
Pembroke	-0.69340	0.57636	-0.39965	0.33220
Perry	10.07320	1.51136	15.22427	2.28422
Sheldon	-13.74900	-11.41364	156.92609	130.27110
Stafford	3.15100	4.01636	12.65556	16.13118
Warsaw	-3.97120	1.53136	-6.08135	2.34507
Wethersfield	5.92880	-8.72864	-51.75034	76.18909
Total			198.2232	817.2105

Partial slope, effect of value per acre on Antimasonic vote, controlling for number of churches:

partial $b = \sum (lm) / \sum m^2$ $m = x_i - \bar{x}$

       $= 198.2232 / 817.2105$ $l = y_i - \bar{y}$

       $= 0.2426$

Note: We have done the calculations to more decimal places than shown here. Consequently, if you use the values presented in the table in your calculations, your results may not correspond exactly with ours.

Source: Authors' calculations from data in Table 9.2.

Table 9.4
Calculation of Partial Slope: Effect of Number of Churches on Antimasonic Vote, Controlling for Value per Acre, Genesee County Data

| Township | (Residuals - Mean of Residual) | | | |
	Antimasonic Vote, with Effects of Land Value Removed (l)	Number of Churches, with Effects of Land Value Removed (m)	(l)(m)	m^2
Alabama	-1.94744	-1.59291	3.10209	2.53737
Alexander	-16.80121	-0.75804	12.73593	0.57462
Attica	-5.53188	-0.85042	4.70442	0.72321
Batavia	-7.32919	-1.93403	14.17487	3.74047
Bennington	-2.52839	-1.54618	3.90934	2.39066
Bergen	-7.98966	-1.04932	8.38369	1.10107
Bethany	-0.59386	1.90612	-1.13197	3.63330
Byron	11.39031	0.81591	9.29348	0.66571
Castile	-5.02019	-1.46784	7.36885	2.15456
China	-2.57383	-0.30380	0.78194	0.09230
Covington	8.85322	0.81048	7.17532	0.65687
Elba	17.35263	2.08871	36.24469	4.36273
Gainesville	-8.75880	0.05386	-0.47171	0.00290
LeRoy	-0.72374	-0.10902	0.07890	0.01188
Middlebury	-4.99892	1.44738	-7.23534	2.09491
Orangeville	18.05158	1.31905	23.81097	1.73990
Pembroke	-6.04980	-1.13526	6.86810	1.28882
Perry	13.59064	0.84526	11.48757	0.71446
Sheldon	-3.83095	1.55599	-5.96092	2.42110
Stafford	1.62065	-0.12105	-0.19618	0.01465
Warsaw	-6.84698	-0.54501	3.73167	0.29704
Wethersfield	10.66550	0.57012	6.08060	0.32504
Total			144.9364	31.5437

Partial slope, effect of number of churches on Antimasonic vote, controlling for value per acre:

$$\text{partial } b = \Sigma(lm) / \Sigma m^2 \qquad\qquad m = x_i - \bar{x}$$

$$= 144.9364 / 31.5437 \qquad\qquad l = y_i - \bar{y}$$

$$= 4.59$$

Note: We have done the calculations to more decimal places than shown here. Consequently, if you use the values presented in the table in your calculations, your results may not correspond exactly with ours.

Source: Authors' calculations from data in Table 9.2.

by 0.24 percent (one quarter of 1 percent) with number of churches controlled. Obviously, the partial effect of a church on the Antimasonic vote is much stronger than that of a dollar's worth of land.

The multiple regression takes the form

$$\hat{y}_i = a + b_{1.2}x_1 + b_{2.1}x_2$$

where $b_{1.2}$ is the partial slope for variable x_1, controlling for x_2
       $b_{2.1}$ is the partial slope for variable x_2, controlling for x_1

To determine the value of the intercept (a), insert the means of the variables into the equation and solve for a. The mean Antimasonic vote is 68.45, the mean value per acre is 16.4241, and the mean number of churches is 4.5455 (see Table 9.1). Thus,

Predicted Antimasonic vote = a + .2426 (value per acre) + 4.5947 (churches)
     a = Antimasonic vote - [.2426(value per acre) + 4.5947(churches)]
       = 68.45 - [.2426(16.4241) + 4.5947(4.5455)]
       = 43.580

The final multiple regression equation is:

Predicted Antimasonic vote = 43.58 + .2426(value per acre)
                                 + 4.5947(churches)

We used this indirect method of calculating the multiple regression equation in order to explain partial slopes and what is meant by controlling a variable or holding it constant. Typically, computer software performs these calculations. There are other, more direct, ways to calculate partial slopes without determining the residuals, however. The procedures used here clearly demonstrate what "adjusting" and "controlling" mean.

EXPLANATORY POWER

As with simple regression, R^2 provides the explanatory power of the equation. R^2 is the ratio of the explained variation in the dependent variable to its total variation

$$R^2 = \frac{explained\ variation}{total\ variation} = \frac{\Sigma(\hat{y} - \bar{y})^2}{\Sigma(y_i - \bar{y})^2}$$

where $\hat{y}_i$ is the Antimasonic vote predicted from the multiple regression equation, as follows:

$$\hat{y}_i = 43.58 + .2426(\text{value per acre}) + 4.59(\text{churches})$$

In Chapter 8, we used simple regression to calculate the total variation in Antimasonic voting and the variation that can be explained by variation in the number of churches in a township.

$$\text{sum of squares unexplained: } \Sigma(y_i - \hat{y}_i)^2 = 1191.49$$

$$\text{sum of squares explained: } \Sigma(\hat{y}_i - \bar{y})^2 = 1266.14$$

$$\text{sum of squares total: } \Sigma(y_i - \bar{y})^2 = 2457.63$$

Solving for R^2, we find that

$$R^2 = \frac{\text{explained variation}}{\text{total variation}} = \frac{1266.14}{2457.63}$$
$$= .5151$$

Therefore, the number of churches explained .5151, or 52 percent, of the variation in the Antimasonic vote.

To calculate the full explanatory power of the multiple regression equation, we need the predicted values from the multivariate equation for each township and the squared difference between each of these predicted values and the mean Antimasonic vote. For Alabama Township, for example, we calculate the predicted value from the multiple regression equation as follows:

$$
\begin{aligned}
\text{predicted} \\
\text{Antimasonic vote} &= 43.58 + .2426\,(\text{value per acre}) + 4.5947\,(\text{churches}) \\
&= 43.58 + .2426(7.66) + 4.5947(2) \\
&= 54.628
\end{aligned}
$$

The mean Antimasonic vote from all twenty-two townships is 68.45, and the difference between the predicted and mean Antimasonic vote in Alabama Township is $54.628 - 68.45 = -13.822$. That value squared is 191.04.

These values for all the townships are shown in Table 9.5.

The explained sum of squares for the multiple regression equation is the squared difference between the predicted value on the dependent variable (Antimasonic voting) and the mean for the dependent variable summed across all cases. These calculations are done in Table 9.5 and the explained sum of squares is 1,314.23.

As we have already calculated the total sum of squares for the Antimasonic vote and the sum of squares explained by churches alone, subtraction can determine the remaining sums of squares. These are the sum of squares unexplained by the multiple regression and the additional explanatory power of value per acre over number of churches alone.

$$
\begin{aligned}
\text{SS (unexplained)} &= \text{SS (total)} - \text{SS (explained)} \\
&= 2{,}457.63 - 1{,}314.23 \\
&= 1{,}143.40
\end{aligned}
$$

$$
\begin{aligned}
\text{SS (added by} \\
\text{value per acre)} &= \text{SS (explained)} - \text{SS (churches alone)} \\
&= 1{,}314.23 - 1{,}266.14 \\
&= 48.09
\end{aligned}
$$

While we do not show the calculations here, the sum of squares explained by value per acre alone is 648.27. From this and the sum of squares explained by the multiple regression equation, we can calculate the sum of squares added by churches over that of value per acre alone.

$$
\begin{aligned}
\text{SS(added by} \\
\text{churches)} &= \text{SS (explained)} - \text{SS (value per acre alone)} \\
&= 1{,}314.23 - 648.27 \\
&= 665.96
\end{aligned}
$$

Table 9.6 presents the various sums of squares and their associated explanatory power (R^2).

Together, the number of churches and the value per acre of land explain 54 percent of the variation in Antimasonic voting. The number of churches and the value per acre in a township, however, are themselves related. The tendency is for townships with more valuable land also to have more churches. (Recall that we have calculated the set of regression equations relating these variables to one another.) All three of the variables—Antimasonic vote, land value per acre, and number of churches—are, therefore, related to one another. In terms of the models in Figure 9.1, there is an

Table 9.5
Calculation of Explained Sum of Squares: Antimasonic Vote
Predicted by Number of Churches and Value per Acre, Genesee
County Data

Township	Antimasonic Vote in 1828, 1830, and 1832	Predicted Antimasonic Vote from Churches and Value per Acre	Predicted Antimasonic Vote - Mean Antimasonic Vote (Mean = 68.45)	Predicted Antimasonic Vote - Mean Antimasonic Vote, Squared
Alabama	60.0	54.62833	-13.82167	191.03853
Alexander	53.1	66.41818	-2.03182	4.12829
Attica	65.0	66.62436	-1.82564	3.33297
Batavia	70.6	69.04269	0.59269	0.35128
Bennington	59.1	54.52403	-13.92597	193.93264
Bergen	63.9	67.06824	-1.38176	1.90925
Bethany	71.6	80.95209	12.50209	156.30222
Byron	84.2	76.55862	8.10862	65.74966
Castile	62.9	61.17575	-7.27425	52.91478
China	57.4	58.57792	-9.87208	97.45802
Covington	81.7	76.57074	8.12074	65.94649
Elba	88.3	80.54459	12.09459	146.27902
Gainesville	55.6	64.60625	-3.84375	14.77441
LeRoy	78.4	78.62281	10.17281	103.48607
Middlebury	63.5	75.14934	6.69934	44.88111
Orangeville	80.6	68.60920	0.15920	0.02534
Pembroke	59.6	60.43351	-8.01649	64.26413
Perry	86.2	76.49312	8.04312	64.69186
Sheldon	57.1	68.08042	-0.36958	0.13659
Stafford	74.0	71.82313	3.37313	11.37803
Warsaw	61.6	65.94276	-2.50724	6.28624
Wethersfield	71.5	63.45409	-4.99591	24.95916
Total	1,505.9			1,314.2261
Mean	68.45			

Note: We have done the calculations to more decimal places than shown here. Consequently, if you use the values presented in the table in your calculations, your results may not correspond exactly with ours.

Source: Authors' calculations from data in Table 9.1.

Table 9.6
**Explanatory Power of Multiple Regression Equation, by Source,
for Genesee County Data**

Source	Sum of Squares	Proportion (for explained variation: R^2)
Value per acre alone	648.27	.27
Added by churches	665.96	.27
Explained variation	1,314.23	.54
Churches alone	1,266.14	.52
Added by value per acre	48.09	.02
Explained variation	1,314.23	.54
Unexplained variation	1,143.40	.46
Total variation (explained + unexplained)	2,457.63	1.00

Note: We have done the calculations to more decimal places than shown here. Consequently, if you use the values presented in the table in your calculations, your results may not correspond exactly with ours.

Source: Authors' calculations from data in Table 9.1.

arrow connecting each variable to each other variable; these arrows reflect the relationships we have just observed. The problem now is to decide whether the relationships are causal or spurious.

A spurious relationship is a noncausal one. Spurious relationships can occur in several ways. If two variables—say, A and B—are themselves both caused by a third—C—then the observed relationship between A and B would be a noncausal or spurious relationship. A famous example of this was the relationship between clergy salaries and the importation of rum in nineteenth-century England. During years in which clergy salaries were high, rum imports were up; in years in which clergy salaries were down, rum sales were down. The conclusion that the clergy were using their money to import rum, however, is incorrect. The relationship is spurious. A third variable—overall economic conditions—was affecting both variables. When times were good, both salaries and rum imports were up. When times were bad, both rum imports and clerical salaries were down. In Figure 9.1, the causal relationships are shown with solid lines, and the spurious relationships with broken lines.

Which model best fits the data in Table 9.6? Model 1 has the religious factor as the cause of the economic factor, which, in turn, affected the Antimasonic vote. If this model is correct, the religious factor should add little to the economic factor in explaining the vote. This did not happen, however. The religious factor added an additional 27 percent to the explained variation, over and above what the economic variable explained. Model 2 has both the religious and economic factors directly influencing Antimasonic voting. If this is the case, the economic factor should add additional explanatory power to that of the religious factor. But the economic factor added only an additional 2 percent to the explanatory power of the religious factor.

It is Model 3 that is most in agreement with the observed data. This model has the religious factor causing both the economic factor and the vote. Here the economic factor should add little to the explanatory power of the religious factor. As we have already noted, this was the case. The religious factor, however, added to the explanatory power of the economic factor, as the model suggests.

SIGNIFICANCE

The question of significance in multiple regression can be addressed several ways, and may be concerned with the regression equation overall or with one or more of its independent variables.

The Significance of the Equation

First there is the significance of the overall equation. Does the equation account for more variation than chance? The F-ratio tests the significance of the equation. The F-ratio is the ratio of the sum of squares explained by the regression analysis divided by the explained degrees of freedom and the unexplained sum of squares divided by the unexplained degrees of freedom. The degrees of freedom (explained) is k, where k is the number of independent variables in the equation. The degrees of freedom (unexplained) is $n - k - 1$, where n equals the number of cases and k is the number of independent variables. The sum of squares are presented in Table 9.6 and the degrees of freedom are:

$$DF(explained) = k$$
$$= 2$$

$$DF(unexplained) = n - k - 1$$
$$= 22 - 2 - 1$$
$$= 19$$

$$F = \frac{SS(explained)/DF(explained)}{SS(unexplained)/DF(unexplained)}$$

$$= \frac{1,314.23/2}{1,143.40/19}$$

$$= 10.92$$

For degrees of freedom two and nineteen, the critical F-ratio for probability .05 is 3.54 (see Table A.4 at the end of the Appendix). Therefore, the observed F-ratio is significant at < .05. Program A.4 calculates the probability to be < .0025. There is a significant amount of variation explained by the multiple regression equation (see Chapter 4 for a discussion of the meaning of significance for population data and Chapter 7 for a discussion of the F-ratio).

The Significance of Partial Slopes

There are several approaches to determining the significance of each of the independent variables in the multiple regression equation. Here we will present the simplest.

The partial slope is the effect of an independent variable on the dependent variable when a third variable is held constant. The sum of squares corresponding to the partial slope for a variable, then, is the sum of squares added to the explanatory power of another variable alone. For Table 9.6, these are:

$$SS(added\ by\ churches) = 665.96$$
$$SS(added\ by\ value\ per\ acre) = 48.09$$

We can calculate an F-ratio for each of these sum of squares. To do this, we divide each sum of squares by its degrees of freedom (here, 1) and divide this in turn by the unexplained sum of squares divided by its degrees of freedom (here, n - k -1 = 19). Thus,

$$Partial\ F(churches) = \frac{SS(added\ by\ churches)\ /\ 1}{SS(unexplained)\ /\ (n\ -\ k\ -\ 1)} = \frac{665.96\ /\ 1}{1143.4\ /\ 19} = 11.07$$

$$Partial\ F(value\ per\ acre) = \frac{SS(added\ by\ value\ per\ acre\ )\ /\ 1}{SS(unexplained\ )\ /\ (n\ -\ k\ -\ 1)} = \frac{48.09\ /\ 1}{1143.4\ /\ 19} = .79$$

The critical F-ratio for DF = 1 and 19 at probability .05 is 4.38 (see Table A.4 in the Appendix). As the F-ratio for the partial effects of churches (controlling value per acre) exceeds the critical F-ratio, the effects are signifiant at .05. Program A.4 calculates the probability to be .0035. The F-ratio for the partial effects of value per acre (controlling for churches) does not exceed the critical F- ratio. Program A.4 calculates this probability to be .3852. Therefore, the partial effects of value per acre (controlling for churches) are not significantly different from zero.

DUMMY VARIABLES

Regression analysis assumes that the variables are measured on an interval-level scale (see Chapter 3). Yet even when variables are not measured on an interval scale, it is still possible to use regression analysis by creating a *dummy variable*. Dummy variables are made by creating a separate variable for each category of the categorical variable. We then assign to a particular case the value one (1) if it is in the category and the value zero (0) if it is not. A dummy variable can either be an independent or dependent variable. In regression analysis, the procedure and interpretation are slightly different, depending on whether the dummy variable is independent or dependent.

Dependent Dummy Variables

Consider the following example. In the nineteenth century, many places in England were underrepresented or not represented in Parliament, while other places with little population were represented. This situation occurred, in the opinion of some, as a result of demographic changes after the boroughs were granted representation. John Cannon, however, argues that even earlier parliamentary representation had little relationship to the importance of a borough. He collected data on the Ship Money Assessment of 1636, which, he believed, conveyed "some idea of the boroughs' importance."[5] We have presented his data in an altered form in Table 9.7.

In this example, the dependent variable is the dummy variable; in regression analysis, it is coded zero (0) if the borough was not represented in 1640, and one (1) if it was. The independent variable is the amount of the Ship Money Assessment of 1636 in pounds sterling. We calculated the regression equation in the usual way for a two-variable equation (see Chapter 8).

$$\hat{y}_i = a + bx_i$$

representation $= .812 + .0000175$ (ship assessment)

One interpretation of the equation is that an increase of one pound in assessment increases the probability of a borough's gaining representation by .0000175 (the slope, b). An increase in assessment of £1,000 (all but three boroughs paid less) would increase the probability of representation by .0175.

Notice that, when a dummy variable coded 0 (absent) and 1 (present) is used as a dependent variable in regression analysis, we can interpret the slope of the independent variable as the increase in probability of the quality's being present for an increase of one in the independent variable. The slope, in this instance, is not significant, and the equation does not explain a significant amount of the variation in parliamentary representation. Cannon's argument was correct: parliamentary representation in 1640 had little relationship to the importance of the borough.

While a dummy dependent variable can be useful in historical research, there are certain problems. In reality, probabilities or proportions only range between zero and one. Yet the values of a regression equation can be outside these limits and produce absurd results. For example, when the ship assessment is zero, the predicted probability of a borough's having representation is .812 (the a intercept). To have a probability of zero, the assessment must be £-46,418.03 (- .812984/.0000175144)—an absurd number. Furthermore, an assessment of £14,000 (London's assessment) results in a predicted probability of 1.057—clearly an impossible result given that probabilities cannot exceed one.

The solution is to write an equation for an "S"-shaped line that cannot go below y = 0 and above y = 1. One method of doing this is through probit or logit analysis—two techniques, however, that we will not demonstrate here, though the logit model is briefly mentioned again later in the chapter.

Table 9.7
The Ship Money Assessment of 1636, by English Borough

Borough	Amount (in £)	Borough	Amount (in £)
London	14,000	Thaxted*	40
Westminster	1,180	Burford*	40
Bristol	1,000	Gravesend*	40
Newcastle	700	Banbury	40
York	520	Monmouth	40
Norwich	500	Ripon	40
Gloucester	500	Higham Ferrers	36
Shrewsbury	456	Bossiney	36
Colchester	400	Plympton	35
Southwark	350	Shaftsbury	35
Exeter	350	Tregony	33
Bury St. Edmunds	330	Walsall*	32
Canterbury	300	Stafford	30
King's Lynn	300	Scarborough	30
Coventry	266	Thetford	30
Chester	260	Eye	30
Reading	260	Chippenham	30
Ipswich	240	Okehampton	30
Salisbury	240	Poole	30
Worcester	233	Lancaster	30
Hereford	220	East Retford	30
Gt. Yarmouth	220	Yeovil*	30
Leicester	200	Ilchester	30
Northampton	200	Axbridge*	30
Nottingham	200	Chipping Norton*	30
Leeds*	200	Grampound	29
Grantham	200	Penzance*	28
Cranbrook, Kent*	200	Kidderminster*	27
Southampton	195	Blandford*	25
Lincoln	193	Berkhampstead*	25
Plymouth	190	Liverpool	25
Wincester	190	Wareham	25
Derby	175	Newcastle-U-Lyme	24
Maidstone	160	Newport, Mon.*	23
Chichester	150	Berwick	20
Barnstable	150	Hedon	20
Lichfield	150	Langport*	20
Durham*	150	Morpeth	20

Table 9.7, continued

Hull	140	Woodstock	20
Bedford	140	Carlisle	20
Tiverton	130	Harwich	20
Totnes	120	Chipping Camden*	20
Peterborough	120	Lostwithiel	20
Hadleigh*	120	Callington	20
St. Albans	120	Wallingford	20
Newark*	120	Bridport	20
Newbury*	120	Arundel	20
Ludlow	102	Bishop's Castle	15
Birmingham*	100	Grimsby	15
Doncaster*	100	Kendal*	15
Warwick	100	Orford	12
Abingdon	100	St. Mawes	10
Oxford	100	Camelford	10
Cambridge	100	Queenborough	10
Taunton	100	Castle Rising	10
Marlborough	100	Shoreham	10
Windsor	100	Aldeburgh	8
Oswaldston*	90	Southwold*	8
Kingston-on-Thames*	88	Newton	7
Bodmin	83	Clitheroe	7
Aylesbury	80	Wilton	5
Launceston	80	Appleby	5
Dartmouth	80	Dunwich	4
Walden*	80	Manchester*	na
Malden	80	Honiton	na
Godmanchester*	80	Cirencester	na
Rochester	80	Lewes	na
Sutton Coldfield*	80	Reigate	na
Buckingham	70	Sudbury	na
Truro	70	Halifax*	na
Padstow*	70	East Grinstead	na
Boston	70	Amersham	na
Bridgwater	70	Great Marlow	na
Bath	70	Wendover	na
Evesham	74	Fowey	na
Bewdley	62	Mitchell	na
Droitwich	62	Newport, Cornwall	na
Portsmouth	60	St. Germans	na
Tewkesbury	60	St. Ives	na
Stamford	60	Cockermouth	na
Wells	60	Ashburton	na

Table 9.7, continued

Torrington*	60	Bere Alston	na
Basingstoke*	60	Christchurch	na
Henley*	60	Lymington	na
Pontefract	60	Newport, IoW	na
Minehead	60	Newtown, IoW	na
Beverly	57	Petersfield	na
Hertford	55	Stockbridge	na
Guildford	53	Whitchurch	na
Bridgnorth	51	Yarmouth, IoW	na
Oswestry*	51	Weobley	na
Wycombe	50	Milborne Port	na
Wokingham*	50	Tamworth	na
Chesterfield*	50	Bletchingley	na
Bradninch*	50	Gatton	na
Andover	50	Haslemere	na
Huntingdon	50	Bramber	na
Richmond	50	Horsham	na
Devizes	50	Midhurst	na
Wigan	50	Steyning	na
Brackley	50	Calne	na
Stratford-on-Avon*	50	Cricklade	na
Daventry*	50	Downton	na
Penryn	48	Great Bedwyn	na
Dorchester	45	Heytesbury	na
South Molton*	45	Hindon	na
Leominster	44	Ludgershall	na
East & West Looe	43	Malmesbury	na
Weymouth	40	Old Sarum	na
Lyme Regis	40	Westbury	na
Preston	40	Wootton Bassett	na
Saltash	40	Aldborough	na
Liskeard	40	Boroughbridge	na
Helston	40	Knaresborough	na
Bideford*	40	Malton	na
Corfe Castle	40	Northallerton	na
		Thirsk	na

* — no parliamentary representation in 1640
na — not assessed

Source: Adapted from John Ashton Cannon, *Parliamentary Reform, 1640–1832* (Cambridge, England: Cambridge University Press, 1973), 269–274. Copyright © 1972. Reprinted with the permission of Cambridge University Press.

Independent Dummy Variables

As was the case with dependent dummy variables, independent dummy variables are created by coding one variable for each category of the original categorical variable: 0 (absent) and 1 (present). One of the dummy variables must be excluded from the analysis. This is because controlling for all but one dummy variable will remove all the variance in the remaining variable. This process, repeated for each possible combination of dummy variables, will prevent estimating the effects of any of them.

Let us consider the differences between the black and white infant mortality rates in the United States in 1850 (see Table 9.8). One concern might be the relationship between white and black infant mortality rates in each state. Another concern might be with the effect of slavery on black infant mortality. We first create a dummy variable coded zero (0) for free states and one (1) for slave states. We calculated a multiple regression equation, using the data in Table 9.8, for the twenty-nine states for which data are available (calculations not shown). This equation is:

$$\hat{y}_i = a + b_{1.2} x_1 + b_{2.1} x_2$$

where $\hat{y}_i$ is predicted black infant mortality for the ith case

a, the y intercept, is calculated to be 42.42

$b_{1.2}$, the partial slope for white infant mortality holding state constant, is calculated to be .70

$b_{2.1}$, the partial slope for slave state holding white infant mortality constant, is calculated to be 23.94

x_1 is white infant mortality for the ith case

x_2 is the dummy variable for the ith state

Thus,
    black infant mortality = 42.42 + .70 (white infant mortality) + 23.94 (slave state)

The effect of living in a slave state was to add 23.94 per 1,000 to the black infant mortality rate, holding the white infant mortality rate constant. We can see this effect in Figure 9.2, which plots the regression line for slave and free states. We have also plotted the line representing equal black and white infant mortality rates. For every value of white infant mortality—both in slave and free states—the black infant mortality is higher. Furthermore,

Table 9.8
U.S. Infant Mortality per 1,000 Births, by State and Race, 1850

State	Slave/Free	Infant Mortality		
		All	White	Black
Alabama	Slave	90.4	64.3	126.7
Arkansas	Slave	73.5	66.5	102.8
California	Free	116.5	114.8	250.0
Connecticut	Free	83.7	83.6	125.8
Delaware	Slave	87.6	87.0	81.0
Florida	Slave	62.5	45.6	83.0
Georgia	Slave	82.7	55.4	125.7
Illinois	Free	78.8	65.7	65.1
Indiana	Free	68.1	78.5	60.4
Iowa	Free	70.0	68.2	—
Kentucky	Slave	80.3	68.9	129.3
Louisiana	Slave	95.1	72.5	121.2
Maine	Free	59.5	61.2	187.5
Maryland	Slave	103.1	113.3	110.5
Massachusetts	Free	108.3	109.7	43.3
Michigan	Free	73.6	72.9	63.3
Mississippi	Slave	104.3	61.6	146.3
Missouri	Slave	80.0	77.0	104.6
New Hampshire	Free	70.4	68.7	66.8
New Jersey	Free	73.4	74.9	54.0
New York	Free	80.1	81.0	66.6
North Carolina	Slave	73.0	51.1	106.5
Ohio	Free	72.3	72.1	76.4
Pennsylvania	Free	72.5	71.3	93.0
Rhode Island	Free	91.6	87.5	164.6
South Carolina	Slave	82.5	48.0	104.5
Tennessee	Slave	79.9	62.1	124.6
Texas	Slave	82.6	71.9	115.0
Vermont	Free	43.5	43.7	40.0
Virginia	Slave	81.2	57.8	118.7
Wisconsin	Free	56.4	58.4	—
Mean		79.92	71.46	105.42
Variance (s^2)		235.59	312.25	2,031.68
n		31	31	29

Source: Authors' calculations from the U.S. Interior Department, Census Office, *The Seventh Census of the United States, 1850* (Washington, DC: Robert Armstrong, 1853), xlii–xliv; U.S. Interior Department, *Mortality Statistics of the United States, 1850* (Washington, DC: A. O. P. Nicholson, 1855), 34, 44.

Figure 9.2
Dummy-variable Multiple Regression Analysis: Black Infant Mortality by White Infant Mortality and Whether or Not a State Was a Slave State, 1850

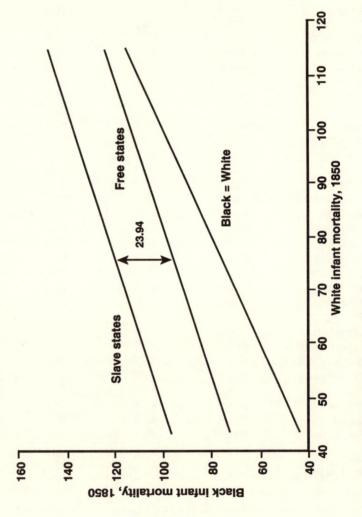

Source: Calculated from data in Table 9.8.

for every value of white infant mortality, the black infant mortality rate in slave states is 23.94 higher than in the free states.

Although useful, there are problems associated with dummy variable regression. It is easy to misinterpret. One might mistakenly conclude, for example, that the effect of slavery is to increase black infant mortality by 23.94 over what it would be if slavery did not exist. The assumption is that the partial slope of the regression line relating white to black infant mortality is the same for slave and free states—that only the intercept of the two lines differs (as in Figure 9.2). Put another way, this mistaken conclusion assumes that the effects of slavery are additive to those of white infant mortality in producing the black infant mortality rate. Thus, the equation adds the partial effects of the white infant mortality rate to the partial effects of slavery and then to a constant (the a intercept) to get a predicted black infant mortality rate.

The effects of the white infant mortality rate and slavery may not be additive, however. Interaction exists if, for example, the relationship between white and black infant mortality rates are different in slave and free states. In Figure 9.3, we calculated and plotted separate regression lines for slave and free states. The equations are:

Slave States: black infant mortality = 118.55 - .07 (white infant mortality)

Free States: black infant mortality = -14.61 + 1.44 (white infant mortality)

In the slave states there is a slight negative slope, indicating that the higher the white infant mortality rate, the lower the black rate. This slope is small, however. It is reasonable to conclude that in slave states there is either no relationship between the white and black infant mortality rates or the rate is negative. In the free states, by contrast, the relationship is strong and positive.

To avoid problems, calculate a regression equation for each dummy variable. If the slopes of each of the lines are similar, the effects are additive and a multiple regression equation with all but one of the dummy variables can represent the relationships. If the slopes are not the same, as was the case with the slave and free states, several two-variable equations will better represent the relationships.

ECOLOGICAL REGRESSION

Frequently, information about individuals living in the past is only avail-

Figure 9.3

Interactive Dummy-variable Regression Analysis: Black Infant Mortality by White Infant Mortality in 1850, Separately Calculated for Slave and Free States

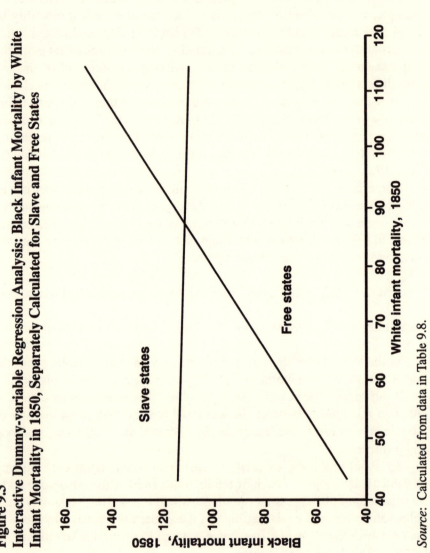

Source: Calculated from data in Table 9.8.

able in the aggregate. Consider, for example, election results. How an individual voted is usually not available; only results by precinct, county, or some other aggregation are preserved. Recent census data give us another example of information gathered about individuals but often only available in aggregated form. *Ecological regression* is a way to extract information about individual-level relationships. "Ecological," in this context, refers to information about individuals aggregated into units like precincts, counties, or states.

While ecological data were always used in regression analysis,[6] William S. Robinson demonstrated in 1950 that aggregate-level relationships cannot necessarily be generalized to the individual level.[7] For example, consider data from some Atlanta, Georgia, precincts during the 1964 presidential election. A regression analysis showed that the larger the black proportion, the larger the vote proportion for Goldwater. Did this mean that blacks were voting for Goldwater? No; such a conclusion would be an example of the *ecological fallacy*. A more plausible explanation would say that most blacks were not voting and that whites living close to blacks at that time were more vulnerable to Goldwater's appeals than whites living far from racial conflict. The possibility of the ecological fallacy caused political scientists and sociologists to shift to surveys in studying the behavior and motives of individuals. Obviously, however, that option is not available to most historians.

Some have misinterpreted the "ecological fallacy" to mean that inferences to individual behavior cannot be made from aggregated data. That is not quite true. If certain assumptions are met, it is possible to infer individual behavior. Techniques of ecological regression were developed in the 1950s[8] and have been subsequently applied to historical and political analysis in the United States,[9] England,[10] Denmark,[11] Sweden,[12] Belgium,[13] Germany,[14] and Korea.[15]

Let us consider a specific example. In the 1850s the American party system changed. Historians of the antebellum era have long been interested in determining where the supporters of the new Republican Party came from, their previous party affiliation (if any), and the rate at which the realignment occurred. William E. Gienapp has examined this process in several states.[16] In Pennsylvania, Gienapp analyzed Republican Party gains between the 1856 presidential election and the 1857 gubernatorial election. The Republican presidential candidate in 1856, John C. Frémont, attracted 32.1 percent of the popular vote in Pennsylvania, while the Republican gubernatorial candidate in 1857, David Wilmot, attracted 40.2 percent. There was, therefore, movement in the electorate between these two elections.

Although aggregate vote totals for Pennsylvania's counties are available, information on how individuals voted is necessary to understand the dynamics of party change. Ecological regression is a technique that can help us do that. The first step is to gather all the necessary data. Here, we need each county's vote total for each party in both elections, the number of people who were eligible to vote but did not, the number of people who were eligible to vote in 1857 but not in 1856 (in other words, new voters), and the number of people who were eligible to vote in 1856 but who were not eligible in 1857 (i.e., some counties experienced population loss). *The Tribune Almanac and Political Register* provides the vote totals for sixty-three of Pennsylvania's sixty-five counties.[17] Two newly formed counties (Forrest and Snyder) are not included. Gienapp has calculated estimates of the total eligible electorate in each of the two elections.

According to Gienapp's estimates, three counties (Clarion, Montour, and Westmoreland) lost a total of ninety-nine eligible voters between the two elections. These voters are assumed to have been nonvoters in 1856. To eliminate them, he subtracted them from the 1856 nonvoters in these counties. The number of new voters in 1857 was calculated by subtracting the eligible voters in 1856 from the 1857 eligible voters. Finally, the 1856 nonvoters were combined with those who were not eligible to vote in 1856 but were eligible to vote in 1857. This left 594,529 Pennsylvanians who were eligible to vote in 1857. The data are presented in Table 9.9.

Table 9.10 is a cross-tabulation of how these 594,529 people voted in 1856 and 1857. The marginal totals and proportions are known. It is now necessary to estimate the unknown cell proportions from these marginals. In Table 9.10, X_1 is the proportion of eligible voters who voted Republican in 1856 and $P_{1,1}$ is the proportion of them who also voted Republican in 1857. The value of $P_{1,1}$ must be estimated. Notice that $P_{1,1} + P_{2,1} + P_{3,1} + P_{4,1} = P_{1,2} + P_{2,2} + P_{3,2} + P_{4,2} = P_{1,3} + P_{2,3} + P_{3,3} + P_{4,3} = P_{1,4} + P_{2,4} + P_{3,4} + P_{4,4} = Y_1 + Y_2 + Y_3 + Y_4 = X_1 + X_2 + X_3 + X_4 = 1$. The several proportions all add up to 1.0. Each of the row cells total the row marginal; for example:

$$Y_1 = P_{1,1}X_1 + P_{1,2}X_2 + P_{1,3}X_3 + P_{1,4}X_4$$

As $X_1 + X_2 + X_3 + X_4 = 1.0$, $X_4 = 1 - (X_1 + X_2 + X_3)$. Substituting for X_4, the row marginal equation becomes:

$$\begin{aligned} Y_1 &= P_{1,1}X_1 + P_{1,2}X_2 + P_{1,3}X_3 + P_{1,4}[1 - (X_1 + X_2 + X_3)] \\ &= P_{1,1}X_1 + P_{1,2}X_2 + P_{1,3}X_3 + P_{1,4} - P_{1,4}X_1 - P_{1,4}X_2 - P_{1,4}X_3 \\ &= P_{1,4} + (P_{1,1} - P_{1,4})X_1 + (P_{1,2} - P_{1,4})X_2 + (P_{1,3} - P_{1,4})X_3 \end{aligned}$$

Table 9.9

Party-tabulated Votes for President and Governor in Pennsylvania, 1856 and 1857, by County

County	Region	Votes for Governor			Votes for President				
		Republican Party Candidate, 1857	Democratic Party Candidate, 1857	American Party Candidate, 1857	Republican Party Candidate, 1856	Democratic Party Candidate, 1856	American Party Candidate, 1856	Eligible Voters, 1856	Eligible Voters, 1857
Adams	W	1900	2363	58	1120	2637	1249	6084	6160
Allegheny	W	7687	6610	856	13671	9062	1488	33672	34341
Armstrong	W	2106	2409	111	2963	2680	188	7039	7148
Beaver	W	1999	1557	20	2658	1905	236	6099	6137
Bedford	W	1568	2338	398	306	2458	1936	5261	5330
Berks	E	2750	8722	874	1037	11272	3586	19299	19656
Blair	W	1450	1819	569	445	2069	2450	5462	5583
Bradford	W	5642	2082	6	6938	2314	101	11005	11169
Bucks	E	4801	5747	101	5048	6517	761	14503	14679
Butler	W	2831	2361	53	3401	2648	67	6938	7037
Cambria	W	1042	2379	165	804	2987	968	5261	5462
Carbon	E	672	1557	153	692	1866	465	4235	4299
Centre	W	2145	2663	35	390	2895	1952	5717	5818
Chester	E	5269	5388	424	5308	6333	1448	15670	15882
Clarion	W	987	2132	23	788	2760	950	5141	5141
Clearfield	W	725	1459	235	718	1978	604	3681	3821
Clinton	W	1083	1464	18	618	1485	682	3456	3618
Columbia	E	1144	2410	30	1239	2889	219	4883	5047
Crawford	W	3514	2576	0	5360	3391	45	10096	10362
Cumberland	W	2466	3078	58	1472	3427	1579	8270	8415

Table 9.9, continued

County	Region	Votes for Governor			Votes for President				
		Republican Party Candidate, 1857	Democratic Party Candidate, 1857	American Party Candidate, 1857	Republican Party Candidate, 1856	Democratic Party Candidate, 1856	American Party Candidate, 1856	Eligible Voters, 1856	Eligible Voters, 1857
Dauphin	E	2656	3109	600	1615	3094	2439	9276	9511
Delaware	E	1614	1598	609	1590	2005	1010	5992	6114
Elk	W	276	502	3	275	575	52	1140	1201
Erie	W	3306	1995	143	5156	2584	289	10260	10495
Fayette	W	2520	3104	80	2089	3554	1174	8068	8085
Franklin	W	3058	3186	91	2446	3469	1233	8637	8688
Fulton	W	570	817	9	142	970	566	1857	1900
Greene	W	1000	2034	8	1321	2747	286	4907	4960
Huntingdon	W	1678	1749	248	926	2164	1645	5977	6034
Indiana	W	2650	1437	0	3612	1762	263	6581	6717
Jefferson	W	1125	1268	54	1063	1463	615	3716	3832
Juniata	W	1035	1108	20	480	1365	747	3266	3346
Lancaster	E	7690	6486	1236	6608	8731	4592	24430	24779
Lawrence	W	1992	993	50	3065	1220	96	4739	4767
Lebanon	E	2664	1980	182	2414	2511	437	6751	6894
Lehigh	E	2957	3805	9	3237	4426	122	9158	9418
Luzerne	E	3536	5268	214	4850	6791	868	16677	17310
Lycoming	W	1684	2824	347	934	3324	1770	7375	7643
McKean	W	565	496	7	812	526	47	1828	1922
Mercer	W	2928	2539	49	3686	2699	118	7555	7628
Mifflin	W	1217	1532	104	216	1491	1050	3437	3461
Monroe	E	504	2254	5	560	2275	69	3360	3438
Montgomery	E	2608	5448	1386	2845	7134	2265	15535	15804

County	Region							
Montour	E	568	1080	71	666	1271	149	2929	2929
Northampton	E	1111	4067	1010	1168	5260	1838	10334	10493
Northumberland	E	974	2821	490	566	3059	1340	5876	6029
Perry	W	1564	1965	161	521	2135	1407	4768	4843
Philadelphia	E	10001	27749	14335	7993	38222	24084	105005	108179
Pike	E	190	758	13	270	862	15	1544	1559
Potter	W	957	495	4	1264	667	6	2226	2360
Schuylkill	E	3079	5980	581	2188	7035	2682	15671	16178
Somerset	W	2277	1741	5	1458	1763	1405	5340	5369
Sullivan	W	3224	2419	8	3861	2548	51	1041	1084
Susquehanna	E	265	494	0	309	538	48	7815	7993
Tioga	W	3284	1193	0	4541	1386	27	6666	6849
Union	W	1275	971	162	1429	1092	186	6126	6219
Venango	W	1790	1900	2	2041	2157	72	5010	5188
Warren	W	1369	899	9	2091	1231	49	4099	4238
Washington	W	3614	3752	142	4237	4288	265	10079	10111
Wayne	E	1691	1992	50	2259	2331	113	6365	6550
Westmoreland	W	3448	4361	24	4091	5172	299	11993	11993
Wyoming	E	995	1226	12	1138	1171	74	2750	2784
York	W	1778	5314	1332	511	6876	4301	14272	14529
Total		145068	187823	28052	147520	229517	81138	582203	594529

Source: Adapted from *The Tribune Almanac and Political Register* (New York: Tribune Publishing, 1858), 53 and authors' communication with William E. Gienapp. See "Nativism and the Creation of a Republican Majority in the North before the Civil War," *Journal of American History*, 72 (December 1985), 529–559; "Nebraska, Nativism, and Rum: The Failure of Fusion in Pennsylvania, 1854," *Pennsylvania Magazine of History and Biography*, 109 (October 1985), 425–471; "'Politics Seem to Enter into Everything': Political Culture in the North, 1840–1860," in Stephen E. Maizlish and John J. Kushma, eds., *Essays on American Antebellum Politics, 1840–1860* (College Station: Texas A&M University Press, 1982), 15–69.

This result is similar in form to the multiple regression equation

$$\hat{y}_1 = a + b_1 x_1 + b_2 x_2 + b_3 x_3$$

with $P_{1,4}$ being estimated by the regression intercept a, $(P_{1,1} - P_{1,4})$ by the partial slope b_1, and so on. With the regression equation, we can calculate the cell proportions by adding the intercept to each of the partial slopes. Thus, if $b_1 = P_{1,1} - P_{1,4}$ and $P_{1,4} = a$, then $P_{1,1} = b_1 + a$.

With regression analysis, one assumes that the change in each county is uniform. $P_{1,1}$, or the proportion of those who voted Republican in 1856 who also voted Republican in 1857, should be the same for each county—at least the average change should be the same for the various possible values of the 1856 Republican vote proportion (X_1). If this assumption is invalid, then regression analysis will yield biased and erroneous results. Doubts about the validity of the assumption of uniform change is one of the main criticisms of ecological regression. There are three approaches to resolving this objection.

First, while change may not be uniform within every county, it may be uniform within regions of the state. There is reason to believe, for example, that voters east of the Susquehanna River acted differently in the 1857 election from voters west of the river. Dividing the sixty-three counties between the twenty-two counties in the east and forty-one in the west will create two regions in which the assumption of uniform change or average uniform change may be valid.

Second, it may be that change for some groups (say, 1856 nonvoters) is not uniform, while change for others (say, 1856 Republicans) is. The ecological regression model may document some changes, while others may be too complex to chart. The solution is to combine categories. For example, in the 1856 presidential election there were two American Party slates: one (which Gienapp calls the "Fillmore Straight") was pledged to Millard Fillmore; the other (which Gienapp calls the "Fillmore Union") was actually pledged to Frémont. Individually, the behavior of these two groups in 1857 might not fit the assumptions of the model, but their joint behavior might. The present analysis combines the two 1856 Fillmore slates into one group, and combines into another group the 1856 eligible but nonvoting citizens along with those who were not eligible to vote in 1856 but were eligible in 1857.

Third, another approach to the problem of uniform change involves the assumption that change is linear: the proportion of 1856 Republican voters voting Republican in 1857 is the same for each level of 1856 Republican voting. This assumption means that the 1857 Republicans gained proportionally the same in counties where their 1856 vote was small as they did

Table 9.10
Finding Unknown Cell Proportions: Party-tabulated Votes in Pennsylvania in 1856 Presidential Election, by Party-tabulated Votes in Pennsylvania in 1857 Gubernatorial Election

Vote in 1857(Y)	Vote in 1856 (X)						
	Republican Party	Democratic Party	American Party	Not Voting & Not Eligible in 1856	Total, 1857	Proportion	(N)
Republican	$P_{1,1}X_1$	$P_{1,2}X_2$	$P_{1,3}X_3$	$P_{1,4}X_4$	Y_1	.2440	(145,068)
Democrat	$P_{2,1}X_1$	$P_{2,2}X_2$	$P_{2,3}X_3$	$P_{2,4}X_4$	Y_2	.3159	(187,823)
American	$P_{3,1}X_1$	$P_{3,2}X_2$	$P_{3,3}X_3$	$P_{3,4}X_4$	Y_3	.0472	(28,052)
Nonvoting	$P_{4,1}X_1$	$P_{4,2}X_2$	$P_{4,3}X_3$	$P_{4,4}X_4$	Y_4	.3929	(233,586)
Total, 1856	X_1	X_2	X_3	X_4			
Proportion	.2481	.3860	.1364	.2294		1.0000	(594,529)
(N)	(147,520)	(229,517)	(81,138)	(136,354)			

X_j is the proportion of the total eligible persons voting for party j in 1856.

Y_i is the proportion of the total eligible persons voting for party i in 1857.

P_{ij} is the proportion of party j voters in 1856 who voted for party i in 1857. The i and j values are (1) Republican, (2) Democrat, (3) American, (4) not eligible or not voting. For example, $P_{2,3}$ is the proportion of 1856 American Party voters who voted Democratic in 1857.

Source: Authors' calculations from data in Table 9.9.

where their vote was large. The proportion is constrained between zero and one; there cannot be negative proportions or proportions exceeding 1.0. Linear regression analysis does not have these constraints, and the results can be absurd proportion estimates.

The solution is the logit model, which produces a curve in which the proportions of 1856 Republican voters, for example, voting Republican in 1857 varies with the proportion of the county voting Republican in 1856. In this way, a county with a small Republican vote in 1856 might have a smaller proportion of 1856 voters voting Republican in 1857, while a county in which the Republican vote in 1856 was high might have a larger proportion of the 1856 Republican voters voting Republican in 1857. Søren Risbjerg Thomsen discusses the logit regression technique.[18] Here, we will confine our analysis to linear regression.

Pennsylvania's counties had varying numbers of eligible voters. In 1857, Philadelphia County had 108,179 eligible voters, while Sullivan County had 1,084. If the assumptions of uniform change are met, then this disparity does not affect the results. To the extent the assumptions are not exactly met, however, the regression equations should be weighted more toward Philadelphia County than Sullivan County. We do this by weighting each county by the number of its eligible voters in 1857. We have calculated the regression results, therefore, as if there were 108,179 Philadelphia counties and 1,084 Sullivan counties.

In all, we calculated eight regression equations for the two regions, with the dependent variables being the Republican, Democratic, American, and nonvoting proportions in 1857, and the independent variables being the Republican, Democratic, and American vote proportions in 1856. The intercepts represent the 1856 nonvoters, whom we omitted from the equations.

The multiple regression equation predicting the 1857 Republican proportion for the twenty-two counties east of the Susquehanna River is:

$$\hat{y} = -.074204 + .9962211x_1 + .075558x_2 + .375644x_3$$

where $\hat{y}$ is the predicted 1857 Republican vote proportion

x_1 is the 1856 Republican vote proportion

x_2 is the 1856 Democratic vote proportion

x_3 is the 1856 American vote proportion

Adding the intercept (-.074204) to each of the partial slopes yields the row entries for the first row in Table 9.10. Thus, the proportion of 1856 Republican voters east of the river who voted Republican in 1857 is -.074204 + .996221 = .922017 (see Table 9.11).

Examine Tables 9.11 and 9.12. First, there are differences in the voter behavior east and west of the Susquehanna River. Eastern Republicans maintained greater party loyalty in 1857 than their counterparts in the west. The western Republicans were three times more likely not to vote in 1857 than those in the east. Another difference involves the 1856 American Party voters. In 1857, twice as many American Party voters in the west switched to the Republican Party than in the east. East of the river, the American Party retained one-half of its 1856 vote, while in the west it retained little more than one-tenth. These differences in voting behavior justify the earlier decision to divide the sixty-three counties into two regions.

The model does produce some impossible estimates. Some of the pro-

Table 9.11
**Making Ecological Estimates of Proportion from Regression
Equations: The Vote East of the Susquehanna River, from the
Pennsylvania Eligible Electorate in 1856 and 1857**

	Estimated Proportion of 1856 Vote				
1857	Republican	Democrat	American*	New and Nonvoters**	(N),1857
Republican	.922017	.001354	.301440	-.074204	(57,739)
Democrat	.035706	.853628	-.150788	-.021123	(99,939)
American	-.049293	-.030439	.503416	.049845	(22,385)
Nonvoters	.091570	.175457	.345932	1.045482	(135,462)
Total	1.000000	1.000000	1.000000	1.000000	
(N), 1856	(53,600)	(125,593)	(48,624)	(87,708)	(315,525)

Regression Equations: Partial Slopes of Predicting Variables (1856)

Predicted (1857)	Republican	Democrat	American	New and Nonvoters (Intercept)	(R²)
Republican	.996221	.075558	.375644	-.074204	(.90)
Democrat	.056829	.874751	-.129665	-.021123	(.91)
American	-.099138	-.080284	.453571	.049845	(.77)
Nonvoters	-.953912	-.870025	-.699550	1.045482	(.92)

*Combines Fillmore Straight and Fillmore Union slates.
**New Voters are those eligible in 1857, but not eligible in 1856.

Source: Authors' calculations from data provided in Table 9.9.

portions are slightly less than zero, while others are slightly in excess of 1.0.
Logit analysis likely would have produced a better fit.

Table 9.13 presents the estimated number of voters in each category by region. To calculate them, take the proportions from Tables 9.11 and 9.12 and multiply them by the column totals in each table. Thus, the estimated number of Republican voters from east of the river in 1856 who also voted

Table 9.12
Making Ecological Estimates and Proportion from Regression Equations: The Vote West of the Susquehanna River from the Pennsylvania Eligible Electorate in 1856 and 1857

	Estimated Proportion of 1856 Vote				
1857	Republican	Democrat	American*	New and Nonvoters**	(N), 1857
Republican	.686690	.065200	.607038	-.075614	(87,329)
Democrat	.026233	.810393	.105974	-.046143	(87,884)
American	.009578	-.007610	.160298	.007124	(5,667)
Nonvoters	.277499	.132017	.126690	1.114633	(98,124)
Total	1.000000	1.000000	1.000000	1.000000	
(N), 1856	(93,920)	(103,924)	(32,514)	(48,646)	(279,004)

Regression Equations: Partial Slopes of Predicting Variables (1856)

Predicted (1857)	Republican	Democrat	American	New and Nonvoters (Intercept)	(R^2)
Republican	.762303	.140814	.682651	-.075613	(.91)
Democrat	.072376	.856536	.152117	-.046143	(.96)
American	.002454	-.014734	.153174	.007124	(.44)
Nonvoters	-.837134	-.982616	-.987942	1.114633	(.95)

*Combines Fillmore Straight and Fillmore Union slates.
**New Voters are those eligible in 1857, but not eligible in 1856.

Source: Authors' calculations from data provided in Table 9.9.

Republican in 1857 is .922017 X 53,600 = 49,420. By adding east and west together, we can determine the number of voters of each type for the entire state (see Table 9.14) and the results percentaged (see Table 9.15).

The Republicans received about the same number of votes in 1857 as they did in 1856 because American Party defections offset Republicans who did not vote in 1857. The Democrats retained a large proportion of

Table 9.13
The 1856 and 1857 Pennsylvania Vote, by Party, Region, and Election Year

Number of Votes in 1857	Number of Votes in 1856				
	Republican	Democrat	American	New and Nonvoters	Total, 1857
East of Susquehanna River					
Republican	49,420	170	14,657	-6,508	57,739
Democrat	1,914	107,209	-7,332	-1,852	99,939
American	-2,642	-3,822	24,478	4,371	22,385
Nonvoters	4,908	22,036	16,821	91,697	135,462
Total, 1856	53,600	125,593	48,624	87,708	315,525
West of Susquehanna River					
Republican	64,494	6,776	19,737	-3,678	87,329
Democrat	2,464	84,219	3,445	-2,244	87,884
American	899	-790	5,212	346	5,667
Nonvoters	26,063	13,719	4,120	54,222	98,124
Total, 1856	93,920	103,924	32,514	48,646	279,004

Source: Authors' calculations from Tables 9.11 and 9.12.

their 1856 votes in 1857 but gained virtually no defections from other parties and lost about 15 percent of their 1856 vote to nonvoters in 1857. As a result, the Democrats had roughly the same vote proportion in 1857 as in 1856. The American Party was the big loser in 1857. It managed to hold only one-third of its 1856 vote; almost one-half voted Republican and one-quarter did not vote. None of the parties were able to mobilize the considerable (22.93 percent of the 1857 electorate) 1856 voters who were not yet eligible to vote or who abstained from voting in 1856.

Here we focused on the realignment of voters during a one-year period. The time was brief and the political units comparatively stable. If the time gap between the first and second elections were increased, the assumptions of the model would be less valid. For example, if the intent was to chart changes in the vote between the 1856 and 1860 Pennsylvania presidential elections, the time difference would increase to four years. Depending on the county, there could be considerable geographical mobility, with voters moving out of one county and into another. The assumption that the eligible voters in 1856 and 1860 represent the same individuals would then be less valid.

Table 9.14
The 1856 and 1857 Pennsylvania Vote, by Party and Election Year

| Number of Votes in 1857 | Number of Votes in 1856 | | | | Total, 1857 |
	Republican	Democrat	American	New and Nonvoters	
Republican	113,914	6,946	34,394	-10,186	145,068
Democrat	4,378	191,428	-3,887	-4,096	187,823
American	-1,743	-4,612	29,690	4,717	28,052
Nonvoters	30,971	35,755	20,941	145,919	233,586
Total, 1856	147,520	229,517	81,138	136,354	594,529

Source: Authors' calculations from Table 9.13.

Table 9.15
The 1856 and 1857 Pennsylvania Vote Percentages, by Party and Election Year

| Vote in 1857 | Percent of Vote in 1856 | | | |
	Republican	Democrat	American	New and Nonvoters
Republican	77.22	3.03	42.39	-7.47
Democrat	2.97	83.40	-4.79	-3.00
American	-1.18	-2.01	36.59	3.46
Nonvoters	20.99	15.58	25.81	107.01
Total	100.00	100.00	100.00	100.00
(N), 1856	(147,520)	(229,517)	(81,138)	(136,354)

Source: Authors' calculations from Table 9.14.

10

Measurement: Scales, Indices, and Historical Demography

Quantitative analysis requires that things be measured or at least counted. Often, however, we need to analyze things that we cannot measure or count directly, but only infer. Examples of such latent (or hidden) aspects include "pro-slavery" attitudes of legislators, "hostility to minorities" within committees, and senatorial "voting blocs." Scales and indices can help measure these difficult-to-count actualities.

In fact, the subject of such measurement is vast, and much discussion of it is highly technical. The historian's interests in the subject are twofold: reading the literature in other disciplines requires some familiarity with these techniques, and application of them to historical research can help in his or her own investigations. All such techniques enable us to organize information, clarify arguments, and compare our results with those of other disciplines. Some of them, such as Guttman Scaling and the Gini Index, have several applications. Others, like the Rice Index of Cohesion and the Success Scores, are intended specifically to study legislative behavior and political parties.

GUTTMAN SCALING

One technique with potential for historical research is Guttman Scaling. Louis Guttman introduced the process in a 1941 article entitled "The Quantification of a Class of Attributes: A Theory and Method of Scale Construction."[1] His proposal was not new; it was based on nearly a century of previous work on external stimuli and latent attitudes.

In 1860 Gustav Theodor Fechner (1801–1887) published *Elemente der Psychophysik*[2] in which he reported his experiments with human perception and sensation. Fechner sought to establish a relationship between the physical magnitude of external stimuli and related human sensations. One of his experiments explored the ability of people to determine the "just noticeable difference" between light intensities as measured in foot-candles. The task was to relate an external or physical scale (i.e., one that instruments could measure) to an individual's internal, subjective scale. Fechner's method of distinguishing the "just noticeable difference" was based on probability theory and a normal distribution. Subjects were asked to indicate which of two light sources was brighter. They occasionally made errors; some indicated one was brighter when it was not, or that it was not brighter when it was.[3]

Hermann Ebbinghaus (1850–1909), in his 1885 book *Über das Gedächtnis*, used Fechner's technique to study memory. Memory and the ability to memorize are latent. Thus, Fechner— in developing a technique of relating an internal scale to a physical scale—allowed subsequent researchers to examine purely internal scales.[4]

Others were interested in measurement. James McKeen Cattell published "Mental Tests and Measurements,"[5] and Alfred Binet studied tests of intelligence.[6] They also placed individuals on scales for which there was no obvious physical measurement. The acceptance of these scales lay in their external validity (e.g., seemingly intelligent people received high scores on IQ tests, and seemingly less intelligent people received low scores) and the pattern of interrelationships among the observations. What began as an attempt to calibrate a latent scale to a physical scale came to be used to measure aspects of human behavior for which there were no external scales.

In 1925, Emory S. Bogardus studied racial attitudes in an article, "Measuring Social Distances," which appeared in the *Journal of Applied Sociology*. Bogardus asked 110 public school teachers and business people to identify activities that they would be willing to participate in with thirty-nine different ethnic and racial groups. The questions ranged from whether the respondent would be willing to admit an individual of that race or ethnicity "to close kinship by marriage" to "would exclude from my country." Bogardus learned that virtually everyone who was willing to admit a person of another race or ethnicity to close kinship by marriage was unwilling to exclude people of that group from the country. But some who were unwilling to exclude a racial or ethnic group from their country were also unwilling to admit a member of that group to kinship by marriage. This led to the formation of a social distance scale that would measure the degrees by which individuals favored (or opposed) ethnic and racial mixing.[7]

Louis Guttman built on this earlier work. His research developed a method that identified gradations of attitudes on a specific topic. By asking questions that involved increasingly difficult choices, he learned more about an individual's attitudes. Although some choices were easy, others challenged the respondent's commitment to a particular belief. Guttman's technique did three things. First, it offered evidence as to whether or not all the items related to a single attitude. Second, it created a scale with interpretable gradations. Third, it enabled the researcher to assign a scale score to each respondent and item. In doing so, Guttman formalized a procedure that could be applied to a variety of research topics.

An example might be helpful at this point. While Guttman's research concerned human attitudes, our initial illustration will discuss something that is not latent: weight. Weight is easily observed and allows us to examine the relationship between a person's response and the external condition being observed. Suppose a group of people was asked to answer yes or no to the following questions: Are you heavier than 150 pounds? Are you heavier than 200 pounds? Are you heavier than 250 pounds? There are eight possible response patterns.[8]

1. yes, yes, yes

2. yes, yes, no

3. yes, no, no

4. no, no, no

5. no, yes, yes

6. no, no, yes

7. yes, no, yes

8. no, yes, no

Some of these patterns (numbers 5 through 8) are not logical; a person cannot be heavier than 200 pounds but not heavier than 150 pounds. Given the nature of the questions, only four response patterns (numbers 1 through 4) are appropriate. Table 10.1 presents an illustration of four people's plausible responses to these questions.

The respective *scale scores* (here, the number of yes answers) determine the order of the respondents and questions in the table. We arranged the questions from high to low or from easy to difficult based on the number of yes responses elicited by the question. Likewise, we arranged the respondents from high to low or from heavier to lighter. If the number of yes responses determine the order of respondents and questions, then anyone responding yes to a higher question will also have responded yes to all the lower questions. Anyone responding yes to a question that another responded

Table 10.1
Scale Scores Derived from Plausible Responses to Questions about Specific Personal Weight

	Are You Heavier than . . .			Scale Score
Person	150 Pounds?	200 Pounds?	250 Pounds?	(Number of yeses)
Sam Smith	Yes	Yes	Yes	3
Ben Mill	Yes	Yes	No	2
Dan Doran	Yes	No	No	1
Jim Jones	No	No	No	0
Scale Score (Number of yeses)	3	2	1	

Source: Adapted from Lee F. Anderson, Meredith W. Watts, Jr., and Allen R. Wilcox, *Legislative Roll-call Analysis* (Evanston, IL: Northwestern University Press, 1966), 91–92.

no to will be as high or higher as that person on all other questions. If a person responded yes to an item, then all persons with a higher scale score will also have responded yes.

These characteristics imply *reproducibility*. Reproducibility is the key concept of Guttman scales. It means the degree to which the actual pattern of responses from the row and column scale scores can be reproduced in an interpretable form. To reproduce Table 10.1 from the responses, we ordered the questions from high to low by their scale scores (here, on the columns) and ordered the individuals from high to low by *their* scale scores (here, on the rows). We assigned yes responses for individuals beginning with the highest-score question and proceeding to lower-score questions until the number of yes responses assigned was equal to the individual's scale score. We then repeated this process for each individual. The same results are achieved when this process is done for each question. Then, we assigned yes responses for each question beginning with the individual with the highest scale score and continuing until the number of yes responses assigned for the question was equal to the scale score. For example, the scale score for the first question—Are you heavier than 150 pounds?—is three. To reproduce the pattern, Smith, Mill, and Doran are assigned yes and Jones no. In Table 10.1, the scale scores permit us to reproduce the table completely and without error.

But weight is not in itself a latent attitude. What if we altered the questions? Instead of asking about specific weights, we could ask individuals to compare themselves to other people. For example, we might ask our four persons the following questions: Are you heavier than Billy Sneed? Are you heavier than Constable Ryan? Are you heavier than Mayor Doe? Respondents might give a pattern of answers as shown in Table 10.2. Now the scale is measured in terms of three people who serve as scale markers. We still order the respondents from heaviest to lightest, but there is no direct relationship with a physical scale (e.g., pounds). Notice we get the same order of persons that we did in Table 10.1, despite the fact we do not know the weight of the individuals who serve as the scale markers.

What evidence is there that we are measuring anything at all? If we consider the number of yes responses to a question as an indication of how hard or easy it is, then no one who said yes to a question could have said no to an easier one. Moreover, we can reproduce each person's responses to the three questions from the scale scores. In sum, we have created a device for measuring the latent dimension of weight, and individuals have been scored on it.

The sequencing of easy to hard questions creates a continuum that ranges from one extreme to the other with a neutral position in the middle.

Table 10.2
Scale Scores Derived from Responses to Questions Comparing Personal Weights

Person	Are You Heavier than . . .			Scale Score (Number of yeses)
	Billy Sneed?	Constable Ryan?	Mayor Doe?	
Sam Smith	Yes	Yes	Yes	3
Ben Mill	Yes	Yes	No	2
Dan Doran	Yes	No	No	1
Jim Jones	No	No	No	0
Scale Score (number of yeses)	3	2	1	

Source: Adapted from Table 10.1.

Persons place themselves on the scale by selecting those alternatives closest to their position. The continuum is cumulative in the sense that each
point on the scale represents an additional increment on that dimension.

Guttman Scaling is one of several forms of continuums. It is a special
type of cumulative scale in which the items are in a particular order; that is,
if a person supports one item, he or she will also support all previous items.
One can then determine, from the scale and the scale score, what items
individuals have and have not supported.

One Application of Guttman Scaling: Roll Call Analysis

In the 1950s, George Belknap suggested a way to apply Guttman Scaling to the study of legislative behavior by identifying blocs of individuals
who voted together on certain issues.[9] This technique is applicable to a
variety of groups that record votes (roll calls): the U.S. Congress, the British Parliament, the UN Security Council, the U.S. Supreme Court, city coun-
cils, and school boards.[10]

Until recently, historians typically determined blocs by examining only
the final recorded vote. That approach led to misleading conclusions, as
legislators did not always vote consistently. At times, they voted one way on
the final vote and another way on the dozens of preliminary and procedural
votes that seldom attracted public attention. Another disadvantage of studying
just the final vote was that only two groups could be identified: those who
supported a position and those who opposed it.

Political scientists have developed an alternative methodological approach—roll call analysis—that applies elements of Guttman Scaling to the
study of recorded votes. Computers would normally do this analysis; here
we have done it by hand to clarify the intermediary steps.

The first step is to select a group of roll calls with a common subject
matter; the content should relate in some way to the same issue. Then, we
assign symbols—a plus (+) or minus (-) for example—to each vote cast. A
plus indicates that the vote was cast in favor, or in support of, a particular
position; and a minus is indicative of opposition to that position. Consider the
following example. Two motions are proposed concerning a declaration of
war. The first stipulates that consideration of the declaration of war be
delayed for one year. In this instance, opponents of the war would vote yes
and proponents no. The second motion is to declare war. Opponents would
then vote no, and proponents yes. A plus signifies a vote on this second
motion cast in support of war, and a minus would indicate opposition to war.
You must consider the wording and intent of each motion. A yes vote is not

necessarily indicative of support for an issue. Yes votes on motions to adjourn or to table, for example, may indicate opposition. Zeros (0) can be used to indicate that no vote was cast.

Traditionally, all votes that attracted unanimous or nearly unanimous (over 90 percent) support or opposition were eliminated because they did not provide any additional insight into the voting blocs. This is true only if the intent is a statistical description of voting correlations, or a regression analysis. If the objective is to create an accurate sense of the past, then all the available information should be included. Likewise, while others suggest eliminating all legislators who failed to vote on at least 50 percent of the roll calls (because they did not vote often enough to ensure accurate placement in a voting bloc), we recommend retaining all of them at least until the final stage of the analysis.

The next step is to order the votes horizontally and the legislators vertically (or vice versa, if more convenient) in descending order of their scale score (see Table 10.3). The number of positive votes determines the preliminary scale score of each roll call and legislator. In effect, this procedure

Table 10.3
Guttman Scaling Applied to Roll Call Analysis: Hypothetical Example Showing Preliminary Scale

Legislators	F	B	C	D	A	E	Scale Score
1	+	+	+	+	+	+	6
f	+	+	+	+	+	+	6
k	+	+	+	+	o	+	5
n	-	+	+	+	+	-	4
c	+	+	+	+	-	-	4
m	+	+	+	+	o	-	4
e	+	+	+	-	-	-	3
h	+	+	+	-	-	-	3
b	+	-	-	-	-	-	1
a	+	-	-	-	-	-	1
g	-	-	o	-	o	-	0
d	-	-	-	-	-	-	0
i	-	-	-	o	-	-	0
j	-	-	-	-	-	-	0
Scale Score	9	8	8	6	3	3	

orders the bills from easiest to hardest and the legislators from most to least supportive. This has been done with imaginary data in Table 10.3.

Some researchers first calculate statistical associations using gamma (see Chapter 6) among all possible combinations of roll calls: Roll Call A and Roll Call B, Roll Call A and Roll Call C, Roll Call A and Roll Call D, and so forth. This step ensures, in effect, that the roll calls involve a common attitude. Those roll calls that do not achieve a certain minimum level of association with all the others are eliminated. However, the automatic elimination of roll calls from further analysis—without considering why they failed to associate—is a mistake for two reasons. First, items that fail to associate may scale. Second, when the researcher begins with a large enough pool of votes, he or she can always form a scale by discarding unsuitable items. The resulting scale, however, will not be evidence of some underlying dimension.

How reproducible is the legislative behavior scale? For the tabulation of legislators, start at the left and assign a plus (+) to the first N roll calls; N here is the scale score of the legislator. For the tabulation of roll calls, start at the top and assign a plus to each legislator until N pluses have been assigned; N is now equal to the roll call scale score. Discrepancies between the preliminary and reproduced scales are "errors" (with absences not counted in the error total). At this point, we adjust the scale scores to reduce errors. In Table 10.3, for example, the scale score for Legislator k is 5, creating one error: vote E. But if Legislator k's scale score is changed to 6, there is no error. That is also the case with vote F: reproducing the responses from a scale score of 9 yields two errors—Legislators n and a— but changing the scale score to 10 eliminates Legislator a as an error, because then the first ten—not nine—legislators will be represented as plus. Changing a scale score may require moving a roll call or legislator. In Table 10.4, we present a new scale in which these changes have been made.

We can now measure the reproducibility of our legislative behavior scale. Recall that reproducibility refers to how much of the scale we can duplicate using row or column scale scores. The *coefficient of reproducibility* (CR) measures this.[11]

$$CR = \frac{(rows \times columns) - errors - absences}{(rows \times columns) - absences}$$

The coefficient of reproducibility is the proportion of responses that can be correctly predicted if we know the scale scores of each legislator and roll call. Consider the example presented in Table 10.4. There are eighty-four votes (six votes times fourteen legislators), five abstentions or no votes, and one error (Legislator n's vote on roll call F).

$$CR = \frac{(14 \times 6) - 1 - 5}{(14 \times 6) - 5}$$

$$= \frac{84 - 6}{84 - 5}$$

$$= .9873$$

We can reproduce almost 99 percent of the nonmissing responses. A rule of thumb is: if the value of the coefficient of reproducibility exceeds .900, then the scale is considered to have the properties of a Guttman scale.

Table 10.4
Guttman Scaling Applied to Roll Call Analysis: Hypothetical Example Showing Final Blocs

Legislators	Roll Calls						Scale Score
	F	B	C	D	A	E	
l	+	+	+	+	+	+	6
f	+	+	+	+	+	+	6
k	+	+	+	+	o	+	6
n	-	+	+	+	+	-	5
c	+	+	+	+	-	-	4
m	+	+	+	+	o	-	4
e	+	+	+	-	-	-	3
h	+	+	+	-	-	-	3
b	+	-	-	-	-	-	1
a	+	-	-	-	-	-	1
g	-	-	o	-	o	-	0
d	-	-	-	-	-	-	0
i	-	-	-	o	-	-	0
j	-	-	-	-	-	-	0
Scale Score	10	8	8	6	4	3	

Source: Based on Table 10.3.

Table 10.5
Scalogram and Analysis of U.S. Supreme Court Civil Liberties Cases from the 1956 Term

Justice	Supreme Court Cases																						Scale Score	Number of +	Number of -
	1	2	3	4	5	6	7	8	9	10	11	12	13	14	15	16	17	18	19	20	21	22			
Douglas	+	+	+	+	+	-	+	+	+	+	+	+	+	+	+	+	+	+	+	+	+	+	22	21	1
Black	+	+	+	+	o	+	+	+	+	+	+	+	+	+	+	+	+	+	+	+	+	+	22	21	0
Warren	+	+	+	+	+	+	+	+	+	+	+	+	+	-	+	+	+	+	+	-	-	-	19	18	4
Brennan	+	o	o	+	+	+	o	+	+	+	+	+	+	+	+	+	+	+	+	-	-	-	19	16	3
Frankfurter	+	+	+	+	+	+	+	+	+	+	+	+	+	+	+	-	-	-	-	-	-	+	14	16	6
Harlan	+	+	+	+	+	+	+	+	+	+	+	+	-	-	-	-	-	-	-	-	+	+	12	14	8
Whittaker	o	o	o	o	o	o	o	o	o	o	o	o	o	o	o	-	-	-	o	o	-	+	11	1	4
Burton	+	+	+	o	+	+	+	-	-	-	-	-	-	-	-	-	-	-	-	-	-	-	5	6	15
Clark	-	-	-	-	-	-	-	-	-	-	-	-	+	-	-	-	-	-	-	-	-	-	0	1	21
Reed	o	o	o	o	o	-	o	o	o	o	o	o	-	o	o	-	-	o	-	-	o	o	0	0	6
Scale Score	8	8	8	8	8	7	6	6	6	6	6	6	5	5	4	4	4	4	4	2	2	2			
Number of +	7	6	6	6	6	6	6	6	6	6	6	6	6	4	5	4	4	4	4	2	4	4			
Number of -	1	1	1	1	1	3	1	2	2	2	2	2	3	4	3	5	5	5	5	7	5	5			

+ Vote in support of civil liberties
- Vote in opposition to civil liberties
o Absent or not voting

Table 10.5, continued

Key to Supreme Court cases:

1. *Jencks v. United States*
2. *Yates v. United States*
3. *Schneiderman v. United States*
4. *Richmond v. United States*
5. *Boviaro v. United States*
6. *Chessman v. Teets*
7. *Watkins v. United States*
8. *Kremen v. United States*
9. *Kinsella v. Krueger*
10. *Reid v. Covert*
11. *Sweezy v. New Hampshire*
12. *Gold v. United States*
13. *Fikes v. Alabama*
14. *Paoli v. United States*
15. *Konigsberg v. State Bar*
16. *Petition of Groban*
17. *Kingsley Books v. Brown*
18. *Nilva v. United States*
19. *Pollard v. United States*
20. *Breithaupt v. Abrams*
21. *Roth v. United States*
22. *Alberts v. United States*

$$CR = \frac{(rows X columns) - errors - absences}{(rows X columns) - absences}$$

$$= \frac{(10 X 22) - 8 - 38}{(10 X 22) - 38}$$

$$= .9560$$

$$MMR = \frac{number\ giving\ modal\ response}{total\ of\ non\text{-}missing\ cases}$$

$$= \frac{114}{(10 X 22) - 38}$$

$$= .6264$$

Source: Adapted from S. Sidney Ulmer, "Supreme Court Behavior and Civil Rights," in *Quantification in American History: Theory and Research*, edited by Robert P. Swierenga (New York: Atheneum, 1970), 173.

Guttman also suggested that the *minimum marginal reproducibility* (MMR) should be low compared to the actual reproducibility. The minimum marginal reproducibility is the reproducibility achieved by simply assigning each vote the modal vote for the entire scale.

$$\frac{\text{number giving modal response}}{(\text{rows X columns) - absences}}$$

This ensures that many cases demonstrating similar behavior—for example, many unanimous votes—do not make the coefficient of reproducibility trivially high. In Table 10.3, the modal response is minus; there are forty-two of them and only thirty-seven pluses. The MMR value for Table 10.3 is:

$$\frac{\text{number of modal responses}}{(\text{rows X columns) - absences}}$$

$$\frac{42}{(6 \text{ X } 14) - 5}$$

$$.5316$$

The reproducibility gained by scaling (CR) is, therefore, substantially better than what one could have reproduced without the scale scores (MMR).

Once the final scores have been determined, additional analysis can begin. For instance, the researcher can combine individuals to form larger blocs sharing the same general attitude. In Table 10.4, Legislators l through n can be labeled "supporters," c through h "moderates," and b through j "opponents." These general categories can be useful in comparing blocs by party, section, and so on.

Now, let us consider a specific example of Guttman Scaling. In a 1960 paper, S. Sidney Ulmer explored the attitudes of U.S. Supreme Court justices by determining how they voted on civil liberties cases.[12] We have reproduced a modified version of his scale in Table 10.5.

The table illustrates several different things. We can determine the voting pattern of individual Supreme Court justices as well as how the justices formed blocs. Some, like Justices Douglas and Black, almost consistently defended civil liberties, while Justice Clark almost consistently opposed them. There were other justices, such as Frankfurter and Harlan, whom we might label "moderates." They supported civil liberties to a point, but then could go no further. The advantages of examining this presentation over analyzing a justice's position on civil liberties based on a single case is obvious.

Another Application of Guttman Scaling

The next example demonstrates a different application of Guttman Scaling. Until now, we have examined Guttman scales for responses in which there were two alternatives: yes and no. It is also possible to form Guttman scales with items that have more than two responses, provided that the alternatives can be interpreted as forming an ordinal scale. Consider Gunnar Myrdal's *An American Dilemma*, published in 1944.[13] One of his interests was to define what constituted "the South." To examine that question, he studied ten variables—some historical (states that seceded during the Civil War), some geographical (states south of 39° 43′26.3, the Mason-Dixon Line), and some involving laws regulating race relations. We have reported a portion of that information, as it relates to how states handled race relations, in Table 10.6. In this table, the data form an ordinal scale from high (h), to medium (m), to low (l) institutional segregation.

Myrdal did not use Guttman Scaling. But we can reorder his data to form a Guttman scale using the following steps:

1. Determine the column and row scale scores. These preliminary scale scores have two components: the number of h and m values.

2. Order the row and column elements from the most to least frequent on the highest alternative (here, h). Within groups having the same number of h values, order those having the most of the next highest alternative (m) first.

3. Change the order of row or column elements if that will reduce errors.

Gilbert Shapiro later used these procedures to examine whether Myrdal's data on institutional segregation formed a single dimension.[14] Shapiro wondered whether the various elements of institutional segregation existed haphazardly in all states or whether they formed a continuum indicating degrees of segregation. If segregation is on a single continuum, we can discuss degrees of segregation, more or less segregated states, and stages in the segregation process. Shapiro's scale, with slight modifications, is reproduced in Table 10.7. One can see that his arrangement of the laws defining race relations resulted in a different grouping of the states from the grouping in Myrdal's findings. Yet even Shapiro's scale can be improved. If the order of "Laws Prohibiting Intermarriage" and "School Segregation Laws" are reversed—as in Table 10.8—we can reduce the number of errors.

What does reproducibility mean, then, in the context of a scale having elements with more than two categories? The scale scores for both the rows and columns are the total numbers for each of the possible responses.

Table 10.6
Various Definitions of the South, Original Scale Based on Myrdal's Categories

State	Laws Prohibiting Intermarriage	School Segregation Laws	Forced School Segregation	Jim Crow Railways	Jim Crow Street Cars	White Primary	Scale Score Total h	Scale Score Total m
OK	h	h	h	h	h	l	5	0
TX	h	h	h	h	h	m	5	1
LA	h	h	h	h	h	h	6	0
AR	h	h	h	h	h	h	6	0
MS	h	h	h	h	h	h	6	0
AL	h	h	h	h	h	h	6	0
TN	h	h	h	h	h	m	5	1
FL	h	h	h	h	h	h	6	0
GA	h	h	h	h	h	h	6	0
SC	h	h	h	h	h	h	6	0
NC	h	h	h	h	h	m	5	1
VA	h	h	h	h	h	h	6	0
WV	h	h	h	l	l	l	3	0
MD	h	h	h	h	l	l	4	0
KY	h	h	h	h	l	l	4	0
DE	h	h	h	m	l	l	3	1
MO	h	h	h	l	l	l	3	0
DC	l	h	h	l	l	l	2	0
NJ	l	l	m	l	l	l	0	1
IN	h	l	m	l	l	l	1	1
KS	l	l	m	l	l	l	0	1
IL	l	l	m	l	l	l	0	1
OH	l	l	m	l	l	l	0	1
PA	l	l	m	l	l	l	0	1

Scale Score:

Total h	18	18	18	14	12	8		
Total m	0	0	6	1	0	3		

h   Present in the state
m   Present only in part of the state or optional within the state
l   Absent from the state

Source: Adapted from Gunnar Myrdal, *The American Dilemma* (New York: Harper and Brothers, 1944), 1072. We added the marginal scale scores for comparison.

Table 10.7
Various Definitions of the South, Shapiro's Scale after Myrdal

State	Forced School Segregation	Laws Prohibiting Intermarriage	School Segregation Laws	Jim Crow Railways	Jim Crow Street Cars	White Primary	Scale Score Total h	Total m
LA	h	h	h	h	h	h	6	0
AR	h	h	h	h	h	h	6	0
MS	h	h	h	h	h	h	6	0
AL	h	h	h	h	h	h	6	0
FL	h	h	h	h	h	h	6	0
GA	h	h	h	h	h	h	6	0
SC	h	h	h	h	h	h	6	0
VA	h	h	h	h	h	h	6	0
TX	h	h	h	h	h	m	5	1
TN	h	h	h	h	h	m	5	1
NC	h	h	h	h	h	m	5	1
OK	h	h	h	h	h	l	5	0
MD	h	h	h	h	l	l	4	0
KY	h	h	h	h	l	l	4	0
DE	h	h	h	m	l	l	3	1
WV	h	h	h	l	l	l	3	0
MO	h	h	h	l	l	l	3	0
DC	h	l	h	l	l	l	2	0
IN	m	h	l	l	l	l	1	1
NJ	m	l	l	l	l	l	0	1
KS	m	l	l	l	l	l	0	1
IL	m	l	l	l	l	l	0	1
OH	m	l	l	l	l	l	0	1
PA	m	l	l	l	l	l	0	1

Scale Score:
Total h	18	18	18	14	12	8		
Total m	6	0	0	1	0	3		

h Present in the state
m Present only in part of the state or optional within the state
l Absent from the state

Source: Adapted from Gilbert Shapiro, "Myrdal's Definitions of the 'South': A Methodological Note," *American Sociological Review*, 13 (October 1948), 621. We added the marginal scale scores for comparison.

Table 10.8
Various Definitions of the South, Final Scale Improvement after Myrdal and Shapiro

State	Forced School Segregation	School Segregation Laws	Laws Prohibiting Intermarriage	Jim Crow Railways	Jim Crow Street Cars	White Primary	Scale Score Total h	Scale Score Total m
LA	h	h	h	h	h	h	6	0
AR	h	h	h	h	h	h	6	0
MS	h	h	h	h	h	h	6	0
AL	h	h	h	h	h	h	6	0
FL	h	h	h	h	h	h	6	0
GA	h	h	h	h	h	h	6	0
SC	h	h	h	h	h	h	6	0
VA	h	h	h	h	h	h	6	0
TX	h	h	h	h	h	m	5	1
TN	h	h	h	h	h	m	5	1
NC	h	h	h	h	h	m	5	1
OK	h	h	h	h	h	l	5	0
MD	h	h	h	h	l	l	4	0
KY	h	h	h	h	l	l	4	0
DE	h	h	h	m	l	l	3	1
WV	h	h	h	l	l	l	3	0
MO	h	h	h	l	l	l	3	0
DC	h	h	l	l	l	l	2	0
IN	m	l	h	l	l	l	1	1
NJ	m	l	l	l	l	l	0	1
KS	m	l	l	l	l	l	0	1
IL	m	l	l	l	l	l	0	1
OH	m	l	l	l	l	l	0	1
PA	m	l	l	l	l	l	0	1

Scale Score:

	Forced School Segregation	School Segregation Laws	Laws Prohibiting Intermarriage	Jim Crow Railways	Jim Crow Street Cars	White Primary
Total h	18	18	18	14	12	8
Total m	6	0	0	1	0	3

h   Present in the state
m   Present only in part of the state or optional within the state
l   Absent from the state

Source: Authors' calculations from data in Tables 10.6 and 10.7.

To reproduce the Myrdal table, we distributed the most extreme responses, followed by the next less extreme responses, and so on, both for the columns and rows. North Carolina has five h values and one m value, so we assigned these by allocating the h values to the first five discrimination practices, followed by the one m value. Likewise, "Jim Crow Railways" has fourteen h values and one m value; we distribute these by assigning h to the first fourteen states, an m to the next state, and 1 to any remaining states. Errors are the discrepancies between the reproduced and actual table. In Table 10.7 there are two errors: one each in the District of Columbia and Indiana. This gives a high coefficient of reproducibility.

$$CR = \frac{(\text{rows X columns}) - \text{errors} - \text{no responses}}{(\text{rows X columns}) - \text{no responses}}$$
$$= \frac{(24 \text{X} 6) - 2 - 0}{(24 \text{X} 6) - 0}$$
$$= .9861$$

By switching the order of the laws as we have done in Table 10.8, however, we have further reduced the errors and increased the value of the coefficient of reproducibility even more.

$$CR = \frac{(\text{rows X columns}) - \text{errors} - \text{no responses}}{(\text{rows X columns}) - \text{no responses}}$$
$$= \frac{(24 \text{X} 6) - 1 - 0}{(24 \text{X} 6) - 0}$$
$$= .9931$$

The column switch also changes the position of the District of Columbia, as we no longer group it with Missouri and West Virginia.

The lesson for historians here is that, while Guttman Scaling can be useful, it should be done carefully. In the half century since Guttman's original work, cumulative scaling has undergone considerable refinement and further development. One limitation to the Guttman approach is that it assumes a deterministic model of a perfect scale. The legislator (in our roll call example) or the state (in our Myrdal example), for instance, has a given position on some dimension, and the response to the items is determined by that position and the content of the items. Another approach is to assume this response to be *stochastic*, or determined by probabilities. A Supreme Court justice, for example, with a certain position on the latent dimension of civil liberties would have a certain probability of voting for or against a particular plaintiff. Justices high on the latent dimension of civil liberties have a higher probability of voting to affirm civil liberties in a particular case than justices lower on the latent dimension. The "Mokken model" is one such approach to scaling.[15] Its value over the Guttman approach is its more realistic mathematical model relating observed indicators to underlying concepts. Other developments in cumulative scaling include expanding the unidimensional analysis to several dimensions.

RICE INDEX OF COHESION

The Rice Index of Cohesion explores collective legislative behavior. Specifically, it measures intraparty cohesion. The Rice Index is equal to the absolute difference (without sign) between the percentage of one group (e.g., a political party) voting yes and the percentage of that same group voting no on one roll call. The value of the Rice Index ranges from 0 (e.g., 50 percent yes minus 50 percent no) to 100 (i.e., 100 percent yes minus 0 percent no).

Consider the following example. On June 17, 1812, the U.S. Senate voted on the question of whether or not to declare war on Great Britain. Nineteen Republicans voted for a declaration of war, and five voted against it. Federalist members of the Senate voted eight to zero against declaring war. The Rice Index of Cohesion for the Republican Party in this instance was 58.4 (the absolute value of 79.2 percent minus 20.8 percent), and 100.0 (the absolute value of 100.0 percent minus 0.0 percent) for the Federalists.

By adding the index for each roll call and dividing that sum by the total number of votes, the researcher can calculate an average index of cohesion for an entire legislative session. The higher the value, the more intraparty unity is indicated.

SUCCESS SCORES

None of the techniques discussed thus far consider who had success in terms of a legislative program; that is another element of legislative behavior. Richard Jensen has proposed one way to calculate the success rate of individual legislators.[16] On each roll call, legislators can vote with the majority (win), vote with the minority (lose), or be absent or abstain. To calculate an individual's success score, subtract the total number of losses from the total number of wins and divide by the total number of roll calls (wins + losses + no votes).

Consider the example presented in Table 10.9. Notice that success scores range from +1 to -1. Legislator a, who voted on all ten roll calls and in each instance voted with the majority, achieved a success score of +1. Legislator f, who also voted on all ten roll calls but each time voted with the minority, achieved a success score of -1.

THE GINI INDEX

The Gini Index measures the amount of inequality existing within a group. In 1905, American statistician Max Otto Lorenz suggested representing inequalities of wealth by a curve.[17] By ordering a group from most to least wealthy, the cumulative proportion of wealth of the first person; the first and second; the first, second, and third; and so on could be calculated and a graph constructed. The horizontal axis (x) of the Lorenz curve represents the cumulative proportion of the population, beginning at zero for the most wealthy and going to 1 for the least wealthy. The vertical axis (y) represents the cumulative proportion of total wealth possessed by a certain proportion of the most wealthy.

The straight line $y_i = x_i$, then, would represent perfect equality: the wealthiest 10 percent of the population owns 10 percent of the wealth, the wealthiest 30 percent owns 30 percent of the wealth, and so on. The extent to

Table 10.9
Another Method of Roll Call Analysis: Examples of Success Scores Tabulated for Hypothetical Individual Legislators

Legislators	Wins	No Votes	Losses	Success Score
a	10	0	0	1.00
b	8	1	1	.70
c	5	0	5	.00
d	4	0	6	-.20
e	3	1	6	-.30
f	0	0	10	-1.00

Source: Authors' calculations.

Figure 10.1
Lorenz Curve of Wealth Distribution

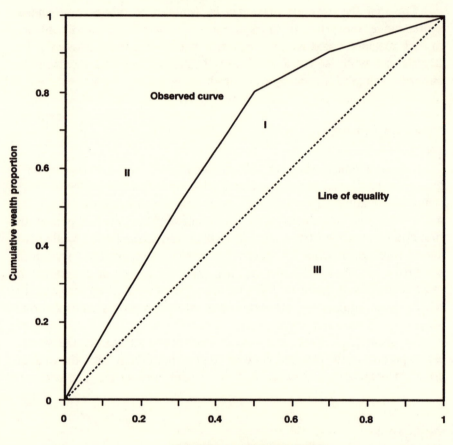

Source: Authors' calculations. See M. O. Lorenz, "Methods of Measuring the Concentration of Wealth, " *Journal of the American Statistical Association,* 9 (June
1905), 209-219.

which the actual distribution of wealth departs from this is the extent of inequality. The Lorenz curve dramatically represents this inequality (see Figure 10.1).

In 1912 Corrado Gini, an Italian economist and statistician, suggested measuring this inequality by computing a ratio of the area between the observed curve and the equality line (area I in Figure 10.1) and the total area away from the equality line (areas I + II).[18] A Gini Index of zero indicates complete equality, and an index of one indicates the theoretical maximum inequality. If the Lorenz curve is known, calculus can determine the areas. For most historians, however, the Lorenz curve can only be roughly approximated. Calculation of the Gini Index, then, begins with the Lorenz curve.

The Lorenz Curve

Before examining specific historical data, a hypothetical example will be used to illustrate the technique. In a fictitious nation there are four regions: the first has 30 percent of the population and 50 percent of the wealth, the second has 30 percent of the population and 10 percent of the wealth, the third has 20 percent of the population and 10 percent of the wealth, and the fourth has 20 percent of the population and 30 percent of the wealth (see Table 10.10). The first step in constructing the Lorenz curve is to calculate the ratio of wealth to population. For the first region, it is 1.666 (.5/.3). The second step is to order the regions from the highest to lowest in the ratio of wealth to population. This step is shown in Table 10.10. The third step is to calculate the cumulative proportions for each variable after reordering the regions. The cumulative proportion is the proportion in the region added to the proportion in all previous regions. We present these cumulative proportions, reordered by the ratios, in Table 10.10.

By setting the cumulative proportion of the population on the horizontal (x) axis and the cumulative proportion of wealth on the vertical (y) axis, we can plot a Lorenz curve. Each region is then plotted and the points connected (see Figure 10.1).

Calculating the Gini Index

Once a Lorenz curve has been plotted from the data at hand, the Gini Index can be calculated several ways (each of which may provide a slightly different value), depending on the nature of the data. If the precise curve is

Table 10.10
Hypothetical Example of Wealth and Population Distribution in Four Regions, Showing the Steps to Producing the Lorenz Curve in Figure 10.1

Region	Population	Proportion of Population	Wealth ($)	Wealth Proportion
A	300,000	.3	50,000,000,000	.5
B	300,000	.3	10,000,000,000	.1
C	200,000	.2	10,000,000,000	.1
D	200,000	.2	30,000,000,000	.3
Total	1,000,000	1.0	100,000,000,000	1.0

Region	Ratio of Wealth to Population
A	.5/.3 = 1.666
B	.1/.3 = 0.333
C	.1/.2 = 0.5
D	.3/.2 = 1.5

Ranked Region	Cumulative Proportion of Population	Cumulative Proportion of Wealth
A	.3	.5
D	.5	.8
C	.7	.9
B	1.0	1.0

Source: Authors' calculations.

known, for example, we can use calculus to determine the index value. If the intervals on the horizontal axis are equal, Simpson's Rule[19] can be used for an approximation (see the Appendix). For most historians, however, the *Trapezoid Rule*—or, the equivalent method of triangles and rectangles—

will prove simplest.

The Trapezoid Rule requires that we divide the area under the curve into N trapezoids. A trapezoid is a four-sided figure—a square or rectangle, for example. The ith trapezoid has a width w_i and two heights defined by the y axis: y_{i-1} (the shorter height) and y_i (the longer height). We can calculate the area of the trapezoid by the Trapezoid Rule as:

$$w_i (1/2(y_{i-1} + y_i))$$

The total area of all the N trapezoids together is the area under the Lorenz curve. We calculate the area of inequality subtracting .5 from this, the area of the lower triangle (area III in Figure 10.1). Let us return to our hypothetical example of a nation with four regions. Figure 10.2 illustrates the basis for the calculations.

In the hypothetical example, the width (w_i) of each trapezoid is the region's population proportion, the first height (y_{i-1}) is the cumulative proportion of wealth for the preceding region (in the case of Region A this is zero as there is no preceding region), and the second height (y_i) is the cumulative proportion of wealth for the ith region. Here there are four trapezoids, one for each region. The areas of each are:

$$
\begin{aligned}
\text{Region A} &= .3 \times (1/2(0 + .5)) &= .075 \\
\text{Region D} &= .2 \times (1/2(.5 + .8)) &= .130 \\
\text{Region C} &= .2 \times (1/2(.8 + .9)) &= .170 \\
\text{Region B} &= .3 \times (1/2(.9 + 1.0)) &= .285 \\
\text{Total} & &= .660
\end{aligned}
$$

The next step is to subtract the area of the lower triangle (area III in Figure 10.1) from the total area of the N trapezoids. The area of the lower triangle is

$$1/2 (1 \times 1) = .5$$

and the area of inequality (area I) is .66 - .5 = .16. The Gini Index is

$$\frac{area\ I}{(area\ I + area\ II)} = \frac{.16}{.5}$$

$$= .32$$

Figure 10.2
Gini Index Calculation from the Lorenz Curve of Wealth Distribution,
Using the Trapeziod Rule

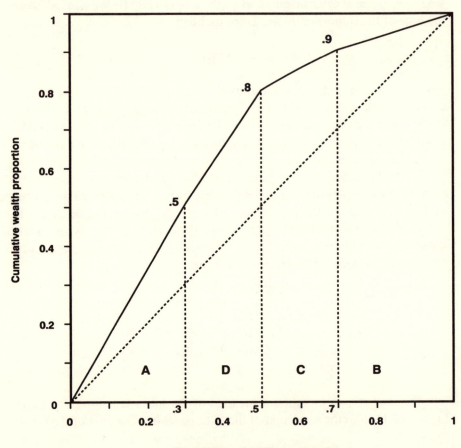

Source: Constructed from Figure 10.1.

The amount of inequality is about a third of the theoretical maximum inequality. The Gini Index has its own intuitive meaning. Zero indicates perfect equality in the distribution of something—in this case, wealth—and one indicates the theoretical maximum possible inequality: in this case, roughly, one person has all the wealth. But a degree of inequality is expected in all societies. The question for historians usually is whether the inequality in one area or year is larger or smaller than the inequality in another. The Gini Index is a useful way to compare inequalities.

The Gini Index Applied to Electoral Apportionment

Now let us consider an actual example. The Electoral College—and not the direct popular vote—elects the president of the United States. Each state is allotted electors equal to the number of senators and members of the House of Representatives apportioned to that state. Votes are cast for members of the Electoral College, who then vote for the president. There are several sources of inequality in this process. For one thing, each state is given two senators regardless of its population. Next, while each state's allotment to the House of Representatives is based on the census, this is not an exact method, because states are given only whole numbers of representatives (3 and not 3.4, as might be required by the state's proportion of the total population). Population shifts produce additional inequality. By the last election after each decennial reapportionment, substantial population shifts can occur. Prior to reapportionment in 1870, another source of inequality was slavery. Before then, three-fifths of a state's slave population were counted in determining a state's representation in the House of Representatives. Additionally, not everyone votes; people in some states vote at higher rates than in others. There are also differences in suffrage requirements among the states. The result is unequal representation of voters by the Electoral College. Voters in some states are better represented in the college than voters in other states.

Now let us apply the Gini Index technique to two presidential elections. Table 10.11 presents the total number of votes cast for president in the 1852 and 1860 elections, the number of electors, and the ratio of electors to votes cast. A computer program in BASIC was used to perform the necessary calculations (see PROGRAM 10.1). Table 10.12 presents the cumulative popular and electoral votes for thirty states in 1860, ordered from highest to lowest by ratio of electoral vote to popular vote. The 1852 data (cumulative proportions not shown) excludes three states not casting popular votes in 1852. (Minnesota and Oregon were not states in 1852, and South Carolina's

Table 10.11

U.S. Presidential Popular Vote and Electoral Vote in 1852 and 1860, by State

State	Electoral Vote 1852 & 1860 No.	Prop.	Popular Votes Cast (in thousands) 1852 No.	Prop.	1860 No.	Prop.	Ratio of Electoral to Popular Vote Props. 1852	1860
Alabama	9	(.03)	44	(.01)	90	(.02)	3.00	1.50
Arkansas	4	(.01)	20	(.01)	54	(.01)	1.00	1.00
California	4	(.01)	77	(.02)	120	(.03)	0.50	0.33
Connecticut	6	(.02)	67	(.02)	80	(.02)	1.00	1.00
Delaware	3	(.01)	13	(.004)	16	(.003)	2.50	3.33
Florida	3	(.01)	7	(.002)	13	(.003)	5.00	3.33
Georgia	10	(.04)	62	(.02)	107	(.02)	2.00	2.00
Illinois	11	(.04)	155	(.05)	337	(.07)	0.80	0.57
Indiana	13	(.05)	184	(.06)	272	(.06)	0.83	0.83
Iowa	4	(.01)	35	(.01)	128	(.03)	1.00	0.33
Kentucky	12	(.04)	111	(.04)	146	(.03)	1.00	1.33
Louisiana	6	(.02)	36	(.01)	51	(.01)	2.00	2.00
Maine	8	(.03)	82	(.03)	101	(.02)	1.00	1.50
Maryland	8	(.03)	75	(.02)	93	(.02)	1.50	1.50
Massachusetts	13	(.05)	125	(.04)	169	(.04)	1.25	1.25
Michigan	6	(.02)	83	(.03)	155	(.03)	0.66	0.66
Mississippi	7	(.02)	45	(.01)	69	(.01)	2.00	2.00
Missouri	9	(.03)	69	(.02)	165	(.04)	1.50	0.75
New Hampshire	5	(.02)	51	(.02)	66	(.01)	1.00	2.00
New Jersey	7	(.02)	84	(.03)	121	(.03)	0.66	0.66
New York	35	(.12)	525	(.17)	677	(.15)	0.705	0.80
North Carolina	10	(.04)	79	(.02)	96	(.02)	2.00	2.00
Ohio	23	(.08)	353	(.11)	443	(.10)	0.72	0.80
Pennsylvania	27	(.09)	386	(.12)	476	(.10)	0.75	0.90
Rhode Island	4	(.01)	17	(.005)	20	(.004)	2.00	2.50
Tennessee	12	(.04)	115	(.04)	144	(.03)	1.00	1.33
Texas	4	(.01)	20	(.01)	63	(.01)	1.00	1.00
Vermont	5	(.02)	44	(.01)	45	(.01)	2.00	2.00
Virginia	15	(.05)	133	(.04)	167	(.04)	1.25	1.25
Wisconsin	5	(.02)	62	(.02)	152	(.03)	1.00	0.66
Total	288	(0.99)	3159	(1.001)	4636	(1.00)		

Source: U. S. Department of Commerce, Bureau of the Census, *Historical Statistics of the United States: Colonial Times to 1970*, pt. 2 (Washington, DC: Government Printing Office, 1975), 1075, 1076, 1080.

Program 10.1
A BASIC Program to Calculate the Gini Index

```
10    PRINT "INPUT THE NUMBER OF CASES"
20    INPUT N
30    DIM W(N+1)
40    DIM H(N+1)
50    DIM R(N+1)
60    DIM P(2,N+1)
70    DIM C(2,N+1)
80    DIM A(N+1)
90    T(1)=0
100   T(2)=0
110   REM READ IN DATA, COMPUTE TOTALS, COMPUTE RATIOS
120   FOR I=1 TO N STEP 1
130   PRINT "ENTER CASE: ",I
140   PRINT "  HORIZONTAL VARIABLE:"
150   INPUT W(I)
160   PRINT "  VERTICAL VARIABLE:"
170   INPUT H(I)
180   T(1)=T(1)+W(I)
190   T(2)=T(2)+H(I)
200   R(I)=(H(I)/W(I))
210   NEXT I
220   REM COMPUTE PROPORTIONS
230   FOR I=1 TO N STEP 1
240   P(1,I)=W(I)/T(1)
250   P(2,I)=H(I)/T(2)
260   NEXT I
270   REM SORT FROM HIGH TO LOW ON RATIO
280   FOR J=1 TO N STEP 1
290   FOR I=1 TO N STEP 1
300   IF R(I)<R(I+1) GOTO 320
310   GOTO 470
320   B=P(1,I)
330   P(1,I)=P(1,I+1)
340   P(1,I+1)=B
350   B=P(2,I)
360   P(2,I)=P(2,I+1)
370   P(2,I+1)=B
380   B=R(I)
390   R(I)=R(I+1)
400   R(I+1)=B
```

```
410    B=W(I)
420    W(I)=W(I+1)
430    W(I+1)=B
440    B=H(I)
450    H(I)=H(I+1)
460    H(I+1)=B
470    NEXT I
480    NEXT J
490    REM CALCULATE CUMULATIVE PROPORTIONS
500    C(1,0)=0
510    C(2,0)=0
520    FOR I=1 TO N STEP 1
530    C(1,I)=C(1,I-1)+P(1,I)
540    C(2,I)=C(2,I-1)+P(2,I)
550    A(I)=P(1,I)*.5*(C(2,I)+C(2,I-1))
560    T(3)=T(3)+A(I)
570    NEXT I
580    G=(T(3)-.5)/.5
590    PRINT "THE GINI INDEX IS: ",G
600    PRINT "X VAR","Y VAR","CUMULATIVE X","CUMULATIVE Y"
610    FOR I=1 TO N STEP 1
620    PRINT W(I),H(I),C(1,I),C(2,I)
630    NEXT I
640    END
```

legislature selected its electors.) Figures 10.3 and 10.4 present Lorenz curves for 1852 and 1860.

Remarkably, the Gini indices for the 1852 and 1860 elections are very similar: .19 for 1852 and .21 for 1860. Thirty-four percent of the popular vote selected 50 percent of the electoral college in both elections. Population shifts and variations in voting rates and requirements apparently offset one another. Only one state had a noticeable shift. Missouri changed from a state with excessive influence (based on its popular vote) in 1852 to being underrepresented in 1860.

HISTORICAL DEMOGRAPHY

One way to investigate the collective experiences of people is demography—the study of human population. The four components of demo-

Table 10.12
**Cumulative Proportion of Popular Votes Cast and Electoral
Votes with States Ordered from Most Overrepresented to
Most Underrepresented in the Electoral College, 1860 Election**

Ranked State	Cumulative Popular Vote Proportion	Cumulative Electoral Vote Proportion
Florida	0.002804142	0.01041667
Delaware	0.006255393	0.02083333
Rhode Island	0.01056946	0.03472223
Louisiana	0.02157032	0.05555556
Vermont	0.03127696	0.07291667
North Carolina	0.05198447	0.1076389
Mississippi	0.066868	0.1319445
Alabama	0.08628128	0.1631945
Georgia	0.1093615	0.1979167
Virginia	0.145384	0.25
Maryland	0.1654444	0.2777778
Tennessee	0.1965056	0.3194445
Kentucky	0.2279983	0.3611111
Maine	0.2497843	0.3888889
Massachusetts	0.2862381	0.4340278
New Hampshire	0.3004746	0.4513889
Connecticut	0.3177308	0.4722223
Arkansas	0.3293788	0.4861112
Texas	0.3429681	0.5
New Jersey	0.3690682	0.5243056
Pennsylvania	0.4717429	0.6180556
Missouri	0.507334	0.6493056
Ohio	0.6028905	0.7291667
New York	0.7489215	0.8506945
Indiana	0.8075928	0.8958334
Michigan	0.8410268	0.9166667
California	0.8669112	0.9305556
Wisconsin	0.8996981	0.9479167
Illinois	0.9723901	0.9861111
Iowa	1.0000000	1.0000000

Source: Authors' calculations from data in Table 10.11.

Figure 10.3
Lorenz Curve: Cumulative Proportion of Popular Votes Cast and
Cumulative Proportion of Electoral College, 1852

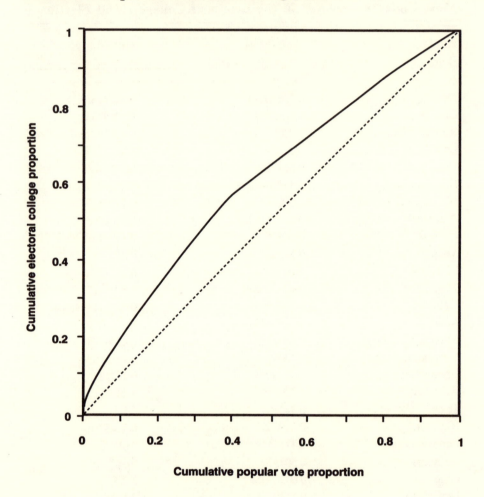

Source: Constructed from data in Table 10.11.

Figure 10.4
Lorenz Curve: Cumulative Proportion of Popular Votes Cast and
Cumulative Proportion of Electoral College, 1860

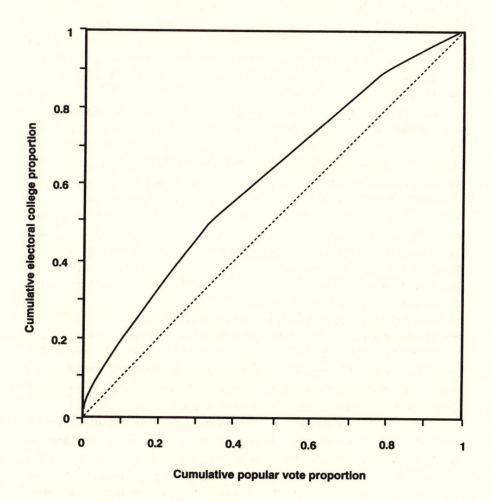

Source: Constructed from data in Table 10.12.

graphy of most interest to historians are characteristics of the population, fertility, mortality, and migration. Historians have only somewhat recently applied demographic techniques to the study of the past. Some journals, like the *Journal of Family History*, devote most of every issue to historical demography. Others, such as the *Journal of Interdisciplinary History*, the *Journal of Urban History, Historical Methods*, and *Social Science History*, occasionally publish articles. Some journals in other disciplines also publish the results of historical demographers' research; consult *Journal of Marriage and the Family, Demography, Population Studies*, and the *American Sociological Review*.

General population characteristics provide aggregate information about a population. Its *size*, or the number of people living in a given area, is the most obvious. Another is *natural increase*, which is calculated by subtracting the number of deaths from the number of births during a given period. The *sex ratio*, or the number of males for every 100 females, is also important. The sex ratio has been of considerable interest to historians of colonial America who study how it affected marriage and remarriage patterns. *Age cohorts* can also describe a population (see Figure 10.5). There are many factors that affect the distribution of ages within a population. Consider the impact of an epidemic, war, baby boom, or extensive in- or out-migration. A population can also be described by its racial, religious, occupational, and educational composition.

Another group of population characteristics involve marriage. One is age at first marriage. It may tell us much about the nature of a society. Delaying marriage may, for example, indicate a period of economic distress. The extent of *exogamy*, or the incidence of marrying outside one's own group, and *endogamy*, or the incidence of marrying within one's own group, is one measure of the rate of assimilation.

The second area of interest to historical demographers is fertility or birth rates. There are several indices of fertility; which one we use depends on the availability of data. The *crude birth rate* (CBR) equals the number of live births in a given year, divided by the midyear population of that year, times 1,000. It is the least exact of the fertility measures because the midyear population includes men, children, and the elderly—few of whom give birth. If more detailed data are available, we should employ more exact fertility measures. One of these is the *general fertility rate* (GFR). It equals the total number of births in a given year, divided by the number of women of childbearing age (fifteen to forty-four, or puberty to menopause), times 1,000. An even better measure considers the birth rates of specific age cohorts. The *age-specific fertility rate* (ASFR) equals the number of births in a given year to women between the ages x and x plus five (five-

Figure 10.5
Example of an Age-Sex Pyramid Useful in Historical Demography

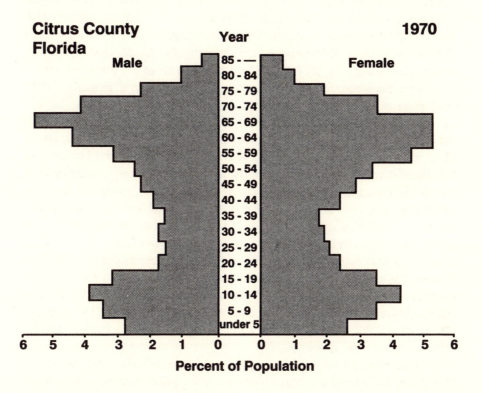

Source: Adapted from U.S. Department of Commerce, *Census '80: Continuing the Factfinder Tradition* (Washington, D.C.: Government Printing Office, 1980), 206.

year age increments are most commonly used); divided by the total number of women between the ages x and x plus five; times 1,000. You then get birth rates for each five-year age cohort (twenty to twenty-four, twenty-five to twenty-nine, etc.). The final measure is the *total fertility rate* (TFR). It is calculated by multiplying each of the age-specific fertility rates by five and then totaling these products. That sum is equal to the total number of children for every 1,000 women of childbearing age. Dividing by 1,000 calculates the average number of children per woman of childbearing age.

The third general area of historical demography is mortality. The most common measure of mortality is the average age at death. Technically, it changes for each age cohort; the life expectancy of newborns is lower than that of ten year olds, for example. The *life table* is a statistical device that provides the average age at death. Englishman John Graunt first developed it in the seventeenth century to delineate varying mortality rates for different sections of London. In the United States, there are separate tables for each year of birth and for both males and females.[20] The *crude death rate* (CDR) is calculated by dividing the total number of deaths in a given year by the average population of that year, times 1,000. One can also compute *age-sex-specific death rates* (ASDR). One calculates them by dividing the number of deaths of one sex or one age cohort or both by the number of people in that age cohort or of that sex. Another index of mortality is *infant mortality*. It is the number of deaths of children less than one year old per 1,000 live births. One can also figure infant mortality rates for different sexes and races.

Another component of demography is migration. *External migration* includes both *emigration* (leaving one's country) and *immigration* (settling in a new country). In determining population change, the researcher must consider the migration rate along with natural increase. Another component of migration is *internal migration*. It includes settlement patterns and the extent of geographical or horizontal mobility within a given geographical area.

There are numerous examples of research that employ historical demography. Gretchen Condran and Ellen Kramarow's research on child mortality among Jewish immigrants to the United States,[21] Anne McCants's research on late eighteenth-century and early nineteenth-century domestic migration in Friesland, the Dutch Republic,[22] and Lee Bean and his co-workers' study of infant mortality and fertility on the American frontier[23] exemplify the diversity of this research.

Concerns of Data Gathering

Sources and accuracy of the data are major concerns for historical demographers.[24] For most countries, only fragmentary demographic data are available before the twentieth century. Annual editions of the United Nations' *Demographic Yearbook* have improved that situation recently. The United States and some countries in Western Europe collected and published census data beginning in the late eighteenth century. At times these data are sufficiently detailed to calculate some demographic characteristics.

The process of gathering information about families and, ultimately, communities to study their demographic characteristics is called *family reconstitution*.[25] Usually it is based on parish church records, which are extant back to the sixteenth century in certain locales in Europe. With this process, the historical demographer can re-create information about individuals, families, and communities in sufficient detail to study them demographically. This procedure provides information that is not easily accessible from the aggregations contained in census records. Parish records typically include three dates for each individual: the dates of baptism, marriage, and death. While it appears that these dates offer scant information, we can determine infant mortality, life expectancy, age at first marriage, delay between marriage and birth of first child, delay between death of first spouse and remarriage, fertility rates, and many other demographic characteristics.

Philip Greven's study of colonial Andover, Massachusetts, provides an example of research based on family reconstitution. In this study, Greven began with the twenty-eight families who were the first permanent settlers of the town. He then reconstituted their families and the families of the next three generations. In all, he studied 247 families and more than 2,000 individuals.[26]

As Greven and others have pointed out, however, these techniques are not without problems. Unfortunately, historical demographers cannot simply identify the appropriate formula and calculate the results. When the sources are fragmentary or biased, these techniques should not be used.[27]

Record Linkage

Record linkage—merging data about an individual (or other unit of analysis) in one source with information about that same individual in other sources —becomes very important in using data for demographic analysis.

Record linkage can be either vertical, linking information about a person over time from different sources, or horizontal, linking information about a person at the same time from different sources. Occasionally, opportunities for both types of linkage are available.

Unfortunately, linking two or more different sources poses problems. Consider the example of using two successive censuses to explore persistence in a particular neighborhood. There are several explanations why an individual might appear in the first census, but not in the second. One explanation is that the individual has moved. But there are also others. One is death. Mistakes by either of the two census enumerators might also make it appear as if an individual no longer resides at the same address. Illegible handwriting, misspelling of surnames, and errors in recording addresses can and do occur. Concluding that a person has moved may, therefore, be unfounded.

Despite these problems, the opportunities for record linkage are too valuable to be ignored. The problem of misspelled names has also arisen in industry; airplane companies and people responsible for keeping medical records, for example, also encounter difficulties with record linkage.[28] These experiences have led to some possible solutions. One is to identify possible matches between names appearing in two or more sources either by hand or with a computer program. Initially, most researchers believed that hand linkage was more accurate. Several studies have demonstrated that one can achieve comparable results with a computer at a significantly reduced cost and in less time.[29] As computerized-record linkage has been more widely accepted, there have been further refinements to improve its accuracy and speed by using either mainframes or personal computers.[30]

One linkage method is a form of SOUNDEX, a procedure that assigns a letter and a three-number code to each surname. For example, the SOUNDEX code for the name Adams is A350. The codes facilitate comparing lists of names. The SOUNDEX method is most appropriate for common names; it has not proved to be applicable for all names. To accommodate these problems, variations have been developed for French-Canadian names[31] and eighteenth-century English names.[32]

Once pairs of surnames are identified, the demographer can compare other variables. It is at this stage that important decisions are made. If not all the variables match up exactly, which ones are more important? How much divergence can we tolerate? Scholars using record linkage have determined that age will not always be a reliable way to generate potential matches. Depending on the month of a census enumeration, there may be a variance of up to two years in a person's age from one decennial census to the next. It is also common for people to round their ages to the nearest decade, making it difficult to locate them in birth registers. Others have suggested relying on information about spouses and children. This procedure, however, is limited to those individuals who were married and had children.

An additional problem involves sampling; one cannot sample each source from which a researcher hopes to link records. One solution is to employ a *letter-cluster sample*. This process involves randomly selecting several letters of the alphabet from the most complete source and compiling information from all the other sources only on those individuals whose surnames begin with those letters. While recognizing that there are some problems inherent with this procedure (some letters of the alphabet will result in an ethnic bias, for example), proponents argue that this solution is the most viable for large groups.[33]

Computers can facilitate record linkage in several ways. For historians who prefer to link records themselves, computers can locate and reorganize records and produce lists. Once entered, records can be recalled, reorganized, matched, and processed easily. Standard statistical analysis programs can be used to match and merge records.

Appendix

Determining Probabilities Associated with Test Statistics: BASIC Computer Programs and Tables of Critical Values

In Chapters 4, 5, 6, 7, 8, and 9 we discussed testing hypotheses using z, t, chi-square, and F. In each instance we explained the formula and technique for calculating the statistic. Associated with each of these statistics is a distribution that takes a certain form if the null hypothesis is correct. To decide whether to accept or reject the null hypothesis, we determined the probability of observing a test statistic as large or larger than the one calculated from observed data if the null hypothesis is correct. Determining this probability involves calculating a certain area under the distribution curve in question. There are two ways to accomplish this. The first uses tables of critical values for certain areas, and the second uses computer programs to approximate the areas directly. Most texts include tables of critical test statistic values, and most statistical-analysis computer packages calculate probabilities.

Here, we do both. Throughout this book we have shown all our calculations and emphasized that all the basic statistical work can be done by hand. The purpose was to demystify the procedures by carefully taking the reader through all the operations. Some brief comments concerning the calculation of areas under a curve will complete this process and serve to introduce the BASIC computer programs.

SIMPSON'S RULE

Integral calculus is a branch of mathematics concerned with determining areas under curves. While there are a number of ways to approach this, here we use Simpson's Rule or Simpson's Method. Thomas Simpson (1710–1761) was a mathematician who taught at the Royal Military Academy in Woolwich, England. To illustrate his method, we begin with a vertical (y) and horizontal (x) axis upon which a standard normal (z) curve is plotted. The goal is to determine the area defined by the interval greater than a z-value of +1.96. We know that half the area under the curve is defined by z-values greater than zero. We will determine the area under the curve from zero to 1.96 and subtract this from .5 to determine the area in question.

Simpson's method divides the interval (here, 0–1.96) into an even number of segments. Each of the segments is treated as the area under the arc of a parabola. A simple formula gives a good approximation of the true area (see Figure A.1). Obviously, the greater the number of the segments, the closer the approximation will be. Here we divide the area under the standard normal distribution from zero to 1.96 into six segments of equal width, each width being (1/6) X 1.96. On the horizontal axis, then, the several z_i values defining the segments are:

$$z_1 = (0/6) \text{ X } 1.96$$
$$z_2 = (1/6) \text{ X } 1.96$$
$$z_3 = (2/6) \text{ X } 1.96$$
$$z_4 = (3/6) \text{ X } 1.96$$
$$z_5 = (4/6) \text{ X } 1.96$$
$$z_6 = (5/6) \text{ X } 1.96$$
$$z_7 = (6/6) \text{ X } 1.96$$

The corresponding y_i values are calculated from the formula for the standard normal distribution, as follows:

$$y = \frac{1}{\sqrt{2\pi}} e^{-z^2/2}$$

We notice that if

$$1/\sqrt{2\pi} = 1/\sqrt{2 \text{ X } 3.141592654}$$
$$= .398942280$$

and e, the mathematical constant, is 2.718281828, then,

$$y_1 = .398942280 \text{ X } 2.718281828^{\,-[(0/6)1.96]^2/2}$$
$$= .398942280$$
$$y_2 = .398942280 \text{ X } 2.718281828^{\,-[(1/6)1.96]^2/2}$$
$$= .378214385$$

Figure A.1
Calculation of Area under Curve Using Simpson's Rule

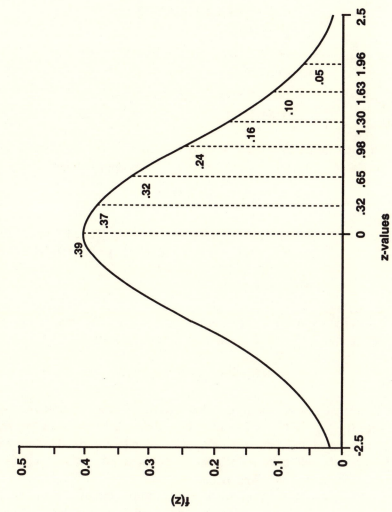

$$y_3 = .398942280 \times 2.718281828^{-[(2/6)1.96]^2/2}$$
$$= .322271553$$

$$y_4 = .398942280 \times 2.718281828^{-[(3/6)1.96]^2/2}$$
$$= .246809491$$

$$y_5 = .398942280 \times 2.718281828^{-[(4/6)1.96]^2/2}$$
$$= .169886039$$

$$y_6 = .398942280 \times 2.718281828^{-[(5/6)1.96]^2/2}$$
$$= .105101637$$

$$y_7 = .398942280 \times 2.718281828^{-[(6/6)1.96]^2/2}$$
$$= .058440944$$

If h is the segment width—here, h = (1/6) X 1.96—then Simpson's Rule calculates the area between zero and 1.96 as approximately:

$$\cong (h/3)(y_1 + 4y_2 + 2y_3 + 4y_4 + 2y_5 + 4y_6 + y_7)$$

$$\cong [(1/6 \times 1.96]/3)[.398942280 + 4(.378214385) +$$
$$2(.322271553) + 4(.246809491) + 2(.169886039) +$$
$$4(.105101637) + .058440944]$$
$$\cong .474995161$$

If the area from zero to 1.96 is approximately .474995161, then the area greater than 1.96—that is, the area of interest—is:

$$.5 - .474995161 = .025004839$$

which is the approximate one-tailed probability. The two-tailed probability is twice this, or .050009678. Simpson's Rule, even with only six segments, gives a very good approximation of areas under the standard normal distribution—the tabulated values being .025 and .05, respectively (see Table A.1 at the end of this Appendix).

Each of our computer programs prompts the user for the number of iterations desired. This determines the number of y_i values calculated; the number of segments will be one less than the number supplied. *The user must supply an odd number* so that there will be an even number of segments—a requirement of Simpson's Method. Generally, 100 segments (101 iterations) will give good approximations when the true probability is .05 or larger, and 500 segments (501 iterations) should give good results for smaller probabilities. Oscar Kempthorne and J. Leroy Folks describe several functions yielding the curves of interest.[1]

Tabulated Values

We used 2,000 segments to determine the tabulated values. The smallest value for the test statistic (before rounding) that has a probability less than the probability of interest was tabulated. For example, the z-value tabulated for a one-tailed probability of .25 is 0.68 (see Table A.1 at the end of this Appendix). The one-tailed probability for 0.6744443 (which rounds to 0.67) is .250014350 (larger than .25), while the one-tailed probability for 0.6844443 (which rounds to 0.68) is .246847350—less than .25. Thus, 0.68 is the smallest value (after rounding) with a one-tailed probability less than .25. If we were testing the significance of the difference between two sample means, and the null hypothesis was that the population means were the same, then—if the null hypothesis was correct—the probability of a z-value of 0.68 or larger would be less than .25.

THE STANDARD NORMAL (z) DISTRIBUTION

Program A.1 at the end of this Appendix calculates the area under the curve from zero (the center of the distribution) to the observed z-value and subtracts this area from .5. The result is the one-tailed probability. Twice this probability is the two-tailed probability. For values of z larger than 6.0, probabilities are not calculated. Instead, the program indicates the one-tailed probability is less than .000000298 and the two-tailed probability is less than .000000596. As mentioned above, the height of the curve (y) for a particular z-value is given by the formula

$$y = \frac{1}{\sqrt{2\pi}} e^{-z^2/2}$$

where e and π are mathematical constants.

THE t-DISTRIBUTION

As with the standard normal (z) distribution, Program A.2 calculates the area from zero (the center of the distribution) to the observed t-value and subtracts this area from .5. The result is the one-tailed probability of t. Twice this area is the two- tailed probability. For degrees of freedom larger than 600, we used the normal (z) distribution, rather than the t-distribution. The height of the curve (y) for a particular t-value is given by the formula

$$y = \frac{\Gamma[(d+1)/2]}{\sqrt{d\pi}\Gamma(d/2)}(1+t^2/d)^{-(d+1)/2}$$

where d represents the degrees of freedom
π is a mathematical constant
Γ is the gamma function[2]

THE CHI-SQUARE DISTRIBUTION

For chi-square with one degree of freedom, Program A.3 converts the observed chi-square value to a z-score (by taking the square root of the chi-square value). We determine the probability associated with the chi-square value using the standard normal (z) distribution. For degrees of freedom from two to sixty, we calculate the area under the chi-square distribution from zero to the observed chi-square value and then subtract it from one to give the probability of a larger value. Probabilities for chi-square values with degrees of freedom larger than sixty should not be calculated with this program. The formula for the height (y) of the chi-square distribution for a given chi-square value and degrees of freedom is:

$$y = \frac{[x^{(d/2)-1}](e^{-x/2})}{(2^{d/2})\Gamma(d/2)}$$

where x is the chi-square value
d represents the degrees of freedom
Γ is the gamma function.[3]

THE F-DISTRIBUTION

The F-distribution involves both explained and unexplained degrees of freedom. When the explained degree of freedom is one, the observed F-value is converted to a t (or z, if the unexplained degrees of freedom exceed

600) value by taking the square root of F. The probability of F is then calculated by Program A.4 using the t (or z) distribution. When the explained degrees of freedom are less than, or equal, to the unexplained degrees of freedom, the reciprocal of the F-value (1/F) is calculated, the degrees of freedom are reversed, and the area under the curve from zero to 1/F determined. That is the appropriate probability. When the explained degrees of freedom are greater than one and less than the unexplained degrees of freedom, the area from zero to the observed F-value is determined and subtracted from one to produce the appropriate probability. The formula for the height (y) of the F-distribution for a given F-value is:

$$y = \frac{a^{a/2} b^{b/2} F^{(a/2)-1}}{B(a/2, b/2)(b + aF)^{(a+b)/2}}$$

where a represents the explained degrees of freedom
b represents the unexplained degrees of freedom
B is the beta function[4]

Program A.1
A BASIC Program to Calculate Areas under the Standard
Normal (z) Distribution

```
10 REM  Z TEST
20 PRINT "input absolute value of z"
30 INPUT Z
40 PRINT "input number of iterations (enter an odd number)"
50 INPUT Q
60 IF (Z>6) GOTO 190
70 S=0
80 FOR J=2 TO (Q-3) STEP 2
90 S=S+4*(.39894228#/(EXP(1)^(((((J-1)*Z)/(Q-1))^2)/2)))
100 S=S+2*(.39894228#/(EXP(1)^((((J*Z)/(Q-1))^2)/2)))
110 NEXT J
120 S=S+4*(.39894228#/(EXP(1)^((((((Q-2)*Z)/(Q-1))^2)/2)))
130 S=S+(.39894228#/(EXP(1)^((((((Q-1)*Z)/(Q-1))^2)/2)))
140 S=S+(.39894228#/(EXP(1)^((((0*Z)/(Q-1))^2)/2)))
150 R=.5-((Z/(3*(Q-1)))*S)
160 PRINT "z = ",Z,"one tail prob. = ",R
170 PRINT "z = ",Z,"two tail prob. = ",2*R
180 GOTO 210
190 PRINT "z = ",Z,"one tail prob. < 2.980232E-07"
200 PRINT "z = ",Z,"two tail prob. < 5.960465E-07"
210 END
```

Program A.2
A BASIC Program to Calculate Areas under the t-Distribution

```
10 REM T TEST
20 PRINT "input absolute value of t"
30 INPUT T
40 PRINT "input degrees of freedom"
50 INPUT G
60 PRINT "input iterations (enter an odd number)"
70 INPUT Q
80 S=0
90 IF (T > 6 AND G > 600) GOTO 550
100 IF (G>600) GOTO 400
110 H(1)=G/2
120 H(2)=(G+1)/2
130 C(1)=.9189385332046727#
140 C(2)=8.333333333333333D-02
150 C(3)=2.777777777777777D-03
160 C(4)=7.936507936507936D-04
170 C(5)=5.952380952380952D-04
180 C(6)=3.141592654#
190 FOR J=1 TO 2
200 V=1!
210 Z=H(J)
220 IF (Z>18#) GOTO 260
230 V=V*Z
240 Z=Z+1
250 GOTO 220
260 U=1#/Z^2
270 B(J)=(Z-.5#)*LOG(Z)-Z+C(1)-LOG(V)+(1#/Z)*(C(2)-
      U*(C(3)+(U*(C(4)-(U*(C(5)))))))
280 NEXT J
290 FOR J=2 TO (Q-3) STEP 2
300 REM ****
310 REM CALCULATION OF AREAS
320 REM ****
330 S=S+4*(((EXP(1)^(B(2)-B(1)))/SQR(C(6)*G))*(1+(((((J-1)*T)/
      (Q-1))^2)/G))^-((G+1)/2))
340 S=S+2*(((EXP(1)^(B(2)-B(1)))/SQR(C(6)*G))*(1+(((((J*T)/(Q-
      1))^2)/G))^-((G+1)/2))
```

Program A.2, continued

```
350 NEXT J
360 S=S+4*(((EXP(1)^(B(2)-B(1)))/SQR(C(6)*G))*(1+(((((Q-2)*T)/
      (Q-1))^2)/G))^-((G+1)/2))
370 S=S+(((EXP(1)^(B(2)-B(1)))/SQR(C(6)*G))*(1+(((((Q-1)*T)/(Q-
      1))^2)/G))^-((G+1)/2))
380 S=S+(((EXP(1)^(B(2)-B(1)))/SQR(C(6)*G))*(1+(((((0*T)/(Q-
      1))^2)/G))^-((G+1)/2))
390 GOTO 470
400 FOR J=2 TO (Q-3) STEP 2
410 S=S+4*(.39894228#/(EXP(1)^(((((J-1)*T)/(Q-1))^2)/2)))
420 S=S+2*(.39894228#/(EXP(1)^((((J*T)/(Q-1))^2)/2)))
430 NEXT J
440 S=S+4*(.39894228#/(EXP(1)^(((((Q-2)*T)/(Q-1))^2)/2)))
450 S=S+(.39894228#/(EXP(1)^(((((Q-1)*T)/(Q-1))^2)/2)))
460 S=S+(.39894228#/(EXP(1)^((((0*T)/(Q-1))^2)/2)))
470 R=.5-((T/(3*(Q-1)))*S)
480 IF (R < 0) GOTO 520
490 PRINT "t = ",T,"DF =",G,"one tail prob. = ",R
500 PRINT "t = ",T,"DF =",G,"two tail prob. = ",2*R
510 GOTO 570
520 PRINT "t = ",T,"DF =",G,"one tail prob. < .001"
530 PRINT "t = ",T,"DF =",G,"two tail prob. < .002"
540 GOTO 570
550 PRINT "t = ",T,"DF =",G,"one tail prob. < 2.980232E-07"
560 PRINT "t = ",T,"DF =",G,"two tail prob. < 5.960465E-07"
570 END
```

Program A.3
A BASIC Program to Calculate Areas under the Chi-Square Distribution

```
10 REM CHI SQUARE TEST
20 PRINT "input value of chi square"
30 INPUT X#
40 PRINT "input degrees of freedom"
50 INPUT D#
60 IF (D#=1 AND X#> 10.828) GOTO 650
70 IF ((D#>1 AND D#<4) AND X#>6*SQR(2*D#)+D#) GOTO 650
80 IF (D#>4 AND X#> 5*SQR(2*D#)+D#) GOTO 650
90 PRINT "input iterations (enter an odd number)"
100 INPUT Q#
110 IF (D#=1) THEN X#=SQR(X#)
120 S#=0#
130 IF (D#=1#) GOTO 300
140 C#(1)=.9189385332046727#
150 C#(2)=8.333333333333333D-02
160 C#(3)=2.777777777777777D-03
170 C#(4)=7.936507936507936D-04
180 C#(5)=5.952380952380952D-04
190 H#=1#
200 E#=D#/2
210 IF (E#>18#) GOTO 250
220 H#=H#*E#
230 E#=E#+1#
240 GOTO 210
250 U#=1#/E#^2
260 G#=(E#-.5#)*LOG(E#)-E#+C#(1)-LOG(H#)+(1#/E#)*(C#(2)-
      U#*(C#(3)+(U#*(C#(4)-(U#*(C#(5)))))))
270 G#=EXP(1)^G#
280 IF (D#=2#) THEN G#=1#
290 IF (D#>1#) GOTO 380
300 FOR J=2 TO (Q#-3#) STEP 2
310 S#=S#+4*(.39894228#/(EXP(1)^(((((J-1)*X#)/(Q#-1))^2)/2#)))
320 S#=S#+2*(.39894228#/(EXP(1)^((((J*X#)/(Q#-1))^2)/2#)))
330 NEXT J
340 S#=S#+4*(.39894228#/(EXP(1)^(((((Q#-2)*X#)/(Q#-1))^2)/2#)))
350 S#=S#+(.39894228#/(EXP(1)^(((((Q#-1)*X#)/(Q#-1))^2)/2#)))
```

Program A.3, continued

```
360 S#=S#+(.39894228#/(EXP(1)^((((0*X#)/(Q#-1))^2)/2#)))
370 GOTO 580
380 FOR J=2 TO (Q#-3#) STEP 2
390 W#=((J-1)*X#)/(Q#-1)
400 A#=(((D#/2#)-1#)*LOG(W#)+(-W#/2#))-((D#/
      2#)*LOG(2#)+LOG(G#))
410 IF (A#<-70.01#) THEN A#=-70.01#
420 S#=S#+4*(EXP(1#)^A#)
430 W#=(J*X#)/(Q#-1)
440 A#=(((D#/2#)-1#)*LOG(W#)+(-W#/2#))-((D#/
      2#)*LOG(2#)+LOG(G#))
450 IF (A#<-70.01#) THEN A#=-70.01#
460 S#=S#+2*(EXP(1#)^A#)
470 NEXT J
480 W#=((Q#-2)*X#)/(Q#-1)
490 A#=(((D#/2#)-1#)*LOG(W#)+(-W#/2#))-((D#/
      2#)*LOG(2#)+LOG(G#))
500 IF (A#<-70.01#) THEN A#=-70.01#
510 S#=S#+4*(EXP(1#)^A#)
520 W#=((Q#-1)*X#)/(Q#-1)
530 A#=(((D#/2#)-1#)*LOG(W#)+(-W#/2#))-((D#/
      2#)*LOG(2#)+LOG(G#))
540 IF (A#<-70.01#) THEN A#=-70.01#
550 S#=S#+(EXP(1#)^A#)
560 IF (D#=2) THEN S#=S#+.5: IF (D#>2) THEN S#=S#+0
570 IF (D#>1#) GOTO 600
580 R#=2*(.5#-((X#/(3#*(Q#-1)))*S#))
590 GOTO 610
600 R#=1#-((X#/(3#*(Q#-1#)))*S#)
610 IF (D#=1#) THEN X#=X#^2
620 IF (R#<0#) GOTO 650
630 PRINT "Chi Square = ",X#,"DF =",D#,"prob. = ",R#
640 GOTO 660
650 PRINT "Chi Square = ",X#,"DF =",D#,"prob. < .001"
660 END
```

Program A.4
A BASIC Program to Calculate Areas under the F-Distribution

```
10 REM F RATIO
20 PRINT "input value of F"
30 INPUT F
40 PRINT "input explained degrees of freedom"
50 INPUT G(1)
60 PRINT "input unexplained degrees of freedom"
70 INPUT G(2)
80 PRINT "input iterations (enter an odd number)"
90 INPUT Q
100 S=0
110 Y=0
120 IF (G(1) >= G(2)) THEN Y=1
130 IF (Y <>1) GOTO 180
140 G(3)=G(1)
150 G(1)=G(2)
160 G(2)=G(3)
170 F=1/F
180 IF (G(1) = 1 AND F>36 AND G(2)>600) GOTO 1010
190 IF (G(1) >1 AND F>(G(2)/(G(2)-2))*15) GOTO 1030
200 IF (G(1) = 1 AND G(2) >600) GOTO 550
210 IF (G(1) > 1) GOTO 260
220 H(1)=G(2)/2
230 H(2)=(G(2)+1)/2
240 H(3)=2
250 GOTO 290
260 H(1)=G(1)/2
270 H(2)=G(2)/2
280 H(3)=H(1)+H(2)
290 C(1)=.9189385332046727#
300 C(2)=8.333333333333333D-02
310 C(3)=2.777777777777777D-03
320 C(4)=7.936507936507936D-04
330 C(5)=5.952380952380952D-04
340 C(6)=3.141592654#
350 FOR J=1 TO 3
360 T=1!
370 Z=H(J)
380 IF (Z>18#) GOTO 420
```

Program A.4, continued

```
390 T=T*Z
400 Z=Z+1
410 GOTO 380
420 U=1#/Z^2
430 B(J)=(Z-.5#)*LOG(Z)-Z+C(1)-LOG(T)+(1#/Z)*(C(2)-
      U*(C(3)+(U*(C(4)-(U*(C(5)))))))
440 NEXT J
450 B(4)=(B(1)+B(2))-B(3)
460 IF (G(1)>1) GOTO 630
470 FOR J=2 TO (Q-3) STEP 2
480 S=S+4*(((EXP(1)^(B(2)-B(1)))/SQR(C(6)*G(2)))*(1+(((((J-
      1)*SQR(F))/(Q-1))^2)/G(2)))^-((G(2)+1)/2))
490 S=S+2*(((EXP(1)^(B(2)-B(1)))/     SQR(C(6)*G(2)))
      *(1+(((((J*SQR(F))/(Q-1))^2)/G(2)))^-((G(2)+1)/2))
500 NEXT J
510 S=S+4*(((EXP(1)^(B(2)-B(1)))/SQR(C(6)*G(2)))*(1+(((((Q-
      2)*SQR(F))/(Q-1))^2)/G(2)))^-((G(2)+1)/2))
520 S=S+(((EXP(1)^(B(2)-B(1)))/SQR(C(6)*G(2)))*(1+(((((Q-
      1)*SQR(F))/(Q-1))^2)/G(2)))^-((G(2)+1)/2))
530 S=S+(((EXP(1)^(B(2)-B(1)))/SQR(C(6)*G(2)))*(1+(((((0*SQR(F))/
      (Q-1))^2)/G(2)))^-((G(2)+1)/2))
540 GOTO 820
550 FOR J=2 TO (Q-3) STEP 2
560 S=S+4*(.39894228#/(EXP(1)^(((((J-1)*SQR(F))/(Q-1))^2)/2)))
570 S=S+2*(.39894228#/(EXP(1)^((((J*SQR(F))/(Q-1))^2)/2)))
580 NEXT J
590 S=S+4*(.39894228#/(EXP(1)^(((((Q-2)*SQR(F))/(Q-1))^2)/2)))
600 S=S+(.39894228#/(EXP(1)^(((((Q-1)*SQR(F))/(Q-1))^2)/2)))
610 S=S+(.39894228#/(EXP(1)^((((0*SQR(F))/(Q-1))^2)/2)))
620 GOTO 810
630 FOR J=2 TO (Q-3) STEP 2
640 W=((J-1)*F)/(Q-1)
650 A=((G(1)/2)*LOG(G(1))+(G(2)/2)*LOG(G(2))+((G(1)/2)-
      1)*LOG(W))
660 IF (A<-70.01) THEN A=-70.01
670 S=S+4*EXP(1)^(A-(B(4)+((G(1)+G(2))/
      2)*(LOG(G(2)+G(1)*W))))
680 W=(J*F)/(Q-1)
690 A=((G(1)/2)*LOG(G(1))+(G(2)/2)*LOG(G(2))+((G(1)/2)-
      1)*LOG(W))
```

Program A.4, continued

```
700 IF (A<-70.01) THEN A=-70.01
710 S=S+2*EXP(1)^(A-(B(4)+((G(1)+G(2))/
        2)*(LOG(G(2)+G(1)*W))))
720 NEXT J
730 W=((Q-2)*F)/(Q-1)
740 A=((G(1)/2)*LOG(G(1))+(G(2)/2)*LOG(G(2))+((G(1)/2)-
        1)*LOG(W))
750 IF (A<-70.01) THEN A=-70.01
760 S=S+4*EXP(1)^(A-(B(4)+((G(1)+G(2))/
        2)*(LOG(G(2)+G(1)*W))))
770 W=((Q-1)*F)/(Q-1)
780 A=((G(1)/2)*LOG(G(1))+(G(2)/2)*LOG(G(2))+((G(1)/2)-
        1)*LOG(W))
790 IF (A<-70.01) THEN A=-70.01
800 S=S+EXP(1)^(A-(B(4)+((G(1)+G(2))/2)*(LOG(G(2)+G(1)*W))))
810 IF (G(1) > 1) GOTO 910
820 R=2*(.5-((SQR(F)/(3*(Q-1)))*S))
830 IF (Y<>1) GOTO 920
840 R=1-R
850 G(3)=G(1)
860 G(1)=G(2)
870 G(2)=G(3)
880 F=1/F
890 IF (R<0) GOTO 1030
900 GOTO 990
910 R=1-((F/(3*(Q-1)))*S)
920 IF (R<0) GOTO 1030
930 IF (Y<>1) GOTO 990
940 R=1-R
950 G(3)=G(1)
960 G(1)=G(2)
970 G(2)=G(3)
980 F=1/F
990 PRINT "F = ",F,"DF =",G(1),",",G(2),"prob. = ",R
1000 GOTO 1040
1010 PRINT "F = ",F,"DF =",G(1),",",G(2),"prob. < 5.960465E-07"
1020 GOTO 1040
1030 PRINT "F = ",F,"DF =",G(1),",",G(2),"prob. <.005"
1040 END
```

Table A.1
Certain Critical z-Values

Critical z-value	Probability	
	One-tailed	Two-tailed
0.68	.25	.5
1.65	.05	.10
1.96	.025	.05
2.24	.0125	.025
2.34	.01	.02
2.58	.005	.01
2.81	.0025	.005
3.29	.0005	.001

Source: Authors' calculations.

Table A.2
Certain Critical t-Values

Degrees of Freedom	Critical t-Values	
	One-tailed Probability <.05 Two-tailed Probability <.10	One-tailed Probability <.025 Two-tailed Probability <.05
1	6.31	12.71
2	2.92	4.30
3	2. 35	3.18
4	2.13	2.78
5	2.02	2.57
6	1.94	2.45
7	1.90	2.37
8	1.86	2.31
9	1.83	2.26
10	1.81	2.23
11	1.80	2.20
12	1.78	2.18
13	1.77	2.16
14	1.76	2.15
15	1.75	2.13
16	1.75	2.12
17	1.74	2.11
18	1.73	2.10
19	1.73	2.09
20	1.73	2.09
21	1.72	2.08
22	1.72	2.07
23	1.71	2.07
24	1.71	2.06
25	1.71	2.06
26	1.71	2.06
27	1.70	2.05
28	1.70	2.05
29	1.70	2.05
30	1.70	2.04
31	1.70	2.04
32	1.69	2.04
33	1.69	2.04
34	1.69	2.03
35	1.69	2.03
36	1.69	2.03
37	1.69	2.03
38	1.69	2.03
39	1.69	2.02
40	1.68	2.02
41	1.68	2.02
42	1.68	2.02
43	1.68	2.02
44	1.68	2.02
45	1.68	2.01
100	1.66	1.98
z	1.65	1.96

Source: Authors' calculations.

Table A.3
Certain Critical Chi-square Values

Degrees of Freedom	Critical Chi-square Values for Probability <.05
1	3.84
2	5.99
3	7.82
4	9.49
5	11.07
6	12.59
7	14.07
8	15.51
9	16.92
10	18.31
11	19.68
12	21.03
13	22.36
14	23.69
15	25.00
16	26.30
17	27.59
18	28.87
19	30.14
20	31.41

Source: Authors' calculations.

Table A.4
Certain Critical F-Values

Unexplained Degrees of Freedom	Critical F-Values for Probability < .05								
	Explained Degrees of Freedom								
	1	2	3	4	5	6	7	8	9
9	5.12	4.29	3.86	3.63	3.48	3.37	3.29	3.23	3.18
10	4.97	4.13	3.71	3.48	3.33	3.22	3.14	3.07	3.02
11	4.84	4.01	3.59	3.36	3.20	3.10	3.01	2.95	2.90
12	4.75	3.91	3.49	3.26	3.11	3.00	2.91	2.85	2.80
13	4.67	3.83	3.41	3.18	3.03	2.92	2.83	2.77	2.71
14	4.60	3.76	3.34	3.11	2.96	2.85	2.76	2.70	2.65
15	4.54	3.70	3.29	3.06	2.90	2.79	2.71	2.64	2.59
16	4.49	3.65	3.24	3.01	2.85	2.74	2.66	2.59	2.54
17	4.45	3.61	3.20	2.97	2.81	2.70	2.61	2.55	2.49
18	4.41	3.57	3.16	2.93	2.77	2.66	2.58	2.51	2.46
19	4.38	3.54	3.13	2.90	2.74	2.63	2.54	2.48	2.42
20	4.35	3.51	3.10	2.87	2.71	2.60	2.51	2.45	2.39
21	4.33	3.48	3.07	2.84	2.69	2.57	2.49	2.42	2.37
22	4.30	3.46	3.05	2.82	2.66	2.55	2.46	2.40	2.34
23	4.28	3.44	3.03	2.80	2.64	2.53	2.44	2.38	2.32
24	4.26	3.42	3.01	2.78	2.62	2.51	2.42	2.36	2.30
25	4.24	3.40	2.99	2.76	2.60	2.49	2.41	2.34	2.28
26	4.23	3.38	2.98	2.74	2.59	2.47	2.39	2.32	2.27
27	4.21	3.37	2.96	2.73	2.57	2.46	2.37	2.31	2.25
28	4.20	3.35	2.95	2.71	2.56	2.45	2.36	2.29	2.24
29	4.18	3.34	2.93	2.70	2.55	2.43	2.35	2.28	2.22
30	4.17	3.33	2.92	2.69	2.53	2.42	2.33	2.27	2.21
31	4.16	3.32	2.91	2.68	2.52	2.41	2.32	2.26	2.20
40	4.09	3.25	2.84	2.61	2.45	2.34	2.25	2.18	2.12
50	4.03	3.20	2.79	2.56	2.40	2.29	2.20	2.13	2.07
60	4.00	3.16	2.76	2.53	2.37	2.25	2.17	2.10	2.04
70	3.98	3.14	2.74	2.50	2.35	2.23	2.14	2.07	2.02
80	3.96	3.12	2.72	2.49	2.33	2.21	2.13	2.06	2.00
90	3.95	3.11	2.71	2.47	2.32	2.20	2.11	2.04	1.99
100	3.94	3.10	2.70	2.46	2.31	2.19	2.10	2.03	1.98
1000	3.84	3.02	2.62	2.39	2.23	2.11	2.02	1.95	1.89
5000	3.84	3.00	2.57	2.35	2.23	2.11	2.01	1.92	1.88

Source: Authors' calculations.

Notes

CHAPTER 1

1. Allan G. Bogue, "The Quest for Numeracy: Data and Methods in American Political History," *Journal of Interdisciplinary History*, 21 (Summer 1990), 89–92.

2. Geoffrey Barraclough, "History," in Jacques Havet, ed., *Main Trends of Research in the Social and Human Sciences* (The Hague, Netherlands: Mouton Publishers, 1978), pt. 2, I:262–273.

3. Robert William Fogel, "The Limits of Quantitative Methods in History," *American Historical Review*, 80 (April 1975), 345.

4. Lawrence Stone, *The Past and the Present* (Boston: Routledge and Kegan Paul, 1981), 15.

5. Allan G. Bogue, *Clio & the Bitch Goddess: Quantification in American Political History* (Beverly Hills, CA: Sage Publications, 1983), 24. See also ibid., 207–213, 217–219, 221–229; Bogue, "The Quest for Numeracy," 89, 92.

6. Lee Benson, *Toward the Scientific Study of History: Selected Essays* (Philadelphia: J. B. Lippincott, 1972), 99.

7. Bogue, *Clio & the Bitch Goddess*, 30.

8. Bogue, "The Quest for Numeracy," 96–97.

9. Stone, *The Past and the Present*, 21. See also Carl Bridenbaugh, "The Great Mutation," *American Historical Review*, 68 (January 1963), 326; Gertrude Himmelfarb, *The New History and the Old* (Cambridge, MA: Belknap Press of Harvard University Press, 1987), 5; Stone, *The Past and the Present*, 31–32.

10. J. Morgan Kousser, "The State of Social Science History in the Late 1980s," *Historical Methods*, 22 (Winter 1989), 14.

11. Ibid., 16, 17.

12. For an interesting overview of the status of quantification, consult Konrad H. Jarausch, "Quantitative History in Transition," American Historical Association

Perspectives, 20 (September 1982), 14–16, 21; Charles M. Dollar and Richard J. Jensen, *Historian's Guide to Statistics: Quantitative Analysis and Historical Research* (New York: Holt, Rinehart, and Winston, 1971); Loren Haskins and Kirk Jeffrey, *Understanding Quantitative History* (New York: McGraw-Hill Publishing, 1990); Konrad H. Jarausch and Kenneth A. Hardy, *Quantitative Methods for Historians: A Guide to Research, Data, and Statistics* (Chapel Hill: University of North Carolina Press, 1991).

13. See G. W. Baethne, ed., *Practical Applications of the Punched Card Method in Colleges and Universities* (New York: Columbia University Press, 1935).

14. See Kenneth Janda, *Data Processing: Applications to Political Research*, 2nd ed. (Evanston, IL: Northwestern University Press, 1969).

15. See Stein Rokkan, "Archives for Secondary Analysis of Sample Survey Data: An Early Inquiry into the Prospects for Western Europe," *UNESCO International Social Science Journal*, 16 (1964), 49–62.

CHAPTER 2

1. For a discussion of polling and how the several populations sampled can produce different results, see Seymour Martin Lipset, "Different Polls, Different Results in 1980 Politics," *Public Opinion*, 3 (August/September 1980), 19–20, 60; Everett C. Ladd and G. Donald Ferree, "Were the Pollsters Really Wrong?" *Public Opinion*, 3 (December 1980/January 1981), 13–20.

2. See S. S. Stevens, "On the Theory of Scales of Measurement," *Science*, 103 (June 7, 1946), 677–680; Ernest Sondheimer and Alan Rogerson, *Numbers and Infinity: A Historical Account of Mathematical Concepts* (Cambridge, England: Cambridge University Press, 1981); H. Graham Flegg, *Numbers: Their History and Meaning* (New York: Schoken, 1983).

3. There are other types of variables defined by the suitable arithmetic operations. Typically, however, they are of little interest to historians. For a further discussion of some of these, see Clyde H. Coombs, *A Theory of Data* (New York: John Wiley and Sons, 1964).

4. See Bill Williams, *A Sampler on Sampling* (New York: Wiley, 1978), 46; Oskar Morgenstern, *On the Accuracy of Economic Observations*, 2nd ed. (Princeton, NJ: Princeton University Press, 1963).

5. See George Horace Gallup and Saul Forbes Rae, *The Pulse of Democracy: The Public-opinion Poll and How It Works* (New York: Simon and Schuster, 1940), 41–43; George Horace Gallup, *The Sophisticated Poll Watcher's Guide* (Princeton, NJ: Princeton Opinion Press, 1972), 64–70.

6. See Leslie Kish, *Survey Sampling* (New York: John Wiley and Sons, 1965), 36–40.

7. See Kish, *Survey Sampling*, 39; William Feller, *An Introduction to Probability Theory and Its Applications*, 2 vols. (New York: John Wiley and Sons, 1950), vol. 1, 164–165.

8. See R. Christian Johnson, "A Procedure for Sampling the Manuscript Census Schedules," *Journal of Interdisciplinary History*, 8 (Winter 1978), 515–530; R. Christian Johnson, "The 1900 Census Sampling Project: Methods and Procedures for Sampling and Data Entry," *Historical Methods*, 11 (Fall 1978), 147–151; Joel Perlmann, "Using Census Districts in Analysis, Record Linkage, and Sampling," *Journal of Interdisciplinary History*, 10 (Autumn 1979), 279–289.

9. The method described on page 15 can be used here to get an approximation.

10. Which sample provides reliable estimates will be considered in Chapter 4. A sample of a few hundred cases will be sufficient in most instances.

11. When computing statistics describing a sample constructed by combining several strata, special formula may be necessary; see Kish, *Survey Sampling*.

12. See John P. Robinson, Robert Athanasiou, and Kendra B. Head, *Measures of Occupational Attitudes and Occupational Characteristics* (Ann Arbor, MI: Institute for Social Research, 1969).

13. Michael B. Katz, "Occupational Classification in History," *Journal of Interdisciplinary History*, 3 (Summer 1972), 63–88.

14. Theodore Hershberg and Robert Dockhorn, "Occupational Classification," *Historical Methods Newsletter*, 9 (March–June 1976), 59–98.

15. Patrick M. Horan, "Occupational Mobility and Historical Social Structure," *Social Science History*, 9 (Winter 1985), 25–47.

16. Hershberg and Dockhorn, "Occupational Classification," 59–98.

17. Matthew Sobek, "Class Analysis and the U.S. Census Public Use Samples," *Historical Methods*, 24 (Fall 1991), 179.

18. David Herlihy and Christiane Klapisch-Zuber, *Tuscans and Their Families: A Study of the Florentine* Catasto *of 1427* (New Haven, CT: Yale University Press, 1985).

19. Theodore Hershberg et al., "Occupation and Ethnicity in Five Nineteenth-century Cities: A Collaborative Inquiry," *Historical Methods Newsletter*, 7 (June 1974), 174–216.

20. For an explanation of coding errors, consult A. Gordon Darroch and Michael D. Ornstein, "Error in Historical Data Files: A Research Note on the Automatic Detection of Error and on the Nature and Sources of Errors in Coding," *Historical Methods*, 12 (Fall 1979), 157–167.

21. Ansley J. Coale and Frederick F. Stephan, "The Case of the Indians and the Teen-age Widows," in Edward R. Tufte, ed., *The Quantitative Analysis of Social Problems* (Reading, MA: Addison-Wesley Publishing, 1970), 426–436.

22. Nancy Shoemaker, "The Census as Civilizer: American Indian Household Structure in the 1900 and 1910 U.S. Census," *Historical Methods*, 25 (Winter 1992), 4–11.

CHAPTER 3

1. A chi-square test (see Chapter 6) shows that it was very unlikely that men and women had the same probability of being literate; chi-square = 9.68, DF = 1, p < .0018.

2. J. M. Thompson, *The French Revolution* (New York: Oxford University Press, 1945), 539.

3. There is a considerable literature on cabinet duration. Here, we will define it as the months served consecutively, and not the period between elections.

4. Sir Maurice G. Kendall and Alan Stuart, *The Advanced Theory of Statistics*, 3 vols., 4th ed. (London: Charles Griffin, 1977–1983), vol. 1, 41.

5. See, for example, Dunham Jackson, "Note on the Median of a Set of Numbers," *Bulletin of the American Mathematical Society*, 27 (January 1921), 160.

6. See R. L. Plackett, "The Principle of the Arithmetic Mean," *Biometrika*, 45 (1958), 130–135.

7. Stephen M. Stigler, *The History of Statistics: The Measurement of Uncertainty before 1900* (Cambridge, MA: Belknap Press of Harvard University Press, 1986), 89–98.

8. Ibid., 158.

9. Quoted in ibid., 14–15.

10. Ibid., 141.

11. Ibid., 137.

12. Ibid., 25–31.

13. Quoted in ibid., 148.

14. Ibid.

15. For a discussion of these techniques, see Bonnie H. Erickson and T. A. Nosanchuk, *Understanding Data: An Introduction to Exploratory and Confirmatory Data Analysis for Students of the Social Sciences* (Milton Keynes, England: Open University Press, 1979), 38–42.

16. R. A. Fisher, "The Correlation between Relatives on the Supposition of Mendelian Inheritance," *Transactions of the Royal Society of Edinburgh*, 52 (1918/1919), 399–433; Kendall and Stuart, *The Advanced Theory of Statistics*, vol. 1, 44.

17. Kendall and Stuart, *The Advanced Theory of Statistics*, vol. 1, 41–42; Stigler, *The History of Statistics*, 265–299.

18. Adolphe Quetelet, *Letters Addressed to H.R.H. the Grand Duke of Saxe Cobourg and Gotha, on the Theory of Probabilities as Applied to the Moral and Political Sciences*, trans. by O. G. Downes (London: Layton, 1849).

19. Stigler, *The History of Statistics*, 271.

20. The issue of whether or not intelligence is normally distributed is a matter of debate.

21. Edward R. Tufte, *The Visual Display of Quantitative Information* (Cheshire, CT: Graphics Press, 1983), 107–121.

CHAPTER 4

1.   See I. Todhunter, *A History of the Mathematical Theory of Probability from the Time of Pascal to That of Laplace* (New York: G. E. Stechert, 1931); Helen M. Walker, *Studies in History of Statistical Method* (Baltimore: Williams and Wilkins, 1929); Ian Hacking, *Logic of Statistical Inference* (Cambridge, England: Cambridge University Press, 1965); and Oscar Kempthorne and Leroy Folks, *Probability, Statistics, and Data Analysis* (Ames: Iowa State University Press, 1971).

2.   See Ludwig Boltzmann, *Lectures on Gas Theory*, trans. by Stephen G. Brush (Berkeley: University of California Press, 1964); A. d'Abro, *The Rise of the New Physics*, 2 vols. (New York: Dover Publishing, 1951).

3.   Werner Heisenberg et al., *On Modern Physics* (New York: Collier Books, 1962), 16.

4.   Emile Durkheim, *Suicide: A Study in Sociology*, trans. by John A. Spaulding and George Simpson (New York: Free Press, 1951).

5.   The frequency theory of probability is associated with John Venn and Richard von Mises. See John Venn, *The Logic of Chance*, 4th ed. (New York: Chelsea Publishing, 1962); Richard von Mises, *Probability, Statistics, and Truth* (New York: Macmillan, 1957).

6.   See Jacob Bernoulli, *Ars conjectandi* (Basil: Thurnisiorum, 1713); Pierre Simon Laplace, *Essai Philosophique sur les Probabilités*, 2nd ed. (Paris: Ve Courcier, 1814); John Maynard Keynes, *A Treatise on Probability* (New York: Harper and Row, 1962).

7.   See Frank Plumpton Ramsey, *The Foundations of Mathematics, and Other Logical Essays* (Paterson, NJ: Littlefield, Adams, 1960), 188–189.

8.   Ibid., 195.

9.   For the subjectivist view, see Leonard J. Savage, *The Foundations of Statistics* (New York: John Wiley and Sons, 1954); D. V. Lindley, *Introduction to Statistics and Probability from a Bayesian Viewpoint* (Cambridge, England: Cambridge University Press, 1965).

10.   A. N. Kolmogorov, *Foundations of the Theory of Probability*, trans. by Nathan Morrison, 2nd ed. (New York: Chelsea Publishing, 1956).

11.   Others include Keynes, *A Treatise on Probability*.

12.   See Kempthorne and Folks, *Probability, Statistics, and Data Analysis*, 69–70; B. V. Gnedenko, *The Theory of Probability*, trans. by George Yankovsky (Moscow: Mir Publishers, 1969), 45–51.

13.   See J. Leroy Folks, *Ideas of Statistics* (New York: John Wiley and Sons, 1981), 64–66.

14.   For a discussion of this and related issues, see R. Darcy, "Position Effects with Party Column Ballots," *Western Political Quarterly*, 39 (December 1986), 648–662; R. Darcy and Anne Schneider, "Confusing Ballots, Roll-off, and the Black

Vote," *Western Political Quarterly*, 42 (September 1989), 347–364; R. Darcy and Ian McAllister, "Ballot Position Effects," *Electoral Studies*, 9 (March 1990), 5–17.

15.   R. Darcy and Charles D. Hadley, "Black Women in Politics: The Puzzle of Success," *Social Science Quarterly*, 69 (September 1988), 629–645; N. J., "Eyes on the Prize: Black Women in Politics," *Psychology Today* (April 23, 1989), 10.

16.   Folks, *Ideas of Statistics*, 107–112; Walker, *Studies in the History of Statistical Method*, 13–16.

17.   Stephen M. Stigler, *The History of Statistics: The Measurement of Uncertainty before 1900* (Cambridge, MA: Belknap Press of Harvard University Press, 1986), 137.

18.   Ibid., 202.

19.   Ibid., 311.

20.   Richard Lowry, *The Architecture of Chance: An Introduction to the Logic and Arithmetic of Probability* (New York: Oxford University Press, 1989), 131.

21.   Ronald A. Fisher, "On Mathematical Foundations of Theoretical Statistics," reprinted in Ronald A. Fisher, *Collected Papers of R. A. Fisher*, vol. 1, *1912–1924*, ed. J. H. Bennett (Adelaide, Australia: University of Adelaide Press, 1971), 275–335.

22.   Charles Sanders Peirce, "Reasoning from Samples," reprinted in Charles Sanders Peirce, *Collected Papers of Charles Sanders Peirce*, vol. 1, *Principles of Philosophy*, eds. Charles Hartshorne and Paul Weiss (Cambridge, MA: Harvard University Press, 1931), 39; Folks, *Ideas of Statistics*, 27–31.

23.   See Leslie Kish, *Survey Sampling* (New York: John Wiley and Sons, 1965), 30.

24.   Frederick F. Stephan, "History of the Uses of Modern Sampling Procedures," *Journal of the American Statistical Association*, 43 (March 1948), 12–39.

25.   J. Neyman and E. S. Pearson, "On the Problem of the Most Efficient Tests of Statistical Hypotheses," *Philosophical Transactions of the Royal Society of London*, A-231 (1932/1933), 289–337.

26.   Ramon E. Henkel, *Tests of Significance* (Beverly Hills, CA: Sage Publications, 1976), 86.

CHAPTER 5

1.   See Chris Curtin and Anthony Varley, "Marginal Men? Bachelor Farmers in a West of Ireland Community," in Chris Curtin, Pauline Jackson, and Barbara O'Connor, eds., *Gender in Irish Society* (Galway, Ireland: Galway University Press, 1987), 287–308.

2.   See Nelson W. Polsby, "The Institutionalization of the U.S. House of Representatives," *American Political Science Review*, 62 (March 1968), 144–168.

3.   Frederick Mosteller and David L. Wallace, *Inference and Disputed Authorship:* The Federalist (Reading, MA: Addison-Wesley Publishing, 1964).

4.   Frederick Mosteller, Stephen E. Fienberg, and Robert E. K. Rourke, *Beginning Statistics with Data Analysis* (Reading, MA: Addison-Wesley Publishing, 1983), 289.

5.   Hubert M. Blalock, Jr., *Social Statistics*, 2nd ed. (New York: McGraw-Hill, 1972), 227.

6.   J. Neyman and E. S. Pearson, "On the Problem of the Most Efficient Tests of Statistical Hypotheses," *Philosophical Transactions of the Royal Society of London*, A-231 (1932/1933), 296.

7.   See Anne L. Schneider and Robert E. Darcy, "Policy Implications of Using Significance Tests in Evaluation Research," *Evaluation Review*, 8 (August 1984), 573–582.

CHAPTER 6

1.   Kathleen Neils Conzen, *Immigrant Milwaukee, 1836–1860: Accommodation and Community in a Frontier City* (Cambridge, MA: Harvard University Press, 1976), 90–92.

2.   See Ronald A. Fisher, *Statistical Methods for Research Workers*, 13th ed. (New York: Hafner Publishing, 1958), 85–86. For a slightly different treatment of degrees of freedom, consult J. Leroy Folks, *Ideas of Statistics* (New York: John Wiley and Sons, 1981), 323.

3.   Melvyn Hammarberg, "Indiana Farmers and the Group Basis of the Late Nineteenth-century Political Parties," *Journal of American History*, 61 (June 1974), 108–109.

4.   There are other topics, such as Yates's Correction, which can be found by consulting Fisher, *Statistical Methods for Research Workers,* 92–95.

5.   Leo A. Goodman and William H. Kruskal, "Measures of Association for Cross Classifications," *Journal of the American Statistical Association*, 49 (December 1954), 732–764.

6.   Stephan Thernstrom, *The Other Bostonians: Poverty and Progress in the American Metropolis, 1880–1970* (Cambridge, MA: Harvard University Press, 1973), 88–89.

7.   See Leo A. Goodman and William H. Kruskal, "Measures of Association for Cross Classifications III: Approximate Sampling Theory," *Journal of the American Statistical Association*, 58 (June 1963), 310–364; Alan Agresti and Barbara Finlay Agresti, *Statistical Methods for the Social Sciences* (San Francisco: Dellen Publishing, 1979), 253–256.

CHAPTER 7

1. Ronald A. Fisher, *Statistical Methods for Research Workers*, 13th ed. (New York: Hafner Publishing, 1958); R. A. Fisher, *The Design of Experiments*, 2nd ed. (Edinburgh, Scotland: Oliver and Boyd, 1937).

2. Several measures of the strength of the relationship have been proposed for use with analysis of variance. Among them is the ratio of explained to a total sum of squares, which we will refer to as E^2. This ratio is referred to as r^2, R^2, $beta^2$, and eta^2 by various authors, depending on the particular explained sum of squares used. Here, the context will make the meaning of E^2 clear.

3. David Herlihy and Christiane Klapisch-Zuber, *Tuscans and Their Families: A Study of the Florentine* Catasto *of 1427* (New Haven, CT: Yale University Press, 1985). See J. Paul Bischoff and R. Darcy, "Reformating the Florentine CATASTO Data for Use by Standard Statistical Analysis Programs," *Computers and Medieval Data Processing* 11 (October 1981), 5–6.

4. George Snedecor, *Analysis of Variance and Covariance* (Ames, IA: Collegiate Press, 1934).

5. See George W. Snedecor and William G. Cochran, *Statistical Methods*, 6th ed. (Ames: Iowa State University Press, 1967), 484–493.

6. See Frank M. Andrews et al., *Multiple Classification Analysis*, 2nd ed. (Ann Arbor, MI: Institute for Social Research, 1973). The SPSS ANOVA procedure calculates adjusted means.

CHAPTER 8

1. Kathleen Smith Kutolowski, "Antimasonry Reexamined: Social Bases of the Grass-roots Party," *Journal of American History*, 71 (September 1984), 279.

2. Stephen M. Stigler, *The History of Statistics: The Measurement of Uncertainty before 1900* (Cambridge, MA: Belknap Press of Harvard University Press, 1986), 321, 352–354.

3. See Karl Pearson, "Notes on the History of Correlation," in E. S. Pearson and M. G. Kendall, eds., *Studies in the History of Statistics and Probability* (London: Charles Griffin, 1970), 185–205.

CHAPTER 9

1. Stephen M. Stigler, *The History of Statistics: The Measurement of Uncertainty before 1900* (Cambridge, MA: Belknap Press of Harvard University Press, 1986), 347–348.

2. William F. Ogburn and Inez Goltra, "How Women Vote: A Study of an Election in Portland, Oregon," *Political Science Quarterly*, 34 (September 1919), 413–433. See also David John Gow, "Quantification and Statistics in the Early Years of American Political Science, 1880–1922," *Political Methodology*, 11 (1985), 1–18.

3. Kathleen Smith Kutolowski, "Antimasonry Reexamined: Social Bases of the Grass-roots Party," *Journal of American History*, 71 (September 1984), 280–281.

4. For a discussion of causal modeling, see Hubert M. Blalock, Jr., *Causal Inferences in Nonexperimental Research* (Chapel Hill: University of North Carolina Press, 1964).

5. John Ashton Cannon, *Parliamentary Reform, 1640–1832* (Cambridge, England: Cambridge University Press, 1973), 269.

6. See, for example, Ogburn and Goltra, "How Women Vote."

7. W. S. Robinson, "Ecological Correlations and the Behavior of Individuals," *American Sociological Review*, 15 (June 1950), 351–357.

8. See Leo A. Goodman, "Some Alternatives to Ecological Correlation," *American Journal of Sociology*, 64 (May 1959), 610–625; W. Phillips Shively, " 'Ecological' Inference: The Use of Aggregate Data to Study Individuals," *American Political Science Review*, 63 (December 1969), 1183–1196; Laura Irwin Langbein and Allan J. Lichtman, *Ecological Inference* (Beverly Hills, CA: Sage Publications, 1978); Søren Risbjerg Thomsen, *Danish Elections, 1920–79: A Logit Approach to Ecological Analysis and Inference* (Aarhus, Denmark: Politica, 1987); James L. Huston, "Weighting, Confidence Intervals, and Ecological Regression," *Journal of Interdisciplinary History*, 21 (Spring 1991), 631–654.

9. J. Morgan Kousser, *The Shaping of Southern Politics: Suffrage Restriction and the Establishment of the One-party South, 1880–1910* (New Haven, CT: Yale University Press, 1974); Eileen L. McDonagh and H. Douglas Price, "Woman Suffrage in the Progressive Era: Patterns of Opposition and Support in Referenda Voting, 1910–1918," *American Political Science Review*, 79 (June 1985), 415–435.

10. Kenneth D. Wald, *Crosses on the Ballot: Patterns of British Voter Alignment since 1885* (Princeton, NJ: Princeton University Press, 1983).

11. Thomsen, *Danish Elections, 1920–79*.

12. Sten Berglund, Søren Risbjerg Thomsen, and Ingemar Worlund, "The Mobilization of the Swedish Vote: An Ecological Analysis of the General Elections of 1928, 1948, and 1968," Paper presented at the ECPR Joint Sessions of Workshops, Bologna (Rimini) Italy, April 5–11, 1988.

13. Raymond Boudon, "Properties Individuelles et Properties Collectives: Une Problème d'Analyse Ecologique," *Revue Française de Sociologie*, 4 (1963), 275–299.

14. Peter Hoschka and Hermann Schunck, "Schatzung von Wahlerwandrungen Puzzlespiel oder gesicherte Ergebnisse?" *Politische Vierteljahrschrift*, 16 (1975), 491–539.

15.   Robert Darcy, Chong-Min Hyun, James Huston, and Hyun-woo Kim, "Political Party Support in the Korean Fifth Republic: An Ecological Analysis, 1981–1985," *Australian Journal of Political Science*, 26 (July 1991), 295–306.

16.   William E. Gienapp: "Nativism and the Creation of a Republican Majority in the North before the Civil War," *Journal of American History*, 72 (December 1985), 529–559; "Nebraska, Nativism, and Rum: The Failure of Fusion in Pennsylvania, 1854," *Pennsylvania Magazine of History and Biography*, 109 (October 1985), 425–471; " 'Politics Seem to Enter into Everything': Political Culture in the North, 1840–1860," in Stephen E. Maizlish and John J. Kushma, eds., *Essays on American Antebellum Politics, 1840–1860* (College Station: Texas A&M University Press, 1982), 15–69.

17.   *The Tribune Almanac and Political Register* (New York: Tribune Publishing, 1858), 53.

18.   Thomsen, *Danish Elections, 1920–79*. See also Sten Berglund and Søren Risbjerg Thomsen, eds., *Modern Political Ecological Analysis* (Åbo, Finland: Åbo Academy Press, 1990).

CHAPTER 10

1.   Louis Guttman, "The Quantification of a Class of Attributes: A Theory and Method of Scale Construction," in Paul Horst, ed., *The Prediction of Personal Adjustment* (New York: Social Science Research Council, 1941), 321–348.

2.   Gustav Theodor Fechner, *Elemente der Psychophysik* (Leipzig: Breitkoph und Härtel, 1860).

3.   Robyn M. Dawes, *Fundamentals of Attitude Measurement* (New York: Wiley, 1972).

4.   See Stephen M. Stigler, *The History of Statistics: The Measurement of Uncertainty before 1900* (Cambridge, MA: Belknap Press of Harvard University Press, 1986), 255.

5.   J. McK. Cattell, "Mental Tests and Measurements," *Mind*, 15 (July 1890), 373–380.

6.   A. Binet and V. Henri, "La Psychologie Individuelle," *L'Année Psychologique*, 2 (1895), 411–465.

7.   Emory S. Bogardus, "Measuring Social Distances," *Journal of Applied Sociology*, 9 (March/April 1925), 299–308.

8.   If there are n questions with r possible responses, the total number of possible response patterns is r^n; here: $2^3 = 8$.

9.   George M. Belknap, "A Method for Analyzing Legislative Behavior," *Midwest Journal of Political Science*, 2 (November 1958), 377–402.

10.   For some examples, consult Allan G. Bogue, *The Earnest Men: Republi-*

cans of the Civil War Senate (Ithaca, NY: Cornell University Press, 1981); Joel H. Silbey, *The Shrine of Party: Congressional Voting Behavior, 1841–1852* (Pittsburgh, PA: University of Pittsburgh Press, 1967); S. Sidney Ulmer, "Supreme Court Behavior and Civil Rights," *Western Political Quarterly*, 13 (June 1960), 288–311.

11.   See Louis Guttman, "The Basis for Scalogram Analysis," in Samuel A. Stouffer et al., eds., *Measurement and Prediction* (Princeton, NJ: Princeton University Press, 1950), 60–90.

12.   S. Sidney Ulmer, "Supreme Court Behavior and Civil Rights," in Robert P. Swierenga, ed., *Quantification in American History: Theory and Research* (New York: Atheneum, 1970), 163–186.

13.   Gunnar Myrdal, *An American Dilemma* (New York: Harper and Brothers, 1944).

14.   Gilbert Shapiro, "Myrdal's Definitions of the 'South': A Methodological Note," *American Sociological Review, 13* (October 1948), 619–621; A. H. G. S. van der Ven, *An Introduction to Scaling* (Chichester, England: Wiley, 1980).

15.   R. J. Mokken, *A Theory and Procedure of Scale Analysis: With Applications in Political Research* (The Hague, Netherlands: Mouton, 1971); Kees Niemöller and Wijbrandt van Schuur, "Stochastic Models for Unidimensional Scaling: Mokken and Rasch," in David H. McKay, Norman Schofield, and Paul Whiteley, eds., *Data Analysis and the Social Sciences* (New York: St. Martin's Press, 1983), 120–170.

16.   Richard Jensen, "Power and Success Scores," *Historical Methods Newsletter*, 1 (June 1968), 1–6.

17.   M. O. Lorenz, "Methods of Measuring the Concentration of Wealth," *Journal of the American Statistical Association*, 9 (June 1905), 209–219.

18.   Corrado Gini, "Variabilità e mutabilità," *Studi economico-giuridici, Università di Cagliari*, 3, 2a, (1912).

19.   See Michael Keane and R. Darcy, "Simpson's Rule: A Simple and Accurate Method for Calculating a Gini Index (or Any Area under a Curve)," Economics Department, University College, Galway, Ireland, July 1988.

20.   John R. Weeks, *Population: An Introduction to Concepts and Issues*, 2nd ed. (Belmont, CA: Wadsworth Publishing, 1981), 371–372.

21.   Gretchen A. Condran and Ellen A. Kramarow, "Child Mortality among Jewish Immigrants to the United States," *Journal of Interdisciplinary History*, 22 (Autumn 1991), 223–254.

22.   Anne McCants, "Internal Migration in Friesland, 1750–1805," *Journal of Interdisciplinary History*, 22 (Winter 1992), 387–409.

23.   Lee L. Bean, Geraldine P. Mineau, and Douglas L. Anderton, "High-risk Childbearing: Fertility and Infant Mortality on the American Frontier," *Social Science History*, 16 (Fall 1992), 337–363.

24.   For one example, consult George Emery, "Incomplete Registration of Births in Civil Systems: The Example of Ontario, Canada, 1900–1960," *Historical Methods*,

23 (Winter 1990), 5–21.

25.   For an introduction to family reconstitution see E. A. Wrigley, "Family Reconstitution," in E. A. Wrigley, ed., *An Introduction to English Historical Demography from the Sixteenth to the Nineteenth Century* (New York: Basic Books, 1966), 96–159; Myron P. Gutmann, "Gold from Dross? Population Reconstruction for the Pre-Census Era," *Historical Methods*, 17 (Winter 1984), 5–19.

26.   Philip J. Greven, Jr., *Four Generations: Population, Land, and Family in Colonial Andover, Massachusetts* (Ithaca, NY: Cornell University Press, 1970), 4–5.

27.   Ibid., 5–8; Lutz K. Berkner, "The Use and Misuse of Census Data for the Historical Analysis of Family Structure," *Journal of Interdisciplinary History*, 5 (Spring 1975), 724, 725; Allan N. Sharlin, "Historical Demography as History and Demography," *American Behavioral Scientist*, 21 (November/December 1977), 255; Daniel Scott Smith, "The Estimates of Early American Historical Demographers: Two Steps Forward, One Step Back, What Steps in the Future?" *Historical Methods*, 12 (Winter 1979), 24–38.

28.   Leon Davidson, "Retrieval of Misspelled Names in an Airlines Passenger Record System," *Communications of the ACM*, 5 (March 1962), 169–171; E. D. Acheson, ed., *Record Linkage in Medicine: Proceedings of the International Symposium, Oxford, July 1967* (Baltimore, MD: Williams and Wilkins, 1968).

29.   Ian Winchester, "The Linkage of Historical Records by Man and Computer: Techniques and Problems," *Journal of Interdisciplinary History*, 1 (Autumn 1970), 107–124; Gretchen A. Condran and Jeff Seaman, "Linkage of the 1880–81 Philadelphia Death Register to the 1880 Manuscript Census: A Comparison of Hand- and Machine-record Linkage Techniques," *Historical Methods*, 14 (Spring 1981), 73–84.

30.   See, for example, Gérard Bouchard, "Current Issues and New Prospects for Computerized Record Linkage in the Province of Québec," *Historical Methods*, 25 (Spring 1992), 67–73; Roger Schofield, "Automatic Family Reconstruction: The Cambridge Experience," *Historical Methods*, 25 (Spring 1992), 75–79; Ian Winchester, "What Every Historian Needs to Know about Record Linkage for the Microcomputer Era," *Historical Methods*, 25 (Fall 1992), 149–165.

31.   Jacques Légaré, Yolande Lavoie, and Hubert Charbonneau, "The Early Canadian Population: Problems in Automatic Record Linkage," *Canadian Historical Review*, 53 (December 1972), 427–442.

32.   Gloria J. A. Guth, "Surname Spellings and Computerized Record Linkage," *Historical Methods Newsletter*, 10 (December 1976), 10–19.

33.   Michael D. Ornstein and A. Gordon Darroch, "National Mobility Studies in Past Time: A Sampling Strategy," *Historical Methods*, 11 (Fall 1978), 152–161; John A. Phillips, "Achieving a Critical Mass while Avoiding an Explosion: Letter-cluster Sampling and Nominal Record Linkage," *Journal of Interdisciplinary History*, 9 (Winter 1979), 493–508.

APPENDIX

1.   Oscar Kempthorne and Leroy Folks, *Probability, Statistics, and Data Analysis* (Ames, IA: Iowa State University Press, 1971), 85-108, 523-526.

2.   Ibid., 106.

3.   Ibid.

4.   Ibid., 107.

Works Cited

Acheson, E. D., ed. *Record Linkage in Medicine: Proceedings of the International Symposium, Oxford, July 1967*. Baltimore, MD: Williams and Wilkins, 1968.

Agresti, Alan and Barbara Finlay Agresti. *Statistical Methods for the Social Sciences*. San Francisco: Dellen Publishing, 1979.

Anderson, Lee F., Meredith W. Watts, Jr., and Allen R. Wilcox. *Legislative Roll-call Analysis*. Evanston, IL: Northwestern University Press, 1966.

Andrews, Frank M., et al. *Multiple Classification Analysis*. 2nd ed. Ann Arbor, MI: Institute for Social Research, 1973.

Annals of Congress, 12th Congress, 1st Session, 1812.

Arnstein, Walter L. *Britain Yesterday and Today: 1830 to the Present*. 4th ed. Lexington, MA: D. C. Heath, 1983.

Baethne, G. W., ed. *Practical Applications of the Punched Card Method in Colleges and Universities*. New York: Columbia University Press, 1935.

Barraclough, Geoffrey. "History." In *Main Trends of Research in the Social and Human Sciences*, ed. Jacques Havet, pt. 2, I:227–487. The Hague, Netherlands: Mouton Publishers, 1978.

Bean, Lee L., Geraldine P. Mineau, and Douglas L. Anderton. "High-risk Childbearing: Fertility and Infant Mortality on the American Frontier." *Social Science History*, 16 (Fall 1992), 337–363.

Becker, Carl Lotus. *The History of Political Parties in the Province of New York, 1760–1776*. 3rd printing. Madison: University of Wisconsin Press, 1968.

Belknap, George M. "A Method for Analyzing Legislative Behavior." *Midwest Journal of Political Science*, 2 (November 1958), 377–402.

Benson, Lee. *Toward the Scientific Study of History: Selected Essays*. Philadelphia: J. B. Lippincott, 1972.

Berglund, Sten and Søren Risbjerg Thomsen, eds. *Modern Political Ecological Analysis*. Åbo, Finland: Åbo Academy Press, 1990.

Berglund, Sten, Søren Risbjerg Thomsen, and Ingemar Worlund. "The Mobilization of the Swedish Vote: An Ecological Analysis of the General Elections of 1928, 1948, and 1968." Paper presented at the ECPR Joint Sessions of Workshops, Bologna (Rimini) Italy, April 5–11, 1988.

Berkner, Lutz K. "The Use and Misuse of Census Data for the Historical Analysis of Family Structure." *Journal of Interdisciplinary History*, 5 (Spring 1975), 721–738.

Bernoulli, Jacob. *Ars conjectandi*. Basil: Thurnisiorum, 1713.

Binet, A. and V. Henri. "La Psychologie Individuelle." *L'Année Psychologique*, 2 (1895), 411–465.

Bischoff, J. Paul and R. Darcy. "Reformating the Florentine CATASTO Data for Use by Standard Statistical Analysis Programs." *Computers and Medieval Data Processing*, 11 (October 1981), 5–6.

Blalock, Jr., Hubert M. *Causal Inferences in Nonexperimental Research*. Chapel Hill: University of North Carolina Press, 1964.

———. *Social Statistics*. 2nd ed. New York: McGraw-Hill, 1972.

Bogardus, Emory S. "Measuring Social Distances." *Journal of Applied Sociology*, 9 (March/April 1925), 299–308.

Bogue, Allan G. *Clio & the Bitch Goddess: Quantification in American Political History*. Beverly Hills, CA: Sage Publications, 1983.

———. *The Earnest Men: Republicans of the Civil War Senate*. Ithaca, NY: Cornell University Press, 1981.

———. "The Quest for Numeracy: Data and Methods in American Political History." *Journal of Interdisciplinary History*, 21 (Summer 1990), 89–116.

Boltzmann, Ludwig. *Lectures on Gas Theory*. Translated by Stephen G. Brush. Berkeley: University of California Press, 1964.

Bouchard, Gerard. "Current Issues and New Prospects for Computerized Record Linkage in the Province of Québec." *Historical Methods*, 25 (Spring 1992), 67–73.

Boudon, Raymond. "Properties Individuelles et Properties Collectives: Une Problème d'Analyse Ecologique." *Revue Française de Sociologie*, 4 (1963), 275–299.

Bridenbaugh, Carl. "The Great Mutation." *American Historical Review*, 68 (January 1963), 315–331.

Bureau of the Census, *Thirteenth Census of the United States Taken in the Year 1910*. 11 vols. Washington, D. C.: Government Printing Office, 1914.

Cannon, John Ashton. *Parliamentary Reform, 1640–1832*. Cambridge, England: Cambridge University Press, 1973.

Cattell, J. McK. "Mental Tests and Measurements." *Mind*, 15 (July 1890), 373–380.

Census and Property Survey of Florentine Domains in the Province of Tuscany, 1427–1480. Data set compiled by David Herlihy and Christiane Klapisch-Zuber.

Center for Political Studies. "American National Election Survey, 1970." ICPSR No. 7298. Inter-university Consortium for Political and Social Research, University of Michigan, Ann Arbor.

Coale, Ansley J. and Frederick F. Stephan. "The Case of the Indians and the Teen-age Widows." In *The Quantitative Analysis of Social Problems*, ed. Edward R. Tufte, 426–436. Reading, MA: Addison-Wesley Publishing, 1970.

Condran, Gretchen A. and Ellen A. Kramarow. "Child Mortality among Jewish Immigrants to the United States." *Journal of Interdisciplinary History*, 22 (Autumn 1991), 223–254.

Condran, Gretchen A. and Jeff Seaman. "Linkage of the 1880–81 Philadelphia Death Register to the 1880 Manuscript Census: A Comparison of Hand- and Machine-record Linkage Techniques." *Historical Methods*, 14 (Spring 1981), 73–84.

Conzen, Kathleen Neils. *Immigrant Milwaukee, 1836-1860: Accommodation and Community in a Frontier City.* Cambridge, MA: Harvard University Press, 1976.

Coombs, Clyde H. *A Theory of Data.* New York: John Wiley and Sons, 1964.

Curtin, Chris and Anthony Varley. "Marginal Men? Bachelor Farmers in a West of Ireland Community." In *Gender in Irish Society,* eds. Chris Curtin, Pauline Jackson, and Barbara O'Connor. Galway, Ireland: Galway University Press, 1987.

d'Abro, A. *The Rise of the New Physics.* 2 vols. New York: Dover Publishing, 1951.

Darcy, R. "Position Effects with Party Column Ballots." *Western Political Quarterly,* 39 (December 1986), 648-662.

Darcy, R. and Charles D. Hadley. "Black Women in Politics: The Puzzle of Success." *Social Science Quarterly,* 69 (September 1988), 629–645.

Darcy, Robert, Chong-Min Hyun, James Huston, and Hyun-woo Kim. "Political Party Support in the Korean Fifth Republic: An Ecological Analysis, 1981–1985." *Australian Journal of Political Science,* 26 (July 1991), 295–306.

Darcy, R. and Ian McAllister. "Ballot Position Effects." *Electoral Studies,* 9 (March 1990), 5–17.

Darcy, R. and Anne Schneider. "Confusing Ballots, Roll-off, and the Black Vote." *Western Political Quarterly,* 42 (September 1989), 347–364.

Darroch, A. Gordon and Michael D. Ornstein. "Error in Historical Data Files: A Research Note on the Automatic Detection of Error and on the Nature and Sources of Errors in Coding." *Historical Methods,* 12 (Fall 1979), 157–167.

Davidson, Leon. "Retrieval of Misspelled Names in an Airlines Passenger Record System." *Communications of the ACM,* 5 (March 1962), 169–171.

Dawes, Robyn M. *Fundamentals of Attitude Measurement.* New York: Wiley, 1972.

Dollar, Charles M. and Richard J. Jensen. *Historian's Guide to Statistics: Quantitative Analysis and Historical Research.* New York: Holt, Rinehart, and Winston, 1971.

Durkheim, Emile. *Suicide: A Study in Sociology.* Translated by John A. Spaulding and George Simpson. New York: Free Press, 1951.

Eleventh Census of the United States, 1890. Federal Population Schedules, MSS.

Emery, George. "Incomplete Registration of Births in Civil Systems: The Example of Ontario, Canada, 1900–1960." *Historical Methods,* 23 (Winter 1990), 5–21.

Erickson, Bonnie H. and T. A. Nosanchuk. *Understanding Data: An Introduction to Exploratory and Confirmatory Data Analysis for Students of the Social Sciences.* Milton Keynes, England: Open University Press, 1979.

Fechner, Gustav Theodor. *Elemente der Psychophysik.* Leipzig: Breitkoph und Härtel, 1860.

Feller, William. *An Introduction to Probability Theory and Its Applications.* 2 vols. New York: John Wiley and Sons, 1950.

Fisher, Ronald A. *Collected Papers of R. A. Fisher,* Vol. 1, *1912–1924.* Edited by J. H. Bennett. Adelaide, Australia: University of Adelaide Press, 1971.

———. "The Correlation between Relatives on the Supposition of Mendelian Inheritance." *Transactions of the Royal Society of Edinburgh,* 52 (1918/1919), 399–433.

———. *The Design of Experiments.* 2nd ed. Edinburgh, Scotland: Oliver and Boyd, 1937.

————. *Statistical Methods for Research Workers.* 13th ed. New York: Hafner Publishing, 1958.

Flegg, H. Graham. *Numbers: Their History and Meaning.* New York: Schoken, 1983.

Fogel, Robert William. "The Limits of Quantitative Methods in History." *American Historical Review,* 80 (April 1975), 329–350.

Fogel, Robert William and Stanley L. Engerman. *Time on the Cross: The Economics of American Negro Slavery.* Boston: Little, Brown, 1974.

Folks, J. Leroy. *Ideas of Statistics.* New York: John Wiley and Sons, 1981.

Gallup, George Horace. *The Sophisticated Poll Watcher's Guide.* Princeton, NJ: Princeton Opinion Press, 1972.

Gallup, George Horace and Saul Forbes Rae. *The Pulse of Democracy: The Public-opinion Poll and How It Works.* New York: Simon and Schuster, 1940.

Gienapp, William E. "Nativism and the Creation of a Republican Majority in the North before the Civil War." *Journal of American History,* 72 (December 1985), 529–559.

————. "Nebraska, Nativism, and Rum: The Failure of Fusion in Pennsylvania, 1854." *Pennsylvania Magazine of History and Biography,* 109 (October 1985), 425–471.

————. " 'Politics Seem to Enter into Everything': Political Culture in the North, 1840–1860." In *Essays on American Antebellum Politics, 1840–1860,* eds. Stephen E. Maizlish and John J. Kushma. College Station: Texas A&M University Press, 1982.

Gini, Corrado. "Variabilità e mutabilità." *Studi economico-giuridici, Università di Cagliari,* 3, 2a, (1912).

Gnedenko, B. V. *The Theory of Probability.* Translated by George Yankovsky. Moscow: Mir Publishers, 1969.

Goodman, Leo A. "Some Alternatives to Ecological Correlation." *American Journal of Sociology,* 64 (May 1959), 610–625.

Goodman, Leo A. and William H. Kruskal. "Measures of Association for Cross Classifications." *Journal of the American Statistical Association,* 49 (December 1954), 732–764.

————. "Measures of Association for Cross Classifications III: Approximate Sampling Theory." *Journal of the American Statistical Association,* 58 (June 1963), 310–364.

Gow, David John. "Quantification and Statistics in the Early Years of American Political Science, 1880–1922." *Political Methodology,* 11 (1985), 1–18.

Greene, Lorenzo Johnston. *The Negro in Colonial New England.* New York: Atheneum, 1969.

Greven, Jr., Philip J. *Four Generations: Population, Land, and Family in Colonial Andover, Massachusetts.* Ithaca, NY: Cornell University Press, 1970.

Guth, Gloria J. A. "Surname Spellings and Computerized Record Linkage." *Historical Methods Newsletter,* 10 (December 1976), 10–19.

Guttman, Louis. "The Basis for Scalogram Analysis." In *Measurement and Prediction,* ed. Samuel A. Stouffer et al., 60–90. Princeton, NJ: Princeton University Press, 1950.

————. "The Quantification of a Class of Attributes: A Theory and Method of Scale Construction." In *The Prediction of Personal Adjustment,* ed. Paul Horst, 319–348. New York: Social Science Research Council, 1941.

Guttmann, Myron P. "Gold from Dross? Population Reconstruction for the Pre-

Census Era." *Historical Methods*, 17 (Winter 1984), 5–19.

Hacking, Ian. *Logic of Statistical Inference*. Cambridge, England: Cambridge University Press, 1965.

Hammarberg, Melvyn. "Indiana Farmers and the Group Basis of the Late Nineteenth-century Political Parties." *Journal of American History*, 61 (June 1974), 91–115.

Haskins, Loren and Kirk Jeffrey. *Understanding Quantitative History*. New York: McGraw-Hill Publishing, 1990.

Heisenberg, Werner, et al. *On Modern Physics*. New York: Collier Books, 1962.

Henkel, Ramon E. *Tests of Significance*. Beverly Hills, CA: Sage Publications, 1976.

Herlihy, David and Christiane Klapisch-Zuber. *Tuscans and Their Families: A Study of the Florentine* Catasto *of 1427*. New Haven, CT: Yale University Press, 1985.

Hershberg, Theodore and Robert Dockhorn. "Occupational Classification." *Historical Methods Newsletter*, 9 (March–June 1976), 59–98.

Hershberg, Theodore, et al. "Occupation and Ethnicity in Five Nineteenth-century Cities: A Collaborative Inquiry." *Historical Methods Newsletter,* 7 (June 1974), 174–216.

Himmelfarb, Gertrude. *The New History and the Old*. Cambridge, MA: Belknap Press of Harvard University Press, 1987.

Horan, Patrick M. "Occupational Mobility and Historical Social Structure." *Social Science History*, 9 (Winter 1985), 25–47.

Hoschka, Peter and Hermann Schunck. "Schatzung von Wahlerwandrungen Puzzlespiel oder gesicherte Ergebnisse?" *Politische Vierteljahrschrift,* 16 (1975), 491–539.

Huston, James L. "Weighting, Confidence Intervals, and Ecological Regression." *Journal of Interdisciplinary History*, 21 (Spring 1991), 631–654.

Jackson, Dunham. "Note on the Median of a Set of Numbers." *Bulletin of the American Mathematical Society*, 27 (January 1921), 160–164.

Janda, Kenneth. *Data Processing: Applications to Political Research*. 2nd ed. Evanston, IL: Northwestern University Press, 1969.

Jarausch, Konrad H. "Quantitative History in Transition." American Historical Association *Perspectives*, 20 (September 1982), 14–16, 21.

Jarausch, Konrad H. and Kenneth A. Hardy. *Quantitative Methods for Historians: A Guide to Research, Data, and Statistics*. Chapel Hill: University of North Carolina Press, 1991.

Jensen, Richard. "Power and Success Scores." *Historical Methods Newsletter,* 1 (June 1968), 1–6.

Johnson, R. Christian. "The 1900 Census Sampling Project: Methods and Procedures for Sampling and Data Entry." *Historical Methods,* 11 (Fall 1978), 147–151.

———. "A Procedure for Sampling the Manuscript Census Schedules." *Journal of Interdisciplinary History*, 8 (Winter 1978), 515–530.

Katz, Michael B. "Occupational Classification in History." *Journal of Interdisciplinary History,* 3 (Summer 1972), 63–88.

Keane, Michael and R. Darcy. "Simpson's Rule: A Simple and Accurate Method for Calculating a Gini Index (or Any Area under a Curve)." Economics Department, University College, Galway, Ireland, July 1988.

Kempthorne, Oscar and J. Leroy Folks. *Probability, Statistics, and Data Analysis*.

Ames: Iowa State University Press, 1971.

Kendall, Sir Maurice G. and Alan Stuart. *The Advanced Theory of Statistics*. 3 vols. 4th ed. London: Charles Griffin, 1977–1983.

Keynes, John Maynard. *A Treatise on Probability*. New York: Harper and Row, 1962.

Kish, Leslie. *Survey Sampling*. New York: John Wiley and Sons, 1965.

Kolmogorov, A. N. *Foundations of the Theory of Probability*. Translated by Nathan Morrison. 2nd ed. New York: Chelsea Publishing, 1956.

Kousser, J. Morgan. *The Shaping of Southern Politics: Suffrage Restriction and the Establishment of the One-party South, 1880–1910*. New Haven, CT: Yale University Press, 1974.

————. "The State of Social Science History in the Late 1980s." *Historical Methods*, 22 (Winter 1989), 13–20.

Kutolowski, Kathleen Smith. "Antimasonry Reexamined: Social Bases of the Grassroots Party." *Journal of American History*, 71 (September 1984), 269–293.

Ladd, Everett C. and G. Donald Ferree. "Were the Pollsters Really Wrong?" *Public Opinion*, 3 (December 1980/January 1981), 13–20.

Langbein, Laura Irwin and Allan J. Lichtman. *Ecological Inference*. Beverly Hills, CA: Sage Publications, 1978.

Laplace, Pierre Simon. *Essai Philosophique sur les Probabilités*. 2nd ed. Paris: Ve Courcier, 1814.

Légaré, Jacques, Yolande Lavoie, and Hubert Charbonneau. "The Early Canadian Population: Problems in Automatic Record Linkage." *Canadian Historical Review*, 53 (December 1972), 427–442.

Lindley, D. V. *Introduction to Statistics and Probability from a Bayesian Viewpoint*. Cambridge, England: Cambridge University Press, 1965.

Lipset, Seymour Martin. "Different Polls, Different Results in 1980 Politics." *Public Opinion*, 3 (August/September 1980), 19–20, 60.

Lorenz, M. O. "Methods of Measuring the Concentration of Wealth." *Journal of the American Statistical Association*, 9 (June 1905), 209–219.

Lowry, Richard. *The Architecture of Chance: An Introduction to the Logic and Arithmetic of Probability*. New York: Oxford University Press, 1989.

McCants, Anne. "Internal Migration in Friesland, 1750–1805." *Journal of Interdisciplinary History*, 22 (Winter 1992), 387–409.

McDonagh, Eileen L. and H. Douglas Price. "Woman Suffrage in the Progressive Era: Patterns of Opposition and Support in Referenda Voting, 1910–1918." *American Political Science Review*, 79 (June 1985), 415–435.

Marey, Etienne Jules. *La Méthode Graphique dans les Sciences Expérimentales et Principalement en Physiologie et en Medecine*. Paris: G. Masson, 1878.

Marx, Karl. *Capital: A Critique of Political Economy*. 3 vols. New York: International Publishers, 1967.

Mokken, R. J. *A Theory and Procedure of Scale Analysis: With Applications in Political Research*. The Hague, Netherlands: Mouton, 1971.

Morgenstern, Oskar. *On the Accuracy of Economic Observations*. 2nd ed. Princeton, NJ: Princeton University Press, 1963.

Mosteller, Frederick, Stephen E. Fienberg, and Robert E. K. Rourke. *Beginning Statistics with Data Analysis*. Reading, MA: Addison-Wesley Publishing, 1983.

Mosteller, Frederick and David L. Wallace. *Inference and Disputed Authorship:*

The Federalist. Reading, MA: Addison-Wesley Publishing, 1964.

Myrdal, Gunnar. *An American Dilemma*. New York: Harper and Brothers, 1944.

Neyman, J. and E. S. Pearson. "On the Problem of the Most Efficient Tests of Statistical Hypotheses." *Philosophical Transactions of the Royal Society of London*, A-231 (1932/1933), 289–337.

Niemöller, Kees and Wijbrandt van Schuur. "Stochastic Models for Unidimensional Scaling: Mokken and Rasch." In *Data Analysis and the Social Sciences*, eds. David H. McKay, Norman Schofield, and Paul Whiteley. New York: St. Martin's Press, 1983.

N. J. "Eyes on the Prize: Black Women in Politics." *Psychology Today* (April 23, 1989), 10.

Ogburn, William F. and Inez Goltra. "How Women Vote: A Study of an Election in Portland, Oregon." *Political Science Quarterly*, 34 (September 1919), 413–433.

Ornstein, Michael D. and A. Gordon Darroch. "National Mobility Studies in Past Time: A Sampling Strategy." *Historical Methods*, 11 (Fall 1978), 152–161.

Ó'Tuathaigh, Gearóid. *Ireland before the Famine, 1798–1848*. Dublin: Gill and Macmillan, 1972.

Pearson, Karl. "Notes on the History of Correlation." In *Studies in the History of Statistics and Probability*, eds. E. S. Pearson and M. G. Kendall, 185–205. London: Charles Griffin, 1970.

Peirce, Charles Sanders. *Collected Papers of Charles Sanders Peirce*, Vol. 1, *Principles of Philosophy*. Edited by Charles Hartshorne and Paul Weiss. Cambridge, MA: Harvard University Press, 1931.

Perlmann, Joel. "Using Census Districts in Analysis, Record Linkage, and Sampling." *Journal of Interdisciplinary History*, 10 (Autumn 1979), 279–289.

Phillips, John A. "Achieving a Critical Mass while Avoiding an Explosion: Letter-cluster Sampling and Nominal Record Linkage." *Journal of Interdisciplinary History*, 9 (Winter 1979), 493–508.

Plackett, R. L. "The Principle of the Arithmetic Mean." *Biometrika*, 45 (1958), 130–135.

Polsby, Nelson W. "The Institutionalization of the U.S. House of Representatives." *American Political Science Review*, 62 (March 1968), 144–168.

Quetelet, Adolphe. *Letters Addressed to H.R.H. the Grand Duke of Saxe Cobourg and Gotha, on the Theories of Probabilities as Applied to the Moral and Political Sciences*. Trans. by O. G. Downes. London: C. and E. Layton, 1849.

Ramsey, Frank Plumpton. *The Foundations of Mathematics, and Other Logical Essays*. Paterson, NJ: Littlefield, Adams, 1960.

Robinson, David J. "Population Patterns in a Northern Mexican Mining Region: Parral in the Late Eighteenth Century." *Geoscience and Man*, 21 (March 17, 1980), 83–96.

Robinson, John P., Robert Athanasiou, and Kendra B. Head. *Measures of Occupational Attitudes and Occupational Characteristics*. Ann Arbor, MI: Institute for Social Research, 1969.

Robinson, W. S. "Ecological Correlations and the Behavior of Individuals." *American Sociological Review*, 15 (June 1950), 351–357.

Rokkan, Stein. "Archives for Secondary Analysis of Sample Survey Data: An Early Inquiry into the Prospects for Western Europe." *UNESCO International Social Science Journal*, 16 (1964), 49–62.

Savage, Leonard J. *The Foundations of Statistics.* New York: John Wiley and Sons, 1954.

Schmidhauser, John R., compiler. "United States Supreme Court Justices Biographical Data, 1789–1958." ICPSR No. 7240. Inter-university Consortium for Political and Social Research, University of Michigan, Ann Arbor.

Schneider, Anne L. and Robert E. Darcy. "Policy Implications of Using Significance Tests in Evaluation Research." *Evaluation Review,* 8 (August 1984), 573–582.

Schofield, Roger. "Automatic Family Reconstruction: The Cambridge Experience." *Historical Methods,* 25 (Spring 1992), 75–79.

Shapiro, Gilbert. "Myrdal's Definitions of the 'South': A Methodological Note." *American Sociological Review,* 13 (October 1948), 619–621.

Sharlin, Allan N. "Historical Demography as History and Demography." *American Behavioral Scientist,* 21 (November/December 1977), 245–262.

Shively, W. Phillips. " 'Ecological' Inference: The Use of Aggregate Data to Study Individuals." *American Political Science Review,* 63 (December 1969), 1183–1196.

Shoemaker, Nancy. "The Census as Civilizer: American Indian Household Structure in the 1900 and 1910 U.S. Census." *Historical Methods,* 25 (Winter 1992), 4–11.

Silbey, Joel H. *The Shrine of Party: Congressional Voting Behavior, 1841–1852.* Pittsburgh, PA: University of Pittsburgh Press, 1967.

Smith, Daniel Scott. "The Estimates of Early American Historical Demographers: Two Steps Forward, One Step Back, What Steps in the Future?" *Historical Methods,* 12 (Winter 1979), 24–38.

Snedecor, George. *Analysis of Variance and Covariance.* Ames, IA: Collegiate Press, 1934.

Snedecor, George W. and William G. Cochran. *Statistical Methods.* 6th ed. Ames: Iowa State University Press, 1967.

Sobek, Matthew. "Class Analysis and the U.S. Census Public Use Samples." *Historical Methods,* 24 (Fall 1991), 171–181.

Sondheimer, Ernest and Alan Rogerson. *Numbers and Infinity: A Historical Account of Mathematical Concepts.* Cambridge, England: Cambridge University Press, 1981.

Stephan, Frederick F. "History of the Uses of Modern Sampling Procedures." *Journal of the American Statistical Association,* 43 (March 1948), 12–39.

Stevens, S. S. "On the Theory of Scales of Measurement." *Science,* 103 (June 7, 1946), 677–680.

Stigler, Stephen M. *The History of Statistics: The Measurement of Uncertainty before 1900.* Cambridge, MA: Belknap Press of Harvard University Press, 1986.

Stone, Lawrence. *The Past and the Present.* Boston: Routledge and Kegan Paul, 1981.

Swierenga, Robert P., ed. *Quantification in American History: Theory and Research.* New York: Atheneum, 1970.

Thernstrom, Stephan. *The Other Bostonians: Poverty and Progress in the American Metropolis, 1880–1970.* Cambridge, MA: Harvard University Press, 1973.

Thompson, J. M. *The French Revolution.* New York: Oxford University Press, 1945.

Thomsen, Søren Risbjerg. *Danish Elections, 1920–79: A Logit Approach to Eco-*

logical Analysis and Inference. Aarhus, Denmark: Politica, 1987.

Todhunter, I. *A History of the Mathematical Theory of Probability from the Time of Pascal to That of Laplace.* New York: G. E. Stechert, 1931.

The Tribune Almanac and Political Register. New York: Tribune Publishing, 1858.

Tufte, Edward R. *The Visual Display of Quantitative Information.* Cheshire, CT: Graphics Press, 1983.

Twelfth Census of the United States, 1900. Federal Population Schedules, MSS.

Ulmer, S. Sidney. "Supreme Court Behavior and Civil Rights." In *Quantification in American History: Theory and Research,* ed. Robert P. Swierenga, 163–186. New York: Atheneum, 1970.

———. "Supreme Court Behavior and Civil Rights." *Western Political Quarterly,* 13 (June 1960), 288–311.

U.S. Department of Commerce. *Census '80: Continuing the Factfinder Tradition.* Washington, DC: Government Printing Office, 1980.

———. Bureau of the Census. *Historical Statistics of the United States: Colonial Times to 1970,* pt. 2. Washington, DC: Government Printing Office, 1975.

U.S. Interior Department. *Mortality Statistics of the United States, 1850.* Washington, DC: A. O. P. Nicholson, 1855.

———. Census Office. *9th Census, 1870: The Statistics of the Population of the United States.* 3 vols. Washington, DC: Government Printing Office, 1872.

———. *The Seventh Census of the United States, 1850.* Washington, DC: Robert Armstrong, 1853.

van der Ven, A. H. G. S. *An Introduction to Scaling.* Chichester, England: Wiley, 1980.

Venn, John. *The Logic of Chance.* 4th ed. New York: Chelsea Publishing, 1962.

von Mises, Richard. *Probability, Statistics, and Truth.* New York: Macmillan, 1957.

Wald, Kenneth D. *Crosses on the Ballot: Patterns of British Voter Alignment since 1885.* Princeton, NJ: Princeton University Press, 1983.

Walker, Helen M. *Studies in History of Statistical Method.* Baltimore: Williams and Wilkins, 1929.

Weeks, John R. *Population: An Introduction to Concepts and Issues.* 2nd ed. Belmont, CA: Wadsworth Publishing, 1981.

Williams, Bill. *A Sampler on Sampling.* New York: Wiley, 1978.

Winchester, Ian. "The Linkage of Historical Records by Man and Computer: Techniques and Problems." *Journal of Interdisciplinary History,* 1 (Autumn 1970), 107–124.

———. "What Every Historian Needs to Know about Record Linkage for the Microcomputer Era." *Historical Methods,* 25 (Fall 1992), 149–165.

Wrigley, E. A., ed. *An Introduction to English Historical Demography from the Sixteenth to the Nineteenth Century.* New York: Basic Books, 1966.

Index

a, the intercept, 181, 183, 185, 204
Absolute difference, 41-43, 250
African-American women in politics, 71-72
Age cohorts, 34, 264
Age heaping, 34, 268-69
Age pyramids, 265
Age-sex-specific death rates (ASDR), 266
Age-specific fertility rate (ASFR), 264-65
Alternative hypothesis. *See* Hypotheses
American colonial trade balances, 148-59
American Sociological Review, 264
An American Dilemma, 245
Analysis of variance (ANOVA), 137-74
  One-way analysis of variance, 137-50, 155, 158, 174
    Category effect, 140-41
    Category mean, 139-40
    Critical F-value, 145
    Explained degrees of freedom, 144
    Explained sum of squares, 143, 145, 148
    F-distribution, 145
    F-ratio, 142, 144-45, 148
    Grand mean, 139-40, 142-44
    Individual effect, 140-41

Mean square, 144-45
Significance: F-test, 141-45
Strength of association, 145-48
Sum of squares, 139, 144
Total sum of squares, 139, 142-43, 145
Unexplained degrees of freedom, 144
Unexplained sum of squares, 143
Two-way analysis of variance with related independent variables, 159-74
  Adjusted category mean, 170-71
  Adjusted grand mean, 170
  Explained degrees of freedom, 172-73
  Explained mean square, 173
  Explained sum of squares, 162-63, 165-66, 172-74
  Hierarchical analysis, 163
  Hierarchical attribution of variation, 166
  Interaction, 160, 163-68
  Interaction degrees of freedom, 171, 173
  Interaction mean square, 173
  Interaction sum of squares, 163, 165-66, 173
  Main effects degrees of freedom, 171, 173
  Main effects mean square, 173

Main effects sum of squares, 166

Multiple classification analysis (MCA), 171
Significance: F-test, 171-74
Critical F-ratio, 172-74
Strength of association: E², 174
Sum of squares, 161-62, 165
Unadjusted category mean, 170
Unadjusted grand mean, 170
Unexplained degrees of freedom, 172-73
Unexplained mean square, 172-73
Unexplained sum of squares, 161, 163, 173
Unexplained variation, 161, 163
Venn diagram, 163, 164
Two-way analysis of variance with unrelated independent variables, 148-59, 162
Additive model, 152
Category mean, 149
Cell mean, 149-50, 152-53
Explained degrees of freedom, 156-57
Grand mean (GM), 150, 152
Interaction, 152-55, 158
Interaction degrees of freedom, 156-57
Interaction sum of squares, 153-55, 157
Main effects, 151, 156
Main effects degrees of freedom, 156-57
Main effects sum of squares, 157
Mean square, 157-58
Significance: F-test, 155-58
Critical F-ratio, 157-58
Strength of association: E², 158-59
Sum of squares, 149-50, 152-55, 157
Total explained variation, 152

Unexplained degrees of freedom, 156-57
Annale school, 1
Annales d'histoire: économique et sociale, 1
ANOVA. *See* Analysis of variance
Antimasonic voting data, 176-211
Aydelotte, William O., 2

b, the slope, 181, 183, 185, 200
Bar charts, 49, 51-56
BASIC programs
Program to calculate areas under the chi-square distribution, 281
Program to calculate areas under the F-distribution, 283
Program to calculate areas under the standard normal (z) distribution, 278
Program to calculate areas under the t-distribution, 279
Program to calculate the Gini Index, 259
Program to generate a set of random numbers, 15
Program to generate a set of random numbers by page, column, and line, 16
Program to generate a set of random numbers for a stratified sample, 23
Program to generate random numbers by volume, page, and line, 18
Bayes, Thomas, 64, 68, 70
Bayesian statistics, 68-71
Bayes's formula, 70-71
Bean, Lee L., 266
Becker, Carl, 148
Belknap, George, 238
Benson, Lee, 2
Bernoulli, Jacob, 64-65, 73, 80
Beta function, 277

Binet, Alfred, 234
Binomial distribution, 73, 77-78, 81
Binomial formula, 73-74, 77, 80, 114
Blalock, Hubert, 106
Bogardus, Emory S., 234
Bogue, Allan, 2
Boltzmann, Ludwig, 62
Bowley, Arthur, 84
Braudel, Fernand, 1

Cabinet durations, 41-44, 46-51
Cannon, John, 211, 215
Cartesian coordinates, 176
Case, 7
Catasto, 33, 137
Categorical variables. *See* Variables
Category mean. *See* Analysis of
  variance
Cattell, James McKeen, 234
Causal model, 196-97, 208-9
Central Limit Theorem, 47, 80-81, 87
Chance model, 59
Checking data, 34-35
Chi-square, 84, 113-20, 122, 145, 170,
  276
  Critical, 116-17
  Distribution, 116-17, 271, 276
Code book, 7, 26
Coding data, 26-34
  Biographical, 28-29
  Occupations, 27, 32, 33
  Religious denominations, 26-27, 30-
    31
  States, 26-29
Coding drift, 34
Coefficient of reproducibility (CR),
  240-41, 243, 249
Coin toss models, 38, 59, 60-67, 73-75,
  78, 81-82, 86, 93
Condran, Gretchen A., 266
Confidence intervals, 59, 87-90
Continuous variables. *See* Variables
Convenience samples, 14

Conzen, Kathleen Neils, 110-11, 113,
  117, 120, 123
"Cookbook" approach, 5, 59
County clerk data, 69-71
Cramér, Harald, 122
Cramér's V^2. *See* Measures of
  association
Cross-classification, 109-35, 232
  Cell frequencies, 111, 115-17, 128
  Cell percentages, 112-13, 115
  Cells, 111
  Column marginals, 111-12, 116
  Column percentages, 111-13
  Columns, 111
  Row marginals, 111-2, 116, 222
  Row percentages, 111-13
  Rows, 111
Crosstabulation. *See* Cross-
  classification
Crude birth rate (CBR), 264
Crude death rate (CDR), 266
Cumulative percentage, 40-41

Darwin, Charles, 175
De Fermat, Pierre, 65
Degrees of freedom, 83
  ANOVA (F-test), 144-45, 148, 155-
    56, 171-72, 276
  Cross-classification (chi-square),
    116-17, 135, 276
  Multiple regression, 209-10
  Regression, 186, 189, 192
  t-test, 94, 96, 98, 102, 105-7, 214
Demographic Yearbook, 267
Demography. *See* Historical
  demography
Demography, 264
De Moivre, Abraham, 78
Dependent variable. *See* Variables
Descartes, René, 175-76
Descriptive statistics, 59
The Design of Experiments, 137
Discrete variables. *See* Variables
Distance, 9-11

Dockhorn, Robert, 27
"Double whammy," 71-72
Dummy variables. *See* Multiple
    regression
Durkheim, Emile, 63
Dykstra, Robert, 2

E^2, 145-48
Ebbinghaus, Hermann, 234
Ecological fallacy, 221
Ecological regression, 219-32
    Logit model, 227
    Weighting, 228
Edgeworth, Francis Ysidro, 81, 179
Election of 1936, 14
Election surveys, 8
Electoral apportionment, 257-63
Emigration, 266
Endogamy, 264
Engerman, Stanley, 53-55
Error, 45
Error sum of squares, 186
Eta. *See* E^2
Ethnicity of spouse among German
    residents of Kingfisher County,
    Oklahoma Territory, 124
Euler, Leonhard, 47
Exogamy, 264
Exogenous factors, 196
Expected frequency, 114, 116-17, 124,
    170
Experimental design, 86-87
External migration, 266

Family reconstitution, 267
F-distribution, 271, 276-77
Fechner, Gustav Theodor, 233-34
The Federalist Papers, 102-8
Fertility, 264, 267
Fienberg, Stephen, 105-6
Fisher, Sir Ronald A., 51, 83, 86, 137

Florentine *Catasto. See Catasto*
Fogel, Robert, 53-55
Folks, J. Leroy, 274
Fortune, 14
F-ratio, 84, 102, 104, 142, 144-45, 209-
    10, 277
Frequencies. *See* Expected frequency
    and Observed frequency
F-test, 106, 148
    Two-tailed, 105

Gallup, George, 14, 83-84, 89
Galton, Francis, 52, 175, 179
Gamma. *See* Measures of association
Gauss, Carl Friedrich, 47, 78, 81
General fertility rate (GFR), 264
Gienapp, William E., 221
Gini, Corrado, 253
Gini Index, 233, 251-63
Goltra, Inez, 195
Goodman, Leo A., 124, 127, 134
Gosset, William S., 82-84
Grand mean. *See* Analysis of variance
Graunt, John, 266
Greven, Philip, 267
Grouped ordinal variables. *See*
    Variables
Guttman, Louis, 233-35
Guttman scaling, 233, 238-250

Hammarberg, Melvyn, 117, 123
Hayes, Samuel, 2
Heisenberg, Werner, 62
Herlihy, David, 33, 137, 139
Hershberg, Theodore, 27, 33
Histograms, 49, 51-56, 75-77
Historical demography, 260, 264-69
Historical Methods, 2-3, 264
*Historical Methods Newsletter. See
    Historical Methods*
*The History of Political Parties in the
    Province of New York, 1760-1776,*
    148-49

Hogg, Margaret, 84
Hollerith, Herman, 3
Hollerith cards, 4, 34
Horan, Patrick, 27
Hyneman, Charles, 4
Hypotheses
    Alternative, 59-61, 85-86, 93, 96, 98,
        101-2, 104-5, 141, 144, 188-89
    Null, 59-61, 81-82, 85-87, 93-96, 98,
        101-2, 104-8, 116, 135, 141-42, 144,
        188-89, 271, 275
    One-tailed, 96-98, 101
    Two-tailed, 96-98

Immigration, 266
Independent events, 66, 73
Independent variable. *See* Variables
Indiana voters' party affiliation, 117-
    20, 123
Infant mortality, 266-67
Infant mortality in 1850, 84-85, 216-19
Inferential statistics, 59-90
Interaction. *See* Analysis of variance
    (two-way)
Internal migration, 266
Interquartile mean, 49
Inter-university Consortium for
    Political and Social Research
    (ICPSR), 2
Interval variables. *See* Variables
Irish immigrants to Worcester,
    Massachusetts, 91-98

Jensen, A., 84
Jensen, Richard, 250
Journal of Family History, 3, 264
Journal of Interdisciplinary History,
    3, 264
Journal of Marriage and the Family,
    264
Journal of Urban History, 264

Katz, Michael, 27
Kempthorne, Oscar, 274
Keynes, John Maynard, 64
Killeshandra, County Cavan, Ireland,
    38
Klapisch-Zuber, Christiane, 33, 137,
    139
Kolmogorov, A. N., 65
Kousser, J. Morgan, 3
Kramarow, Ellen A., 266
Kruskal, William H., 124, 127, 134
Kutolowski, Kathleen Smith, 176-77,
    188, 190, 193, 195-96

Laplace, Pierre Simon, 47, 64, 68, 70, 80-
    81, 107
Law of Large Numbers, 80-81, 87
Least squares, 45-47
Legendre, Adrien Marie, 45-46
Letter-cluster sample, 269
Life table, 266
Literary Digest, 14, 89
Logit regression, 227, 229
Lorenz, Max Otto, 251
Lorenz curve, 253, 255, 260
Lowry, Richard, 82

McCants, Anne, 266
Marital status, 10-11
Marx, Karl, 48
Mean, 37, 39, 44-50, 53, 75, 78, 81-82,
    87, 96, 101-2, 106, 139, 148, 181
Measures of association, 120-35, 148
    Chi-square based, 126-27, 135
        Cramér's V^2, 122-24
        Phi-square, 123-24
    for ANOVA. *See* E^2
    for Regression. *See* Regression
        analysis
    Proportional Reduction in Error
        (PRE) measures, 124-34

gamma, 128, 130-32, 134,
  Tau$_b$, 128, 131-32, 134-35
Measures of dispersion, 49-58
Median, 37, 39-44, 47-49
Migration, 264, 266
Milwaukee school attendance, 84-85,
  110-17
Minimum marginal reproducibility
  (MMR), 243-44
Micegenation among racial groups
  in Parral, 131-32
Missing values, 26
Mode, 37, 39-40, 47-48, 244
  Bi-modal, 39
  Multi-modal, 39
  Tri-modal, 39
Mokken model, 250
Monotonic relationships, 128-29
  Negative, 129
  Positive, 128-29
Mortality, 266
Mosteller, Frederick, 102, 105-6
Mu. *See* Population mean
Multiple classification analysis
  (MCA). *See* Analysis of variance
Multiple regression, 194, 195-232
  Dummy dependent variables, 211-
  12, 216, 219
  Dummy independent variables, 216-
  19
  Explanatory power: R^2, 204-9
  Multiple regression equation, 204-
  6, 210, 216, 219, 226, 228
  Partial slopes, 200, 202-4, 210, 216,
  219, 226, 228
  Residuals, 196, 199-201
  Significance: F-ratio, 209-11
  Degrees of freedom, 209-11
  Significance of the partial slopes,
  210-11
Multivariate analysis, 175
Mutually exclusive events, 66, 74
Myrdal, Gunnar, 245-49

Natural increase, 264, 266
Newton, Isaac, 45, 62, 73
Neyman, Jerzy, 84, 87, 107
Nominal variables. *See* Variables
Normal or Gaussian distribution, 52,
  78-83, 88, 94, 134, 234, 271, 272, 274-
  77
Null hypothesis. *See* Hypotheses

Observed frequency, 114, 124, 170
Occupations. *See* Coding data
Ogburn, William F., 195
Order, 9-11, 13
Ordinal variables. *See* Variables
The Other Bostonians, 129
Ó'Tuathaigh, Gearóid, 40

Partial slopes. *See* Multiple regres-
  sion
Pascal, Blaise, 65
Pearson, Egon, 84, 107
Pearson, Karl, 49, 84, 114, 123, 190
Pearson's r. *See* Regression analysis
Peirce, Charles Sanders, 84
Pennsylvania election data, 1856,
  1857, 221-32
Percent, 37, 49, 57-58, 109
Percentiles, 49, 51-56
Philadelphia Social History Project, 33
Polsby, Nelson, 98
Pooled variance estimate of t. *See*
  t-test
Population, 7-8, 14, 19, 37-39, 83-84, 87,
  93, 96
Population mean, 44, 46-47, 50-51, 78,
  82, 87-88, 96, 141-142, 144
Population parameter, 38-39
Population standard deviation. *See*
  Standard deviation

Population Studies, 264
Population variance, 51, 101, 142, 144
Presidential vetoes, 159-74
Probability, 59, 61-62, 65-68, 93
  Classical, 66
  Conditional, 67-68, 71
  Empirical, 66
  Equally likely events, 64
  Expected, 71-72
  Feature of the physical world, 62-63
  Observed, 71-72
  One-tailed, 98, 102, 105, 135, 189,
    274-76
  Relative frequency, 63
  Subjective assessment, 64-65
  Two-tailed, 90, 98, 102, 105, 107, 189,
    274-76
Probability of error, 45, 47-49
Proportional Reduction in Error
  measures of association (PRE).
  See Measures of association

Quartiles, 49, 51-56
Quetelet, Adolphe, 52

R^2. *See* Regression analysis
Ramsey, Frank, 64
Random samples, 13, 77, 84-85, 87, 93,
  188
Random starting points (seed), 20
Ranked ordinal variables. *See*
  Variables
Record linkage, 267-69
Regression analysis, 91, 175-94, 212,
  226-27
  Exogenous variables, 193-94
  Interpretation of the regression
    equation, 183-85

Measures of association, 189-92
  Pearson's product moment
    correlation coefficient (r), 91,
    189, 191-92
  R^2, 189-91
Negative slope, 183, 192, 219
Nonlinear relationships, 193-94, 227
Plotting the line, 182
Positive slope, 183, 192
Regression equation, 179-91, 193,
  196, 200, 212, 228
Scatterplots, 175-79, 191-93
Significance of r, 192
Significance of slope (b), 189, 192
Significance of the equation, 185-88
Slope, 181, 183, 185-86, 188-89, 191,
  200
Standard deviation of the residuals,
  186
Standard error of the slope, 188
Variation, sources of
  Explained, 190-91, 204
  Total, 190-91, 204-5
  Unexplained, 190-91, 193
y intercept, 183, 186, 216
Rejection region, 96, 101-2
Religious denominations. *See* Coding
  data
Reproducibility, 236-37, 240-41, 244-45
Residuals. *See* Multiple regression
Rice Index of Cohesion, 233, 250
Robinson, William S., 221
Roll call analysis, 238-44
Rourke, Robert, 105-6

Samenow, Charles, 4
Sample mean, 44, 51, 87, 142, 275
Sample size, 87, 89
Sample standard deviation. *See*
  Standard deviation
Sample statistic, 37
Sample variance, 51

Sampling, 13-26
SAS (Statistical Analysis System), 5
Scale scores, 235-36, 238, 240
Scatterplots. *See* Regression analysis
Segregation, 245-50
Separate variance estimate of t. *See* t-test
Sex ratio, 264
Shapiro, Gilbert, 245, 247-48
Ship money assessment of 1636, 211-15
Shoemaker, Nancy, 34
Significance, 85, 107, 109, 120, 192
Significance tests, 59, 73, 84-87
    ANOVA (F-test), 155-58
    Cross-classification (chi-square), 113-20, 134
    Multiple regression, 209-11
    Regression, 192
    t-test, 93, 106
Silbey, Joel, 2
Simple descriptive statistics, 37-58
Simple random samples, 14-19
Simpson, Thomas, 45, 271
Simpson's Rule, 254, 271-72, 274
Skip interval samples, 14, 19-20
Slope. *See* Regression analysis
Snedecor, George, 142
Social mobility, 27, 33
Social Science History, 3, 264
Sons' and fathers' occupations, 129-31
SOUNDEX, 268
SPSS (Statistical Package for the Social Sciences), 5
Spurious relationship, 196, 208-9
Squared error, 47-49, 179
Standard deviation, 37, 49-50, 75, 77-78, 80-82, 87-88, 93, 101, 186
    Population, 50, 87
    Sample, 50, 87
States. *See* Coding data
Statistical Methods for Research Workers, 137

Statistics
    Central tendency, 37, 39-49
    Descriptive, 37-59
    Dispersion, 37, 49-58
    Inferential, 59-90
Stephan, Frederick F., 84
Stochastic, 250
Strata, 21-26
Stratified cluster samples, 14, 21-26
Success scores, 233, 250-51
Sum of squares, 45, 47, 49, 51, 83, 186, 188
Swierenga, Robert, 2

t´, 105-6
Tags, 9-10, 13
Tau$_b$. *See* Measures of association
t-distribution, 82-83, 94, 96, 114, 271, 275-77
    One-tailed, 99, 276
    Two-tailed, 97, 276
Thernstrom, Stephan, 129
Thompson, J. M., 39-40, 58
Thomsen, Søren Risbjerg, 227
Time on the Cross, 53-55
Total fertility rate (TFR), 266
Trapezoid Rule, 254-255
Trimean, 49
t-test, 91-108, 148, 189
    Independent observations, 91, 98-107
    Paired cases, 91-98
    Pooled variance estimate, 101-2, 106
    Separate variance estimate, 102, 105
Tufte, Edward R., 53
Turner, Frederick Jackson, 1
Tuscans and Their Families: A Study of the Florentine Catasto *in 1427,* 137
t-value, 93-96, 101-2, 188-89, 192, 276
    Critical, 96, 98, 102, 106-7
Type I error, 107-8
Type II error, 107-8

Ulmer, S. Sidney, 243, 244
Unit of analysis, 7
United States census, 4, 17
United States Declaration of War, June
    1812, 133-34, 250
University of Iowa, 2
University of Michigan, 2

Variables, 7-8
    Categorical, 8, 137, 152, 156, 216
    Continuous, 8
    Dependent, 113, 176, 185, 190-91,
        193, 196, 200, 206, 212
    Discrete, 8
    Independent, 113, 152, 160, 162, 165,
        168-70, 176, 185, 190, 193, 195-96,
        200, 209-10, 212, 228
    Interval, 9-11, 13, 51, 137, 145, 152,
        175, 179
    Nominal, 9-11, 13, 109
    Ordinal, 9-11, 13, 109, 129
        Grouped ordinal, 11
        Ranked ordinal, 11, 41-42
Variance, 37, 49, 51, 77-78, 82-83, 101-2,
    104-6
    Population, 51, 82-83
    Sample, 51, 82-83, 114
Venn diagram. *See* Analysis of
    variance

Wallace, David, 102
Weighting, 25

y intercept. *See* Regression analysis
Yule, George Udny, 179, 195
Yule's Q, 131

z-distribution. *See* Normal distribution
z-scores, 84, 90, 272-73

About the Authors

R. DARCY is Regents Professor of Political Science and Statistics at Oklahoma State University and co-author of *Women, Elections, and Representation* (1994), along with over 100 journal articles, book chapters, reviews, notes, and academic papers.

RICHARD C. ROHRS is Associate Professor of History at Oklahoma State University. He is the author of a book on ethnicity in Oklahoma and has published articles in such journals as *Historical Methods, Diplomatic History, Journal of the Early Republic, The Historian*, and *Immigration History Newsletter*.

ISBN 0-275-94897-8

90000>

EAN

9 780275 948979

HARDCOVER BAR CODE